Developing a Winning J.I.T. Marketing Strategy

The Industrial Marketer's Guide

Developing a Winning J.I.T. Marketing Strategy

The Industrial Marketer's Guide

Charles O'Neal

Kate Bertrand

Prentice Hall, Englewood Cliffs, New Jersey 07632

Library of Congress Cataloging-in-Publication Data

O'Neal, Charles R.
    Developing a winning J.I.T. marketing strategy : the industrial
marketer's guide / Charles R. O'Neal, Kate Bertrand.
        p.   cm.
    Includes bibliographical references.
    ISBN 0-13-205303-9
    1. Marketing--Management--Handbooks, manuals, etc. 2. Industrial
marketing--Handbooks, manuals, etc. 3. Just-in-time systems-
-Handbooks, manuals, etc.   I. Bertrand, Kate. II. Title.
HF5415.13.O58 1990
658.5'6--dc20   89-71065
                                                                     CIP

Editorial/production supervision
  and interior design: **Karen Bernhaut**
Cover design: **George Cornell**
Manufacturing buyer: **Kelly Behr**

 © 1991 by Prentice-Hall, Inc.
A division of Simon & Schuster
Englewood Cliffs, New Jersey 07632

The publisher offers discounts on this book when ordered
in bulk quantities. For more information, write:

Special Sales/College Marketing
Prentice-Hall, Inc.
College Technical and Reference Division
Englewood Cliffs, NJ 07632

Printed in the United States of America

10 9 8 7 6 5 4 3 2 1

ISBN   0-13-205303-9

Prentice-Hall International (UK) Limited, *London*
Prentice-Hall of Australia Pty. Limited, *Sydney*
Prentice-Hall Canada Inc., *Toronto*
Prentice-Hall Hispanoamericana, S.A., *Mexico*
Prentice-Hall of India Private Limited, *New Delhi*
Prentice-Hall of Japan, Inc., *Tokyo*
Simon & Schuster Asia Pte. Ltd., *Singapore*
Editora Prentice-Hall do Brasil, Ltda., *Rio de Janeiro*

To
Anette
and
Mary

Contents

Preface

The decade of the 1980s brought unprecedented change to the U.S. industrial marketplace. Organizations in most final-product industries—many former leaders in their fields—found they could no longer match the quality, cost, and customer responsiveness of global competitors.

A new class of competitor, dubbed "world class," was emerging. William Weisz, CEO of Motorola, aptly defined the world-class organization as one "aggressively striving for perfect quality, leading edge technology, just-in-time manufacturing, and cost-competitive servicing." These companies compete globally.

A dominant approach they use to develop their competitive edge is the triple-threat just-in-time/total quality commitment/total people involvement (JIT/TQC/TPI) process.

But to benefit from the triple threat, final-product manufacturers need world-class suppliers, which we call "world-class industrial marketers." The final-product manufacturer cannot rise above the quality, cost, or responsiveness levels of the industrial marketers that supply it with materials. Because of that, final-product manufacturers that are adopting JIT, TQC, and TPI approaches are making extraordinary demands of their suppliers. Industrial marketing is a new ball game with a brand new set of rules.

The JIT/TQC/TPI process, as developed by leading final-product manufactuers, has been documented in excellent books. The implications for industrial marketers, or suppliers, serving these producers, have not been well-defined or systematically discussed, however. This book is designed to fill the gap. The title *Developing a Winning JIT Strategy* capsulizes our approach.

"JIT" describes the purchasing organization's orientation, which pushes the marketer to develop a world-class capability. It is a management philosophy that focuses on eliminating waste internally and in upstream relationships with suppliers and downstream relationships with final-product buyers. It also implies total quality commitment and total people involvement in the process.

"Marketing" describes the process of determining customer requirements—the voice of the customer—and designing, developing, producing, delivering, and servicing products that meet these requirements precisely. Marketing must be customer driven.

In this book, marketing is the task of one business striving to develop a relationship with another. The final-product buyer is another step or two downstream. The industrial, or business-to-business, marketer is a supplier whose materials, components, and other products are incorporated into final-product manufacturers' offerings. Industrial marketing has general applicability, as explained in Chapter 12, but we emphasize the relationships and activities as they relate to the supplier serving the final-product original equipment manufacturer (OEM) of industrial and/or consumer goods. After incorporating the industrial marketer's products into their own offerings, original equipment manufacturers sell the final product to end customers.

The phrases "industrial marketer" and "JIT marketer," used throughout the book, refer to the entire industrial organization, not just the marketing function. And in discussing the marketing department or function, we include all units with direct responsibility for serving the customer—sales, product management, physical distribution, and customer service—as well as the marketing support functions of market research, communications, and administration. The resources of all units that communicate with and serve the customer are required to make JIT marketing work.

Developing a Winning JIT Strategy emphasizes that we're dealing with an ongoing process, not a final result. Its objective is continuous improvement, and its ideal output is:

- Perfect quality products, in
- Exact quantities needed, at the

- Precise time needed, at the
- Lowest total delivered cost.

Developing such a strategy presents a tremendous challenge to the industrial marketer. But it's worth the effort. It gives the marketer a competitive advantage that sets it apart as a world-class organization that can compete effectively in the global marketplace.

ACKNOWLEDGMENTS

This book represents the contributions of many individuals and organizations. We would like to recognize those who have had a direct impact on its development.

The seed was planted in the spring of 1984 when Chuck attended a conference co-sponsored by the Illinois Institute of Technology and the Chicago chapter of the American Marketing Association. The theme of the conference was: "The Factory of the Future, How It Works, and Why Marketing Will Never Be The Same Again." The manufacturing concepts of flexible automation, computer-integrated manufacturing, and just-in-time production were exciting and well-presented. The presentations dealing with the marketing implications of this new environment were vague and tentative—presenting a major challenge.

Chuck acknowledges the significant contribution of the General Electric Company in giving him the broad-based experience and training as an industrial marketer needed to tackle this challenge—an assignment that required an understanding of manufacturing, materials management, and distribution systems, as well as the industrial marketing process.

The American Production and Inventory Control Society (APICS) provided the first national forum for testing these marketing implications, the Zero Inventories Conference of Fall 1984. It also marked the beginning of associations with key industry leaders involved in the just-in-time process; Len Ricard, formerly of General Motors Corporation, Ernest Huge of FMC Corporation, and Indiana University's Robert Hall, who "wrote the book" on just-in-time manufacturing.

The Association for Manufacturing Excellence (AME), a spin-off of the repetitive manufacturing group of APICS, has been a significant information source. The organization's philosophy of information-sharing and its outstanding conferences, workshops, and publications have allowed us to interact with many individuals on the cutting edge of just-in-time/total quality technology. Special recognition should be given to past presidents Ken Stork, of Motorola; Lee Sage, of Arthur Young and Company; and Rolland "Mac" McCulloch, of Briggs and Stratton; as well as to Steve

Tierney and Tony Pollock, of Xerox Corporation; Pete Landry, of Landry and Associates (formerly of Xerox); Lewis Stowe, of Arthur Young and Company; Chris Fossee, of Omark Industries; and John Kenfield, of Hewlett-Packard Company.

Special thanks are due to Mike Bungo, a "just-in-time industrial marketer" from Eaton Corporation who served as mentor in the early phases of the research project and critiqued much of the work.

Several professional colleagues have either collaborated on certain concepts in this book or provided the foundation upon which they are built. These individuals include: Gary Frazier and Robert Spekman, of the University of Southern California; Mike Hutt, of Arizona State University; and Larry Guinipero, of Florida State University.

A special thanks also to the University of Evansville, which funded two industry research projects: one focusing on the purchasing behavior of just-in-time final equipment OEMs, and one on the manufacturing, distribution, and marketing behavior of the first-tier suppliers (industrial marketers) serving these OEMs.

And finally, many thanks to Daniel Livak for his support during the preparation of this book, and to Michael Bertrand, for sharing his microcomputer expertise whenever disaster struck.

Perhaps the greatest contribution was made by Anette O'Neal, who waded through reams of hieroglyphics in typing the original manuscript and its numerous revisions and patiently endured endless hours of research and writing to make this book a reality.

Charles O'Neal
Kate Bertrand

Chapter 1

The Comeback Trail

U.S. industry is engaged in a championship competition in the global arena. One of the toughest conflicts is now under way, and the very large domestic market is at stake. The game is in the third period, with the U.S. championship on the line. Let's briefly replay the first two periods and the third period to date.

THE FIRST PERIOD (1945–1965): FRIENDLY DOMESTIC COMPETITION

The two decades following World War II can truly be characterized as friendly competition. Most U.S. teams were winning the battle for the marketplace, which was mainly confined to the United States because no one needed to look further. There was a pent-up demand for products that had not been widely available when production was focused on military products—and five years worth of spending power among potential consumers. Those factors led to a lush market for products of almost any quality. This affluent market was crying for products, and that lasted several years.

Because the United States had most of the resources and technical capabilities to meet these demands, and overseas competitors were in no shape to put up a fight, American manufacturers didn't worry about foreign competition after the war. In contrast to U.S. factories, which the ravages of World War II hadn't touched, Japan's and Western Europe's production systems were essentially destroyed. The Japanese had two additional strikes against them: a reputation in the United States for producing and marketing shoddy products, and very little knowledge of American culture and how to appeal to American consumers.

International competition during this period could be considered "no contest." As Tom Peters so aptly put it in addressing the subject of "The Forgotten Customer," "During these two decades the year-by-year score was 20–0, with the United States winning by forfeit,"[1]

Consequently, American producers and consumers started to take rapid U.S. market growth for granted. Formidable American producers— General Motors, United States Steel, General Electric, and others—all had access to abundant labor, material, and financial resources. What could stop them from continuously improving the U.S. consumer's living standard? The game was confined to the home field, with all the advantages of local officiating, comfortable facilities, and familiar, loyal fans.

THE SECOND PERIOD (1965–1975): ENTRY OF FOREIGN COMPETITION

By the mid-1960s, the competitive arena had started to move beyond domestic boundaries. Volkswagen had established a presence in the United States with its attack on the low-end automobile market; the emphasis was low price, low-cost operations, and quality. Toyota's first attempt to broach the U.S. market, in 1957, failed. It couldn't attract American buyers because of poor quality. When Toyota returned in the mid-1960s, with Nissan, both adopted the Volkswagen (VW) strategy. Consequently, both Nissan and Toyota made substantial inroads into the American small-car market.

Detroit's response to the influx of small cars included a token offering of new, smaller designs—the Corvair, Valiant, and Falcon. These were larger, heavier, and more expensive than their foreign counterparts and posed a nominal threat to the German and Japanese producers. Fortunately, the small-car market was a relatively minor part of the total U.S. auto market between 1965 and the early 1970s, when gasoline was still bargain priced.

Japanese firms were quietly racking up points in several U.S. markets during those years. They moved into the copier market by targeting customers who needed low-volume copiers. Canon, Minolta, Ricoh, and

Sharp chipped away at that segment of the market with low-cost, high-quality machines. Xerox, though aware of the situation, didn't see the Japanese producers as a threat. Believing the low-volume market had relatively little potential, Xerox concentrated on the high-volume market and the "real" competition: IBM and Kodak.

Similarly, Honda entered the U.S. motorcycle market in 1960 with a very small, lightweight motorcycle. The product had a three-speed transmission, five-horsepower engine, electric starter, and step-through frame for female riders. It was truly superior to the U.S. equivalent and sold for about 75% less than the larger American and British motorcycles. Honda also mounted a major campaign to change the image of motorcycle ownership; the theme was, "You meet the nicest people on a Honda." The company's sales mushroomed from $500,000 in 1960 to $77 million by 1965. Harley-Davidson, the traditional leader in the heavyweight motorcycle segment, didn't consider Honda a threat. And in fact, as recently as 1972, Harley-Davidson still enjoyed a more than 99% share in the heavyweight market.

Honda's approach typified the Japanese strategy for entering U.S. markets. By broaching America with products the Japanese market had already accepted—nearly to the point of saturation—Japanese marketers gained economies of scale and could provide a high quality level for features important to customers. At the same time, the Japanese were tapping relatively unserved market segments. The strategy usually included establishing a strong regional position that could be used as a springboard for growth.

As the Japanese chipped away at U.S. market share, American firms were preoccupied with the larger, more lucrative customers and with their major U.S.-based competitors.

Beginning in the mid-1960s, the growth rate of U.S. productivity slowed. By 1973, the 3% growth rate of the 1950s and early 1960s had dropped to 2%. That decline was very disappointing in light of other industrial nations' productivity rates. The following productivity growth rates (1960–1978) tell the story:[2]

United States	2.8%
West Germany	5.4%
France	5.5%
Japan	8.2%

Although several factors caused this condition, there's no doubt the leading factor was U.S. industry's complacency, which had grown out of strong profit performance during the 1960s. Even after it stopped being appropriate, the emphasis continued to be on short-term profits rather than long-term development of product and process technologies. U.S.

manufacturing technology started to lose its leadership position as American executives turned to new strategic management techniques that stressed financial control through portfolio analysis. Financially oriented top managers treated the corporation as a set of profit-generating business units whose destinies were based on short-term financial performance. Manufacturing technologies were neglected and manufacturing bases were eroded as firms shifted to competitive strategies that were "less mundane" than manufacturing competence.

In contrast, economic necessity was propelling Japan's postwar industrial miracle. Japanese industry, with its limited domestic market and strong reliance on imported materials, was forced to vigorously develop international markets through exporting and foreign-based manufacturing. It did so, with the help of borrowed technology, highly motivated and disciplined managers and workers, and government-industry cooperation.

By the mid-1970s, the arena had expanded moderately and foreign competitors were challenging the competitive position of U.S. firms in certain industries.

THE THIRD PERIOD (1975–present): INTENSE GLOBAL COMPETITION

U.S. firms began feeling the effects of foreign competition in the mid-1970s, but the real impact was yet to come. The arena was quickly taking on global dimensions, and those foreign competitors were learning how to win both at home and in the opponent's court. In fact, the boundaries between the two courts were blurring more and more.

The consumer electronics industry provides a vivid illustration. U.S. dominance in that market started to erode during the 1960s as Southeast Asian countries' low labor costs enticed U.S. producers. American manufacturers went offshore—to Hong Kong, Taiwan, Korea, and Singapore—to produce or assemble basic products such as portable radios and TVs for the U.S. market. Gradually, Asian firms acquired product and processing technology and became active manufacturers. In addition to entering the United States with products marketed as low-priced lines of major U.S. consumer electronics companies, these Asian companies sold their own private label products directly to major U.S. retail chains.

Meanwhile, Japanese producers that had already captured the lion's share of the radio, stereo, and portable TV markets with lower priced, quality products were upgrading to take advantage of their emerging reputation for quality. Brand names such as Sony and Panasonic became synonymous with quality and reliability and often commanded a premium price.

Ultimately, the Japanese and other Southeast Asian producers' combined force was too powerful for American producers to overcome. Many long-established consumer electronics manufacturers, including Sylvania, Warwick, Admiral, Motorola, and Philco, were either taken over by Japanese or European firms or dropped by the wayside. By the early 1980s, Japanese firms dominated the color-TV industry RCA had spawned in the 1950s when it developed the color picture tube. U.S. firms gradually withdrew from the color-TV market, with General Electric finally selling its GE-RCA television division to Thomson of France in 1987. Zenith became the sole survivor.

The automotive industry has been the most talked about victim of global competition in the third period. In the 1970s, as total U.S. demand for cars jumped 30%, U.S. demand for Japanese-made cars exploded. The 500% increase in demand for those cars translated into sales of two million units in the United States in 1980. In the early 1980s, Japan voluntarily limited auto exports to the United States, which amounted to a hold-the-line policy. But then Japan altered its strategy for penetrating the U.S. market; it switched to foreign direct investment. Consequently, Japanese automotive plants are currently in production in Ohio, Kentucky, Tennessee, Illinois, Indiana, and Michigan. Automotive industry analysts expect these facilities' output to reach two million units in 1990.

In addition, Korean auto makers are building a strong position in the U.S. subcompact market using the Japanese strategy of low-priced, high-quality offerings. All this is happening when the U.S. auto market is at best stable and suffers from substantial unused capacity.

The assault of Honda, Suzuki, Kawasaki, and Yamaha on the U.S. motorcycle market, and specifically on Harley-Davidson, also intensified in the mid-1970s as those firms built production facilities in the United States to provide better access to the market. Honda continued upgrading its motorcycles to compete head on with the larger models. The strategy was so successful that Harley-Davidson petitioned the U.S. International Trade Commission in 1983 for relief—increased import duties on the larger motorcycles. The government responded with a five-year tariff beginning at 45% in 1983 and phasing down to 10% by 1988.

Japanese copier producers also stepped up U.S. marketing activities in the mid-1970s. Xerox, the industry giant, watched its worldwide share of the copier market plummet from 82% to 41% between 1976 and 1982 as Japanese competition intensified. In a nutshell, the Japanese were building products higher in quality and lower in price than Xerox's. During that period, Ricoh, winner of the coveted Deming Prize for quality in 1975, marketed a machine in the United States that averaged 17,000 copies between machine failures—compared with Xerox's 6,000 to 10,000. And the Ricoh copier took half as long to repair when it did break down.

In the United States, the third wave's competitive assault—especially from Japan—has devastated industry after industry. American manufacturers virtually abandoned the microwave oven, a U.S. innovation whose popularity grew phenomenally in the 1980s. Machine tools have felt the dual impact of German, then Japanese, competition. Manufacturers of forklifts, lawn mowers, cameras, electric motors, automobile tires, appliances, commercial aircraft, and numerous other consumer and industrial products have also suffered.

Summarizing the situation, Akio Morita, Sony's co-founder, was quoted in *Business Week*'s March 3, 1986, cover story: "American companies have either shifted output to low-wage countries or come to buy parts and assembled products from countries like Japan that can make quality products at low prices. The result is a hollowing of American industry. The United States is abandoning its status as an industrial power."[3] There's certainly an element of truth in Morita's statement. In a 1985 Harris poll of U.S. executives facing Japanese competition, 40% of the respondents admitted they had no plan for competing with the Japanese.[4]

A major problem for U.S. producers is that their products just aren't as good as those of Japanese competitors. The typical U.S. factory invests 20% to 25% of its operating budget in finding mistakes (inspection), and fixing them (rework). At any one time, up to 25% of a factory's workers are reworking products that weren't made right the first time.

Japanese manufacturers' strategy has been to produce superior-quality products *that meet the needs of the customer* and sell at attractive prices—which are often less than those of U.S. competitors. The Japanese will forego short-term profits to gain a solid foothold in a product market, recognizing that larger market share leads to lower costs and higher profits in the long run. They also reinvest profits in programs that further increase share and reduce costs. That increases profits in a continuing upward spiral referred to as the "winners' competitive cycle" by James Abegglen and George Stalk, Japan-based management consultants.[5]

Japanese firms depended heavily on U.S. know-how to establish their quality and productivity leadership position. Twenty years ago, two of the world's leading quality experts, Joseph M. Juran and W. Edwards Deming, started working with the Japanese after failing to find American executives interested in boosting product quality and solving quality problems. Only recently have U.S. firms, desperately in need of guidance, started to seek out these experts.

The lower costs of Japanese products—apart from currency exchange rates—aren't based on lower wages. They spring from the efficient use of production resources: labor, materials, and money. The scarcity of these resources has conditioned the Japanese to be very conscious of waste and make every effort to eliminate it. They are meticulous in this respect. Their processes and technology focus on maximum output with minimum input. The only constraint is that products conform to the customer's requirements every time.

Global competition is fierce, with the Japanese currently leading. Newly developed nations are copying their success pattern and maintaining a distinct labor-cost advantage. The major developing nations—China, India, and Malaysia—are waiting in the wings. Can U.S. industry succeed against such formidable competition? Some rays of hope are emerging.

THE U.S. RESPONSE

Frederick Stratton, Briggs and Stratton Corporation's chief executive officer, aptly described the condition of U.S. industry in *Target*. He said, "I think the competitive shock of the early 1980s is a second Pearl Harbor, and the slumbering (U.S.) giant is awakening."[6]

Top managers in leading U.S. industrial firms are indeed waking up, and they are producing results that prove the task is not impossible. There are dozens, perhaps hundreds, of examples of U.S. firms that were reeling from the blows of global opponents but have now turned around. Their response should set the tone for America's response.

Updating the Xerox and Harley-Davidson examples, we find encouraging developments. It took Xerox ten years to wake up to the fact that it was facing unprecedented competition. By 1980, the situation in the copier market had reached crisis proportions, and Xerox finally realized how good its Japanese competitors were. They provided customers with small copiers of higher quality than Xerox's and prices equal to the U.S. firm's *manufacturing cost*.

Xerox responded. The changes started in 1981 as the company tried to gain insight into its problems by analyzing Japanese product and processing technology, quality concepts, and manufacturing philosophy. Fuji Xerox, a Japanese-based joint venture between Xerox and Fuji Electric, provided an excellent vehicle for this analysis.

In this period, Xerox launched a program of *competitive benchmarking*, which it defines as the continuous process of measuring its products, services, and practices against its toughest competitors, or those companies renowned as leaders. The company observes what companies are doing now and projects their future performance. External benchmarks that exceed the performance of Xerox or its suppliers create the "competitive gap" and are targets for future achievement. Fuji Xerox and Rank Xerox, a joint venture between Xerox and Rank, Ltd. of England provide Xerox with benchmarking windows on the Far East and Western Europe.

Between 1980 and 1986, Xerox made tremendous strides in quality, cost, and product delivery. The company reduced the line fallout rate of supplier parts from 10,000 to 450 parts per million defective and set a new benchmark of 125. Quality defects per 100 machines fell from 91 to 12, with a new benchmark set at four. Direct material cost shrank 50%, and the company targeted an additional 50% reduction as the new benchmark. It also reduced labor overhead rates from 380% to 189%; manufacturing lead time from nine to five months; and inventory from 99 to 33 days' stock, with a new target of nine days.

The 10-series copier Xerox introduced as a part of this program became the most successful new copier in history. By the end of 1985, the company had leased or sold more than 750,000 of the new machines; that represented 38% of the Xerox machines in use worldwide. The 1075 model, built in Webster, New York, was the first Xerox copier made in the United States and shipped into Japan. The Japanese Ministry of Trade and Industry awarded that model the Grand Prize for Good Design. Because of its efforts, Xerox didn't just maintain its global market position. It made modest market share gains.[7]

Harley-Davidson's (HD) response to foreign competition resembles Xerox's in many ways. In the late 1970s, HD representatives visited Japanese motorcycle factories to learn about their approach to manufacturing. They returned with several new concepts that lowered HD's break-even volume from 53,000 to 35,000 motorcycles per year. Between 1981 and 1986, HD reduced in-process inventory by $22 million; increased annual inventory turns from six to twenty-one; reduced machine setup times an average of 75%; increased productivity 30%; and reduced scrap and rework 60%. By mid-1986, the company had spent $160 million on improving its manufacturing capabilities. After losing $30 million in 1981–1982, the company made a modest profit in 1983 and $10 million profit in 1985.[8]

Reflecting on that progress, Vaughn Beals, HD's chief executive officer, said in his keynote address at the 1987 AME Conference, "We are really just starting to understand the potential for improvement in the *nonmanufacturing* parts of the company." He added that this area is about five years behind manufacturing. Beals went on to say, "It is harder to see, but I know the quality and productivity improvement activity will invade our marketing and service areas." So confident was Beals in HD's ability to compete that he asked the U.S. government to lift the elevated import tariff on large motorcycles in 1987—a year ahead of schedule. He believed the company was ready to meet global competition head on.[9]

Ford Motor Company has certainly responded to the changing competitive environment. Some observers have called the firm's response "the comeback story of the decade." After losing $3 billion in 1980, Ford dramatically restructured, lowering costs and pushing responsibility down to the line worker. The company emphasized teamwork and quality. By 1987, Ford was the world's most profitable car company, having moved from 17% share in the U.S. market to 20%. Meanwhile, General Motors had lost nine percentage points. Ford also topped other U.S. producers in quality ratings for its cars. Donald Peterson, Ford's chief executive officer, explained the reason behind this dramatic turnaround: "The principle by which we live and die is that once we do something well, we have to figure out how to do it even better." The Japanese word describing this philosophy is "kaisen," meaning continuous improvement.[10]

Black and Decker (B&D) was severely challenged by the Japanese invasion of the professional power tool market in the late 1970s. By 1980, Japan's Makita Electronic Works Ltd. alone controlled 20% of the world market with its high-quality, low-priced tools. This new competition rolled B&D's world market share back from 20% to 15%. B&D responded by cutting its work force 40%, investing $80 million in plant modernization, adopting Japanese manufacturing techniques in the United States, and making tools overseas in attempts to become a more effective competitor in the global market. By 1985, B&D had regained its 20% market share, albeit at reduced profit levels.

In discussing Motorola's competitive situation, chief executive officer William Weisz said, in his keynote address at the 1986 AME Conference, that he had concluded many years ago that Motorola was in a battle for survival. That just deepened his determination to be a winner. Motorola's success with its radio-paging products illustrates what that determination did for the company.[11]

Weisz went on to explain that in 1979 Motorola decided that selling to sophisticated Japanese customers *in Japan* would be crucial in the company's future success. It decided to sell radio pagers to Nippon Telephone and Telegraph Company (NTT), which relied on five suppliers—all Japanese. Motorola placed the highest priority on this project, monitoring progress weekly. He emphasized that Motorola became NTT's first foreign communications equipment supplier. By 1986, the company had delivered more than 300,000 pagers to NTT. Today Motorola enjoys the largest share of NTT's business, and it has been a top supplier for delivered quality and field reliability for some time.

In 1981, Motorola's Policy Committee set out to improve quality ten times over in every part of the organization within five years. It even included the many departments whose existing quality levels were the best in the industry. By 1986, the company had met or exceeded its goal in most organizational units. More recently, Motorola launched a much more ambitious plan: a 100-times improvement in quality by 1992. That translates into a quality level of 99.9997% defect-free parts, or three defective parts per million!

U.S. firms in other industries offer similar success stories. Hewlett-Packard, Timken, 3M, Deere, Parker-Hannifin, Omark, Davidson Instruments, Johnson Control, and Sheller-Globe are all leaders in the race toward global competitiveness. Their strategy is to provide products and services of world-class quality at competitive prices, and their operational philosophy centers on the dynamic trio of just-in-time manufacturing, total quality, and total employee involvement. The success of each of these factors hinges on the other two.

Two groups aggressively promoting these concepts among American manufacturers are the Automotive Industry Action Group (AIAG) and the Association for Manufacturing Excellence (AME). The stated mission of the AIAG, which is a group of middle managers in the U.S. automotive industry formed in 1980, is to increase the U.S. automotive industry's productivity and competitiveness. The group brings manufacturers and suppliers together to improve material management and operations management, using project teams that investigate topics such as just-in-time manufacturing, statistical process control, quality control, schedule stabilization, communications, employee involvement, physical packaging, and logistics. The goal is to develop better methods and standardize them across the industry, with special emphasis on supplier–final assembler coordination. The AIAG currently has several thousand members and is actively developing new operational techniques.

AME was formed in 1984, also in response to intensifying global competition. It is a spin-off of the Repetitive Manufacturing Group of the American Production and Inventory Control Society (APICS). AME originally focused on just-in-time manufacturing systems, but its goals are now broader. Its present mission is to "enable members' companies to achieve excellence and competitive advantage" through education, research, and experience sharing. AME concerns itself with all functions of manufacturing enterprises and doesn't confine itself to a specific industry. Its efforts cut across the complete spectrum of industries. One of AME's more effective educational techniques is the on-site workshop. The association conducts workshops within the facilities of firms that are successfully applying advanced operational concepts. The workshops are conducted frequently and are restricted to fairly small groups to help participants share their experiences. AME also provides case studies in its quarterly journal, *Target*.

Both AIAG and AME have been major forces in helping U.S. manufacturers become more effective global competitors. The two groups draw heavily on Japanese operational methods, adapting those techniques to American practice.

JUST-IN-TIME/TOTAL QUALITY MANUFACTURING IN THE UNITED STATES

Japanese firms, namely Toyota, adopted the just-in-time/total quality control (JIT/TQC) approach to manufacturing nearly thirty years ago. In contrast, U.S. firms started using these techniques around 1980.

Several industry studies have tried to measure the number of U.S. companies developing and implementing JIT/TQC. In a study of automotive industry final product assemblers—original equipment manufacturers (OEMs)—that Dr. O'Neal conducted in 1985, 85% of the respondents were implementing JIT programs. Almost three quarters of these programs were less than three years old, and 40% had been operating less than a year. A second study, which Dr. O'Neal conducted the same year, evaluated the OEMs' first-tier suppliers. The goal was to learn how many of the suppliers' deliveries to OEMs were just-in-time and to quantify the number of suppliers with in-house JIT programs. Although 55% said they were JIT suppliers, only 39% had internal JIT programs.

Using JIT techniques in-house affected both the OEMs and suppliers quite positively, as shown in Table 1-1.

The automotive industry—stimulated by fierce competition and supported by AIAG's efforts to educate firms on JIT techniques—pioneered the use of JIT programs in the United States in the early 1980s. Since then, manufacturers in other industries have followed the automotive firms' lead.

Purchasing magazine conducted its first JIT survey in September 1985, polling purchasing executives in a broad spectrum of industries.[12] More than 400 responded; 20% said they had a program in place, 10% were getting ready to implement one, and 25% were studying the situation. Only 40% had no plans to develop a program. In *Purchasing*'s 1987 follow-up survey of 1,000 purchasing managers, 72% of the respondents either had a program in place or were planning to develop one.[13] Sixty-two percent of these firms stressed that they were facing increased foreign competition, and 82% of the firms with JIT programs in place reported strong foreign competition.

Clearly, U.S. OEM and supplier firms are boosting productivity and product quality using JIT/TQC programs. As we saw earlier, these efforts have dramatically improved the competitive standing of Xerox, Harley-Davidson, Ford, and other JIT pioneers.

TABLE 1-1   JIT Effect on Performance

Performance Measure	Much Higher (%)	Higher (%)	Same (%)	Lower (%)	Much Lower (%)
Productivity					
OEMs	44	35	21	—	—
Suppliers	21	55	18	6	—
Product Quality					
OEMs	36	50	14	—	—
Suppliers	12	64	25	—	—

But the number of firms, especially supplier organizations, that are aggressively developing JIT/TQC programs is still much too small and generally confined to companies facing competitive crises. And the evidence shows that many firms using these methods aren't benefiting fully in either productivity or product-quality gains.

The final-product producer—the OEM—generally initiates the JIT process, usually in response to an external threat or crisis. Initially, the OEM factory tries to reduce costs by eliminating activities that don't add value to the product (see Fig. 1-1). As the OEM streamlines its operations to produce in smaller lots, it requires materials of much higher quality, delivered more frequently.

At that point, the emphasis switches to the OEM's purchasing and materials management functions. Purchasing carefully evaluates suppliers to find those that can meet the rigorous requirements of JIT production. This is a time-consuming process because suppliers must often develop the ability to meet the OEM customer's requirements. It is a critical step, however, because purchased materials represent about half the cost of the final OEM product and at least half the cost of quality.

To meet the OEM's needs, the first-tier supplier must develop an internal JIT program. As with the OEM, this starts in the factory and flows backward to the purchasing department, which implements a similar supplier evaluation and selection process. Because the first-tier supplier depends on its own suppliers for materials, second-tier suppliers must also learn to meet new quality-delivery-service requirements. If they don't, the first-tier supplier ends up grappling with the traditional incoming-materials quality and delivery constraints as well as increasingly stringent OEM quality specifications.

To put it in context, consider how OEMs' quality analysis has changed. Instead of evaluating incoming materials based on acceptable quality levels (AQLs) measured in percent-defective per hundred units, as they used to, leading high-volume OEMs are measuring the number of defective parts per *million* (PPM) in incoming materials shipments.

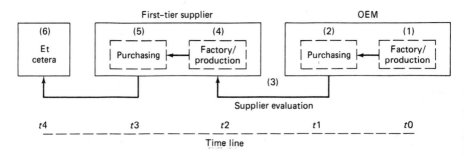

Figure 1-1   The organizational progression of the just-in-time process.

Recent industry studies show that suppliers are the weak link in the JIT process. A study of AIAG members reported in the Winter 1986 issue of the *Journal of Purchasing and Materials Management* revealed that 50% of JIT OEM respondents said poor supplier quality was a problem; and was their second most frequently reported problem.[14] Another study included in the same issue of the publication, covering several industries, indicated "lack of support from suppliers" as the most "significant and severe" problem JIT OEMs face; "the difficulty of obtaining high-quality materials from suppliers on a consistent basis" was their third most "significant and severe" problem.[15]

Speaking at the 1987 AME national conference, Harley-Davidson's Vaughn Beals told attendees, "The easy one-half of the job of implementing JIT is doing it inside. The tough one-half is doing it with suppliers." This reinforces the automotive industry study mentioned earlier, which showed that 85% of final-product OEMs—but *only 39%* of their first-tier suppliers—had JIT programs.

One reason OEMs are further along with JIT manufacturing than their suppliers is that first-tier suppliers usually enter the process much too late and don't really understand the JIT process or their OEM customers' requirements. To solve this problem, leading OEMs are "training" their first-tier suppliers to bring them on stream more quickly.

The "OEM as initiator–trainer" approach to supplier relationships has become quite popular in recent years, as have concepts such as "supply management" and "supplier development." These are all variations on one theme. The OEM is so desperate for suppliers that can satisfy its JIT requirements—equipping it to respond to a competitive crisis—that it is willing to go out and bring suppliers up to speed. Based on their knowledge of the market, suppliers should be able to take a much stronger role in this process. But because many industrial suppliers are not customer oriented, there's a wide gap between what customers want and what suppliers provide.

The supplier development approach may solve the OEM's problem but isn't the ideal solution for either the supplier or the customer. In relinquishing its marketing responsibilities, the supplier foregoes the chance to develop a competitive advantage in serving JIT OEMs. For the OEM, reverse marketing is less efficient than dealing with a market-driven, customer-oriented supplier. Manufacturers simply don't have the time or internal resources to take full responsibility for their suppliers' capabilities.

Ideally, the supplier shoulders much of the responsibility for transforming itself and its customers into world-class marketers. Rather than waiting for the JIT/TQC process to travel backward from the OEM, as in Fig. 1-1, the world-class supplier aggressively moves forward with those

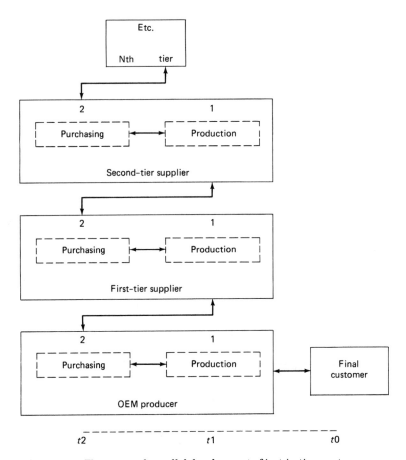

Figure 1-2   The proposed parallel development of just-in-time systems.

concepts. Its goal is to move, in parallel with customers, toward JIT operations, as shown in Fig. 1-2.

Marketers in all tiers can learn, develop, and implement JIT systems even as their common OEM customers gear up. This lets the supplier phase in its own JIT/TQC system to meet the JIT OEM customer's delivery and quality requirements. It also compresses the OEM's lead time in becoming a global competitor.

The customer-oriented supplier doesn't wait for key OEM accounts to initiate strategic partnerships. It takes—or at least shares—the initiative with the prospective OEM partner. This requires a "commitment to change" at all levels of the supplier organization. The change marshalls the *full* capabilities of *each* employee and uses them to create new products and services that ensure customer satisfaction.

The supplier's commitment to change hinges on several tasks, including the following:

• **Customer selection.** The supplier should evaluate potential customer partners as rigorously and comprehensively as the OEM evaluates suppliers; the stakes are just as high.

• **Determining customers' needs and requirements.** The supplier should echo the voice of the customer internally and to its own suppliers regarding costs, quality levels, function and performance of products and services, logistical requirements, and service delivery needs.

• **Planning to meet customer needs.** The up-front work needed to meet customer needs includes joint product design and value analysis/engineering, with the supplier and OEM both participating, and a quality assurance system keyed to the *final* customer's needs. The supplier also needs an in-house JIT/TQC system, fine tuned to customer requirements, and cooperative programs with second- and third-tier suppliers. They, like the first-tier supplier, should also initiate partnerships.

The industrial supplier is a critical contributor in its OEM customers' race to become effective global competitors; the stakes are very high for both organizations. To succeed, the supplier must forge a set of internal and external partnerships. These include the following:

• **Internal partnerships** among corporate functions that have direct stakes in the customer–supplier relationship. Because the supplier's sales and marketing department has the most significant stake in that relationship, it is the natural function to catalyze the suppliers' internal JIT/TQC program. Natural partners in the program include the supplier's research and development, product design, production, process engineering, purchasing, quality assurance, materials management, accounting, and information management departments. The partners' roles vary with the phase of the customer's product develoment cycle, which extends from the supplier's initial customer evaluation to post-sale service.

• **External partnerships** between the supplier functions noted above and their counterparts in the OEM customer organization. Again, their roles and levels of involvement vary with the product–development cycle. The customer function that naturally catalyzes or coordinates partnerships with suppliers is purchasing.

- **The supplier-carrier-customer partnership,** which carries the logistical burden for delivering the supplier's products and service. This partnership is critical because of the rigorous logistical requirements associated with successful JIT/TQC systems.

Each of these partnerships must be built on a philosophy of openness, trust, and cooperation. The supplier and OEM customer must tear down the traditional barriers, with each partner entering the arrangement much as they would a long-term marriage.

INTO THE FOURTH PERIOD

The opposing team—foreign competition—has run up an impressive third-period score. Underestimating the competition's strength, we in the United States have stuck with an outmoded game plan in which each player—OEM and supplier—strives for individual stardom. Our starters, the OEMs, are fatigued from playing so long with little relief. As we enter the game's fourth and final period, it is crucial that the American team modify its game plan to focus on world-class performance, with *all* players operating as a *team*.

Before the industrial marketer can work cooperatively with JIT OEMs, it must learn about JIT/TQC manufacturing and purchasing, and—equally important—develop its own game plan for becoming a world-class just-in-time industrial marketing organization.

NOTES

1. Tom Peters in a video presentation "The Forgotten Customer" broadcast on Public Television Network in 1987.
2. Robert H. Hayes and William J. Abernathy, "Managing our Way to Economic Decline," *Harvard Business Review*, July–August 1980, pp. 67–77.
3. Norman Jonas, "The Hollow Corporation," *Business Week*, March 3, 1986, p. 57.
4. Patrick Houston, "Fighting Back: It Can Work," *Business Week*, August 26, 1985, pp. 62–68.
5. James C. Abegglen and George Stalk, Jr., *Kaisha: The Japanese Corporation* (New York: Basic Books, 1985).
6. Frederick P. Stratton, Jr., "The Slumbering Giant is Awakening," *Target*, Summer 1986, p. 11.

7. John Hillkirk and Gary Jacobson, *Xerox: The American Samurai* (New York: Macmillan, 1986).

8. Rod Willis, "Harley Davidson Comes Roaring Back," *Management Review*, March 1986, pp. 20–27; and Gene Schwind "MAN Arrives Just in Time to Save Harley-Davidson," *Material Handling Engineering*, August 1984, pp. 28–36.

9. Vaughn Beals, in a presentation at 1987 Association For Manufacturing Excellence, "What the World Needs ... Manufacturing Excellence," October 1987, Orlando, Fla.

10. Masaaki Imai, *Kaisen: The Key to Japan's Competitive Success* (New York: Random House, 1986).

11. William J. Weisz, Keynote Presentation at the 1986 Association for Manufacturing Excellence Conference, "Strategies for World Class Manufacturing Excellence," October 1986, Chicago, Ill.

12. This study was reported in the article "American Industry Goes Ape over Just-in-time Strategy," *Purchasing*, September 12, 1985, pp. 21–23.

13. This follow-up study was reported in "Competitive Jitters Fuel JIT Movement in U.S.," *Purchasing*, January 15, 1987, pp. 33–34.

14. Albert F. Celley, William H. Clegg, Arthur W. Smith, and Mark A. Vonderembse, "Implementation of JIT in the United States," *Journal of Purchasing and Materials Management*, January 1987, pp. 9–15.

15. A. Ansari and Batoul Modaress, "Just-in-Time Purchasing: Problems and Solutions," *Journal of Purchasing and Materials Management*, August 1986, pp. 11–15.

PART 1: ADDITIONAL SUGGESTED READINGS

William Abernathy, Kim Clark, and Alan Kantrow, *Industrial Renaissance: Producing a Competitive Future for America* (New York: Basic Books, Inc., 1983).

Joseph Callahan, "Automotive Industry Action Group: Middle Management Takes Charge," *Automotive Industries*, March 1983, pp. 31–32.

Judith Dobrinski and Thane Peterson, "Fighting Back: It Can Work," *Business Week*, August 26, 1985, pp. 62–68.

Brian Dumaine, "Donald Petersen: A Humble Hero Drives Ford to the Top," *Fortune*, January 4, 1988, pp. 23–24.

"JIT Hits American Industry—But Not Without Drawbacks," *Purchasing*, September 11, 1986, pp. 18–19.

"MAN Arrives Just in Time to Save Harley-Davidson," *Materials Handling Engineering*, August 1984, pp. 28–34.

James P. Morgan, "The Facts about Just-in-Time, Japan, and Japanese Business," *Purchasing*, December 19, 1985, pp. 43–50.

Sylvia Nasar, "America's Competitive Revival," *Fortune*, January 4, 1988, p. 44.

Joe Quinlan, "Just-in-Time—It's Seeping into Every Cell," *Handling and Shipping Management,* September 1984, p. 7.

John Ryan, "Vaughn L. Beals: The Man Who Made the Eagle Soar," *Quality Progress,* May 1986, pp. 84–88.

Richard Schonberger, *World Class Manufacturing* (New York: The Free Press, 1987).

Sherry Siegel, "Competing Through Manufacturing: Robert Hayes on Revitalizing America," *Management Review,* March 1985, pp. 21–23.

Arthur Spinella, "Toyota City," *Ward's Auto World,* June 1983, pp. 31–33.

"Xerox Preaches the Gospel of Just-in-Time to Suppliers," *Purchasing,* October 24, 1985, pp. 21–23.

Rod Willis, "Harley-Davidson Comes Roaring Back," *Management Review,* March 1986, pp. 21–27.

All the Rules Change

Chapter 2

Just-in-Time Operations Philosophy

When companies choose to adopt the JIT philosophy, they may not realize just how different it is from what they're used to: JIT runs counter to most traditional practices. That makes it very difficult to implement, because everyone involved needs to change his or her mindset. Achieving that new attitude—which is really just an openness to change—is without a doubt the toughest obstacle to successful implementation.

Experts on the subject have defined and interpreted just-in-time systems in many ways. We would like to offer three simple but profound concepts that characterize the just-in-time industrial marketer's operating philosophy.

1. Definition. Just-in-time is a business *philosophy* that focuses on removing waste from all the organization's *internal* activities and from *external* exchange activities.

This definition establishes the basic thrust of just-in-time—*waste elimination*—which requires removing *all* resource inputs that don't add value to the product or service. It also hints at its scope. Discussion of JIT systems tends to center on the production process. This is a very important aspect of just-in-time, but our definition is broader. We include linkages forward to customers, and backward to suppliers, which are equally important in implementing the JIT philosophy.

2. Objective. The goal is to provide customer satisfaction while minimizing total cost. This is the essence of a just-in-time process that integrates *total quality commitment.* We equate customer satisfaction with total quality, because both require conformance to requirements. By the same token, a JIT/TQC program, well designed and implemented, continuously reduces costs.

3. Strategy. Through a program of *continuous improvement,* the JIT marketer provides:

- perfect quality products, in
- exact quantities needed, at the
- precise time needed, at the
- lowest total delivered cost.

That's a challenging assignment and one that can't be completed quickly. Some may see it as a pie-in-the-sky strategy, especially those who aren't yet JIT/TQC advocates. It's true that the marketer won't conform perfectly to customer requirements for product quality, delivery, service, and cost. However, state-of-the-art JIT/TQC organizations are approaching that level. Continuous improvement is the strategy's key goal.

A critical element in achieving that goal is *total player involvement,* which starts with top management committing to this rather revolutionary philosophy. The JIT philosophy must filter down from the top, because it usually requires a complete change in corporate culture. To successfully implement a JIT system, the company needs an environment in which "the players"—employees—are intimately and continuously involved in working out the game strategy and the game plan's details.

To lead the way, top management must understand the basics of just-in-time processes, total quality control, and total people involvement. Senior managers must become the catalyst for change within the organization, providing motivation and resources for employee education and training, and process development and implementation.

The most crucial aspect of total people involvement is allowing all employees to work at their full potential. By providing incentives for innovative solutions, management can help employees find creative ways to do their jobs. The really important people in this process are the front-line employees—line operators, sales and customer-service reps, buyers, materials handlers, and so on. JIT/TQC education develops these people's skills and fosters their creativity.

In addition to training and educating employees, top managers must reshape the corporate culture. The goal is to tear down barriers that inhibit communication and keep workers from cooperating and trusting each other and their customers and suppliers. Internal barriers are common and may separate departments such as marketing, engineering, manufacturing, purchasing, and quality control.

There are often barriers between the company and major customers and suppliers as well. Those barriers make external relationships adversarial rather than cooperative and stifle creativity in serving the final product marketer—the common customer. Figure 2-1 presents a conceptual overview of the just-in-time operating philosophy, showing its scope and outlining opportunities for eliminating waste.

Management must ask three questions to evaluate internal operations as well as customer and supplier linkages. We will study supplier linkage in depth in Chapter 4 and focus on customer linkage in the following chapters, but a brief overview of the customer's and supplier's role will help put things in perspective.

Poor customer linkage can cause massive waste. Because the system's goal is to provide customer satisfaction, or conformance to requirements, the marketer must carefully determine and specify buyer requirements *from the customer's viewpoint.* Herein lies the problem. The offering—physical product plus delivery plus service—that the marketer designs as it believes the customer wants it, generally causes a lot of waste in design, production, delivery, and/or post-sale service (which may be needed to "make it fit" the customer's specifications).

The loudest voices in such cases are usually those of the marketer's engineering, manufacturing, or marketing departments rather than of

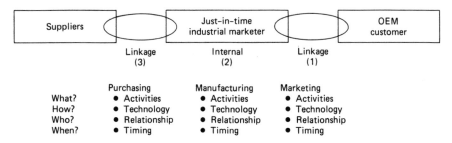

Figure 2-1 Scope of JIT operations, and waste elimination opportunities.

customers. The answer is a system that amplifies the customer's voice, with everyone in the JIT industrial marketing firm hearing and responding to it.

On the supply side, a prime goal for the JIT industrial marketer is to receive purchased materials at lowest total delivered cost. This is critical in controlling final product cost. If the just-in-time OEM emphasizes unit price instead of total delivered cost, it wastes money. The JIT manufacturer may also foster waste by failing to clearly communicate product, delivery, and service requirements to suppliers; insisting on arms-length negotiations; or demanding just-in-time service before the supplier and its own organization can accommodate it.

The JIT OEM customer sets the pace for the just-in-time process by anticipating and responding to final product demand. Upstream channel members and the JIT marketer itself adjust their timing and quantities to meet the market's needs as demand pulls their products through the system. The objective is to mesh the upstream flows precisely with final demand, providing products that meet the customer's requirements every time and at the lowest possible total delivered cost.

The next section, "Getting Started," paints with a broad brush the changes that must take place within the JIT marketer's organization to meet this goal. It also documents companies that have adopted the dynamic trio of just-in-time, total quality commitment, and total people involvement (TPI).

For excellent detailed accounts of the JIT manufacturing process, see Robert Hall's *Zero Inventories,* and Richard Schonberger's *Japanese Manufacturing Techniques.* Broader, more current insights are included in Hall's *Attaining Manufacturing Excellence,* and Schonberger's *World Class Manufacturing.*[1]

GETTING STARTED

A successful JIT/TQC/TPI process starts with people, namely people with the motivation, basic understanding, and authority to commit necessary resources to process development. This group must include an untiring champion of the cause, ideally the organization's CEO.

Perhaps the greatest barrier to starting a JIT program is employees' initial resistance, which may reflect complacency. The company is performing acceptably, so why change? Typically, the complacent attitude changes to urgency as a competitive crisis erupts. Companies that haven't experienced a domestic or international competitive crisis yet soon will—though perhaps not soon enough to avoid severe market share erosion. That's a real waste because, as we all know, it takes much less effort and fewer resources to maintain share than to regain it.

Another common reason for delay is fear of the unknown, particularly if the organization has no positive data on similar firms with JIT programs. The risk of breaking new ground, and possibly threatening the business in the process, holds companies back.

A third barrier is management's unwillingness to scrap time-proven operational techniques. This is a tough one to overcome. After years of success, it's hard to justify:

- Letting expensive equipment sit idle just because the manufacturer doesn't currently need its output.

- Making frequent setups when economies of scale suggest long production runs.

- Cutting back work-in-process buffer stocks when, based on historical problems in quality, machine breakdown, and numerous other areas, the manufacturer could expect to need that stock.

- Working as a long-term partner with a single supplier for purchased materials when we know multiple sourcing more nearly assures delivery as needed and certainly yields the lowest unit price.

- Eliminating incoming and in-process inspections when defective products will clearly result.

These are just a few of the traditional practices that created yesterday's market leaders. How can a manufacturer reverse those to gain a leading role today—and tomorrow? The first step is convincing top management of the need for a change. To eliminate waste, the organization's leaders must remove the formidable barriers of complacency, uncertainity, and unwillingness to revamp traditional practice.

Only committed managers can change those attitudes. Commitment at the top motivates employees and sets the tone for change, starting with education and training for everyone from senior managers to line workers. In addition to moral support, top management supplies the financial and human resources needed to overhaul the organization.

But commitment alone is not enough. Top managers must understand the broad philosophy of JIT, TQC, and TPI. They need to grasp the basic concepts behind eliminating waste and boosting performance. One of the best ways for them to learn is to study successful JIT/TQC/TPI programs in operation. The Association for Manufacturing Excellence is an excellent resource for such learning; managers may attend workshops on key JIT topics at plants with world-class just-in-time capabilities.

After top management understands and commits to the new philosophy, the challenge is to convert everyone else in the organization. Education is the secret behind most successful JIT marketers' operations. Firms
that are gaining market share via JIT marketing invest significant
amounts to teach *all* employees how to eliminate waste. They reinforce
that education with training in JIT practices. In addition to imparting
specific how-to skills, the educational process generates companywide
enthusiasm for the new methods.

Because it's not feasible to educate and train the entire work force
all at once, the marketer should focus on one work group and set up a pilot
operation. This limits the number of employees who need immediate
training and makes for a faster start-up. The initial training motivates
and educates the pilot group, but other organizational units also benfit as
the initial trainees go on to educate others. That multiplies the initial
training's results and accelerates the educational process. On a less
quantifiable plane, this approach gets all employees deeply involved and
committed to developing creative solutions to operational problems. The
waste elimination process requires interaction between the four key elements shown in Fig. 2-2.

These four elements must be carefully coordinated so the right people are doing the right things (activities) the right way (technology) at the
right time (timing). All the elements focus on one thing: eliminating
waste.

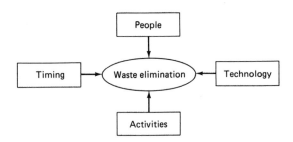

Figure 2-2   Waste elimination through interaction of people, activities, technology, and timing.

FLESHING OUT THE FRAMEWORK

Tables 2-1(a) and 2-1(b) add a first level of detail to the just-in-time
process by considering important production issues and the equally critical issues of demand scheduling and product design. Table 2-1(a) considers the activity, responsibility, timing, and technology, while Table 2-1(b)
includes the waste reduction elements.

TABLE 2-1(a) Resource Elements of the JIT/TQC/TPI Waste Elimination Process

	Product		P R O C E S S				Demand
Activity	**Design**	**Housekeeping**	**Equipment maintenance**	**Layout**	**Model changeover**	**Quality**	**Scheduling**
Responsibility	Team	Work team	Team	Team	Work team	Work team	Team
Timing	Customer determined	Continuous	On-and off shift	Transitional	Frequent	Continuous	Daily
Technology	DFA standardization Taguchi Valve engineering	Keep it visible	Preventive	Group (cell)	SMED	SPC QFD	Computer pull system

TABLE 2-1(b) Waste Reduction Elements of JIT/TQC/TPI

	Product		P R O C E S S				Demand
Waste reduction elements	Incorrect designs	Space Clutter	Downtime Defective products	Material handling People utilization	Setup times Quality costs	Inspection Production disruption	Scheduling variability
	Complexity	Searching		Work center flexibility	Inventory reduction		Back orders
	Non-std	Image				Scrap and rework	Lack of synchronization
	Not cost-optimized			Rework space	Handling		Overproduction

PRODUCT DESIGN

The activity with the most potential for waste elimination is undoubtedly product design. Products have a lot of built-in waste when they're designed by the research and development function to meet what the engineering department *thinks* are customer requirements, and are then handed over to manufacturing to produce.

To eliminate that waste, marketers must design their products to meet customer needs as the customer sees them. It must also keep simplicity, cost, and ease of manufacturing and service in mind. This is a tall order—one beyond the capabilities of the design engineer working alone. A design *team* is required. The team should include representatives from the customer's company, including someone from purchasing, as well as the marketer's design and process engineers.

The customer representatives can provide data on required product features and characteristics that go far beyond the printed specification. The emphasis is on critical dimensions and performance characteristics rather than detailed product specifications. This frees the designer to select materials and design features that provide the necessary functions at minimum cost.

The customer design representatives need to understand the JIT marketer's internal processes and capabilities. Similarly, the marketer's design and process engineering representative must understand how the OEM customer will further process the material or component. And the JIT marketer's purchasing representative needs to know the capabilities and limitations of second- and third-tier suppliers that will supply materials and parts.

The JIT marketer's process engineer makes sure the product is easy to manufacture by encouraging simple designs that use fewer, and standard parts, referred to as design for assembly (DFA). Incorporating fewer parts means fewer steps in manufacturing. It also means fewer part numbers, which cuts the number of suppliers the manufacturer must certify and communicate with. The JIT marketer may eliminate even more waste by standardizing parts across the various models it produces.

For example, General Electric Company totally redesigned its dishwasher line to accommodate new production technology, including just-in-time processes. By switching to one standard tub and frame, GE reduced the number of parts in its fifteen models by 25%, and reduced product weight by fifteen to twenty-five pounds per unit. The company now uses 850 parts and assemblies to produce these fifteen models—down from 5,600.[2]

A technology that focuses on product design quality, called the Taguchi Methods (TM), has recently been introduced into the United States. Named for Genichi Taguchi, the technology's developer and winner of four Deming prizes for quality, the TM combine engineering with statistics to rapidly create optimal product and process designs. Two of the TM techniques are particularly relevant: quality evaluation and quality improvement.

In *quality evaluation*, TM uses the "loss function" to define and evaluate quality. Loss refers to costs the producer incurs, and cost benefits it foregoes, relative to baseline values. Quality loss is proportional to deviation from the target value, which is ideal performance (see Fig. 2-3). This means that conformance within arbitrary specification limits, or tolerances, isn't a meaningful measure of quality. The producer's primary consideration should be the variation of performance around the target, or nominal value.

Let's assume the design characteristic of interest is the diameter of the front door hinge pins of a two-door automobile. This characteristic is specified for processing with a target (nominal) value and a tolerance (range) on either side of the target value, for example, a target of 0.5 inches and tolerance of ± .05 inches. Products falling within the limits—from .45- to .55-inch diameters—will be acceptable. Conventional quality methods would consider all hinge pins falling within the stated control limits as equally acceptable—of equal value.

The TM approach doesn't accept the conventional idea that everything within the established specifications is equally good and everything outside them is equally bad. Instead it says anything deviating from the target value—even within the specifications—causes loss. In the hinge pin example, the loss may be measured in terms of extra friction from a pin on the high side; with additional wear, and added effort to open and close the door. The greater the deviation, the greater the loss. Based on this idea, all quality improvements can be measured in cost savings.

TM also offers new ideas for *quality improvement*. The approach that U.S. companies most commonly use to reduce loss through product design is called "parameter design." This relies on experimental design methods to find the optimal product design: one that makes the product insensitive to manufacturing and field variables, such as excessive opening and closing of the automobile door.

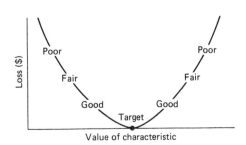

Figure 2-3 The Taguchi continuous
loss function.

In contrast, TM can substantially improve design using relatively few experiments. For example, if a manufacturer wanted to find the best combination of four product variables, the traditional approach would require trying eighty-one different combinations, or experiments. TM would use only nine. ITT, one of the pioneers in Taguchi Methods, used TM to increase the weld-splice strength in wire harness assemblies until it exceeded the wire's core strength. Those results saved the organization $300,000 per year in testing and reduced field failures.[3]

TM is new to America, but Japanese companies, specifically Toyota, have used them for more than a decade. This approach is responsible for a significant share of Toyota's quality improvement in the past ten years. ITT has reported cost savings of $35 million thanks to these methods.[4] Ford Motor Company, which started using the Taguchi Methods in 1982, is another U.S. pioneer. Other American firms are also starting to apply the Taguchi approach, spurred on by the American Supplier Institute, which provides information and training in the methods.

The just-in-time process requires extremely high quality; perfect quality is the goal. Quality begins with product and process design. Design simplicity and standardization, and ease of manufacturing, measurement, and service are all key quality concepts. Some of the more important JIT processing concepts follow.

WORK CENTER PREPARATION

"A place for everything and everything in its place" is an appropriate motto for the conventional work center, but not for the just-in-time workplace. The JIT work center has room for only the bare essentials needed to do the job effectively and efficiently. This means all unnecessary items must go. The company should ask a few basic questions in evaluating the items in its work centers. After asking, "Why is it here?", planners should ask, "Is it adding value to the product?" This is the acid test. If the item doesn't add value, it shouldn't be in the work center. And if it can't add value in another location, get rid of it.

After identifying essential items, the company should assign them to specific locations. That requires careful study to determine where they can provide the most value at least cost. Once the items are moved, they should *always* remain in their new locations, unless the company identifies a better place or finds a way to eliminate them altogether.

In planning a work center, as in product design, the manufacturer should "keep it simple," removing unnecessary items and placing necessary ones in defined locations. These steps eliminate the waste associated with poorly planned work centers. In addition to wasting space, poorly laid out work areas interfere with the efficient flow of materials. And that wastes time and effort, because workers must locate materials, tools, and equipment as needed.

The quality of the workplace often drives the entire quality process. A quality work environment gives all materials and processes *high visibility* and provides *shorter distances* for materials and workers to move and a *smoother flow* of materials throughout the process.

The work center team—comprised of the line workers operating the process—is responsible for workplace preparation. This team, though it needs help from manufacturing engineering and industrial engineering, is primarily responsible for the workplace. That area's appearance reflects the team members' quality attitude. That attitude, and good housekeeping, are critical to just-in-time quality.

The JIT philosophy makes each member of the line operation team highly responsible: total responsibility for total quality. The team members are responsible for preparing, for doing, for correcting, and for cleaning up. Each team member must understand how to do each of the team's tasks.

Because these concepts represent a complete reversal of the traditional approach—worker specialization—education and training are crucial. The workers need to understand how they'll benefit from a broader approach to work. For example, as generalists, they may contribute more fully to the total value-added process, and that is fulfilling. A broader view also gives them more flexibility within the organization. The team leader, who already knows how to do all the required tasks, can train workers to do everything from workplace preparation to cleanup.

U.S. firms are applying this approach to team member total responsibility. NUMMI, the Toyota/General Motors joint venture that produces Nova and Toyota automobiles in Fremont, California, has been very successful in using a team approach.[5] Management expects team members to do their assigned jobs, but also to learn other team members' jobs. The company also asks them to follow the "kaisen" continuous improvement approach, which means workers constantly search for better ways to do each task involved in their operations.

NUMMI applies the team concept throughout its organization. The results speak for themselves: NUMMI's productivity is the highest of any U.S. GM facility, and its quality levels rival those of world-class Toyota.

EQUIPMENT MAINTENANCE

The two goals of equipment maintenance are to extend the equipment's useful life and to assure the quality of products the equipment processes. Both are important, but the latter is critical.

The just-in-time process doesn't allow defectives, which means preventive maintenance for processing equipment, fixtures, and the instruments used to measure and test performance is particularly important. If test equipment used to monitor quality is improperly calibrated, it may generate two kinds of waste: The manufacturer may accept products that fall outside the specification, or reject products that meet it.

It's best to leave preventive maintenance, except major overhauls, to the line operator who uses the equipment. This can eliminate a great deal of waste. The manufacturer may change the maintenance workers' role, using them primarily to train line operators. Line operators responsible for their equipment's maintenance and the quality of goods it produces generally treat the machinery with tender loving care, reducing maintenance needs. They are also available when needed, which eliminates the delay of waiting for a maintenance specialist.

The JIT manufacturer may schedule major maintenance activities for off-shift hours to avoid disrupting production. That may require revamping some production practices. Manufacturers such as Ford Motor Company are starting to move from three shifts per day to two. That allows plenty of off-shift time for equipment maintenance and changeover. The Japanese generally use this approach. And they generate about the same output in the two-shift operation because of reduced downtime and higher product quality.

LAYOUT

The traditional factory is separated into departments, each specializing in a particular processing operation: stamping, forming, cleaning/coating, assembling, and so forth. These processes, especially assembly, are usually laid out in a line, with the product moving from one work station to the next, sequentially. Each preassembly department may process large lots and feed assembly lines dedicated to various different models. The company justifies its large lot sizes on the basis of the expense—in downtime and humanpower—of changing over the equipment.

This departmental approach, with its large lot sizes and linear processing, generates a lot of waste. Materials and work-in-progress must be transported and handled frequently. Raw and in-process materials travel great distances to get from one processing department to the next. The quantities moved are often large and require handling equipment such as forklifts. Those, in turn, require large aisles and turnaround areas to maneuver. Neither transporting nor handling in-process material adds value to the final product.

It also takes a lot of space to hold in-process inventory, which can't be moved to the next department until the entire lot is processed. Taking up space are incoming materials, not yet processed, and outgoing materials awaiting the completion of the rest of the lot. Each department also holds a buffer inventory just in case a disruption of upstream processing or defective incoming materials interrupts the materials supply chain. Because this work-in-process inventory consumes so much floor space, processing units must be widely separated, making quality problems hard to detect.

Finally, this system is not very flexible. The equipment is set up to run large lots. The workers are trained to do a specific operation. The maintenance staff maintains the equipment; the custodial staff cleans; every worker has a specific assignment and job classification.

There are several alternatives to this layout approach, but the cellular approach, also called "group technology," prevails among just-in-time producers.

The cellular or cell layout groups production equipment by family. All the equipment needed to manufacture a particular part or assembly is clustered together, generally in a "U" shape. Materials move from station to station around the U, with each station performing a specific operation. This approach is especially useful when parts or assemblies are small enough to move by hand from station to station. The mechines are placed close enough for hand transfer.

Each manufacturing cell becomes a minifactory. Each cell concentrates on producing families of products—parts, assemblies, or final products—that share configurations, materials, technologies, or skill requirements.

The cellular approach to JIT processing provides many advantages. It reduces work-in-process inventory, materials transportation and handling, and time in storage. At the same time, this approach increases processing flexibility and improves quality.

With the cell approach, work stations are close together, eliminating buffer inventory space and minimizing the distance materials, work-in-process, and personnel must travel. The preferred approach is a continuous process in which each station processes a single unit and passes it to the next station, eliminating the need for in-process inventory buildup. If the completed units are components or assemblies, workers transport them in very small lot sizes to the next cell for final processing or preparation for shipment.

The approach reduces transportation and handling by locating production materials and tooling near the cell. Delivery of production materials directly to the point of use by suppliers eliminates the circuitous path from the stockroom to the processing department. The direct flow of materials to, and through, the cell minimizes travel distance and rehandling during the manufacturing process.

A key JIT objective is to eliminate any time during which value is not added to the product. Receiving material at the exact time needed is a major step toward this goal. Adding value to the product without interruption is also a goal of the cellular approach. Materials do not sit between operations with this method. And the completed units move quickly to the external or internal customer.

The cell approach offers both equipment and personnel flexibility. To maintain flexibility, each cell should be autonomous. Its equipment must be simple, standard, easy to set up, and have a short cycle time, and it shouldn't be constrained by a large, expensive, complex feeder. On the people side, all of a cell's team members must know how to do each of the cell's tasks. To help workers learn all those jobs, management should keep the total number of tasks reasonably small. The company may adjust the cell's output by adding or removing team members.

Quality improvement naturally results from the cell arrangement. Because buffer stock is limited—preferably eliminated—and because each work station processes a single unit before passing it on, cells produce in very small lot sizes. Consequently, quality problems are immediately apparent. Because all team members inspect their own output, the cellular approach minimizes the number of defective units.

In fact, a cell's processing stops when a defective emerges; team members determine and correct the problem before processing any more units. This reduces the defective lot size to one item, rather than 100 or 1,000, which conventional systems often produce. This eliminates a lot of rework and scrap. But to achieve this ideal, materials delivered to the cell must be perfect or near perfect. Quality problems quickly become visible when they can't hide in large lots of incoming materials and work-in-process stocks.

Many U.S. companies have moved, or are moving to, the cell manufacturing arrangement. Eastman Kodak Company (EK) began a program in 1985 to apply the just-in-time and cellular production approaches to its slide projector product line. This line includes sixteen different models and 565 different parts and subassemblies.

The company's previous system was inventory driven, with the plants holding tremendous inventories at all manufacturing points to assure quality products. Under that system, line operators thought their work was redundant; the average operation was about three minutes long. To shift from traditional assembly to the cellular approach, the company chose volunteers from the lines and told them to develop teams that would be responsible for building the entire projector.

To complete that assignment, the volunteers developed expectations of daily output and concentrated on quality. They felt individual ownership of their work. Quality increased immediately, moving within two years from 97% to 99.6% defect-free units. The cell approach also boosted throughput. By late 1987, the company's ten internal (intracompany supplier departments) suppliers were daily delivering 565 discrete parts—

100% of the internally manufactured parts—to the cells on a just-in-time basis, up from ten parts initially.[6]

Eastman Kodak's Circuit Board Assembly Operation illustrated the value of the product-family approach to cellular manufacturing. This EK operation produces about 700 active circuit board assemblies. As in its slide projector program, EK adopted the cell approach as it developed a JIT program. The operation moved from a linear series of process steps with queuing of in-process inventory at each step, which took more than sixty days to complete, to a "total build cell" with five-day cycle time. The first 600 circuit boards produced earned 95% customer acceptance, versus the usual 44% rate.

Eastman's initial cell approach routed any circuit board to an assembly team. This made it hard for the teams to learn how to assemble the boards and produced quality fluctuations. The company solved the problem by creating circuit board "families": groups of circuit boards with similar characteristics. Each cell became responsible for one or more families. Consequently, EK reduced learning curves and defect rates for assembled products.[7]

MODEL CHANGEOVER

Ideally, just-in-time producers should manufacture products as needed by customers, in the exact quantities needed. This presents a dilemma for firms using traditional manufacturing techniques, especially as the variety of products that customers require multiplies.

Historically, manufacturers have satisfied customer demand via long production runs of single models. The company either stored the excess until needed or made large monthly or quarterly stocking shipments to customers. They justified this approach using two production concepts: fixed-cost allocation and the learning curve.

With fixed-cost allocation, the manufacturer treats setup cost as a fixed cost. As the number of units produced per setup grows, the setup cost per unit decreases.

The learning curve concept maintains that workers "learn" during production runs. The first units produced are usually processed at a *slower rate,* because start-up adjustments are needed. Those units are of lower quality—often defectives, in fact—because the process isn't fine tuned yet.

These large lot sizes also boost inventory carrying costs for the producing firm, the customer, or both. The manufacturing community has only recently recognized these costs' magnitude. Inventories' annual carrying cost can reach 30% to 45% of the product's total value.

Manufacturers have justified those carrying costs by viewing them as a trade-off. They considered the setup cost a "given" fixed cost and said the lower setup costs per unit associated with large production runs offset the high carrying costs. What they didn't consider were other cost elements, such as quality, scrap, and overall productivity.

In 1972, Toyota Motor Corporation tackled this problem in earnest. The company made Shigeo Shingo, the pioneer in setup time reduction, responsible for reducing Toyota's setup time. Between 1972 and 1973, Shingo reduced a tooling setup from two hours to less than ten minutes; he reduced it further still, to less than a minute, by 1975. That's more than a 100:1 reduction. This allowed Toyota to handle many different products with existing equipment.

Shingo's creative efforts in setup time reduction destroyed many long-held manufacturing myths. He makes several points that are critical to improving the model changeover process:

- Workers must believe dramatic reductions are possible. This is a tough one. It's easy for people to think, "It won't work in our shop." Shingo suggests starting the process on one production line to gain experience, then transferring that experience to other lines.
- Involve the machine operators in the process. Use their ideas. Train them. Let the operator be part of the setup process.
- Avoid adjustments that are aimed at positioning the part. Parts should be positioned on contact, eliminating the need for adjustment. Adjustments depend on the right "touch," and that varies by operator, thus, they should be avoided.
- Setup changes should produce defect-free products, starting with the first unit.

Shingo has developed five simple but effective rules for reducing setup time. They are:

1. Separate internal setup activities—which require shutting down operations—from external setup tasks.
2. Move as many of the internal activities as possible to external activities. For example, preheating molding dies (external activity) before they are attached, rather than attaching cold dies which must be gradually heated to the appropriate temperature (internal activity).
3. Minimize the time required to make the internal setup.
4. Minimize the time required to make the external setup.
5. Repeat the first four steps to ensure continuous improvement.

Shingo documents this process, the "single minute exchange of die" (SMED),[8] very well in his book, *A Revolution in Manufacturing: SMED*. By trusting in the system and following these simple rules, just-in-time manu-

facturers have virtually destroyed the learning-curve and economies-of-scale myths.
Using these techniques, U.S. firms are achieving results similar to Toyota in Japan. There are hundreds of examples. Consider the following:

- NUMMI can change all the dies on one press line in about fourteen minutes. The process takes a typical U.S. plant a few hours.
- After Omark Corporation introduced a SMED program, its Oroville, Oregon, plant reduced setup time on press dies from six-and-one-half hours to forty seconds.
- Richardson-Vicks Home Care Products, Torshalla, Sweden, cut changeover time on coughdrop lines from one complete eight-hour shift to eighteen minutes.
- FMC Corporation, Aiken, South Carolina, cut setup times in its cargo hatch shop by 60% to 90%.

In 1986, *Automotive Industries* magazine issued a Quick Die Change challenge to the automotive industry.[9] Five U.S. stamping plants participated in the competition. To evaluate the plants, the judges started the stopwatch when the last good piece came off the line, let the watch run as workers changed the die, and stopped the watch when the first *quality* piece came off the line. It typically takes eight hours to change dies in a U.S. stamping plant, and less than fifteen minutes in Japan.

Participants competed in three categories, as defined by the line's automation level: "fully automated," "semiautomated," and "manual." The results are summarized in Table 2-2.

TABLE 2-2   Automobile Industry Die Change Comparison 1985–1987

Competition Category	1985	1986	% Change 1985–1986	1987	% Change 1986–1987
Fully Automated					
Nissan	25 min	13 min 17 sec	47%	6 min 33 sec	50%
GM-BOC	4 hr	10 min 36 sec	95%	9 min 31 sec	10%
Semiautomated					
Honda	8 min	5 min 14 sec	34%	4 min 38 sec	11%
GM-BOC	90 min	13 min 7 sec	85%	10 min 44 sec	17%
Manual					
GM	12 hr	26 min	96%	23 min 53 sec	8%

In the fully automated category, Nissan's Smyrna, Tennessee, facility changed the die in thirteen minutes and seventeen seconds. In 1985, the process took twenty-five minutes. General Motors' fully automated Buick-Oldsmobile-Cadillac (BOC) facility in North Lansing, Michigan, took ten minutes and thirty-six seconds, versus four hours in 1985.

In the semiautomated category, Honda's Maryville, Ohio, plant took just five minutes and fourteen seconds—versus eight minutes in 1985. And GM's South Lansing, Michigan, BOC team changed the die in thirteen minutes and seven seconds. That was down from ninety minutes in 1985.

In the manual category, GM's Lordstown, Ohio, BOC plant took twenty-six minutes, compared with twelve hours in 1985. These tremendous improvements in die change times, ranging from 47% to 96% reductions from 1985 levels, are certainly a reason for celebration by the participants. The new levels of achievement would have been considered impossible just a few years ago. But rather than resting on their laurels, these just-in-time enthusiasts are committed to kaisen—as demonstrated in the results achieved one year later—in the 1987 competition. In every instance, the 1987 times were below those of 1986, with year-to-year reductions ranging from 8% to 50%.[10] The substantially lower times by the Japanese producers—Nissan and Honda—in 1985 reflect previous commitments to kaisen and application of Shingo's SMED principles.

As these results indicate, manufacturers can substantially reduce waste by reducing changeover times and switching to small lot production that is keyed to customer demand.

SCHEDULE STABILITY

A consistent production schedule is essential in just-in-time manufacturing. With JIT, there's no buffer inventory sitting around "just-in-case" of a schedule change. Unfortunately, a stable schedule has traditionally been the exception rather than the rule in most industries. Auto makers have historically stabilized schedules only two or three days in advance—which is obviously insufficient lead time for their suppliers to plan production schedules. Consequently, their suppliers either overproduced, causing waste, or didn't produce enough.

Because the just-in-time system is keyed to final demand, a solid final demand forecast is critical. This provides the basis for the schedules of the JIT manufacturers, their suppliers, and their suppliers' suppliers. Producing high-quality customer demand forecasts requires close working relationships between suppliers and customers at all linking points in the supply chain, from raw materials processor to final product dealer. Each supplier must understand its customer's business and the forces that shape short- and long-term demand. The supplier organizations must also learn to minimize cycle times, within practical limits.

Industrial customers must give their suppliers fixed schedules with advance warning at least equal to the suppliers' delivery lead time. If there is a substantial gap between these two periods—the fixed-schedule length and supplier lead time to delivery—both organizations must focus on reducing it.

The automotive industry, with AIAG's leadership, is making major strides in schedule stabilization.[11] Auto firms have focused on:

- improving the scheduling system
- reducing transportation uncertainty
- developing more reliable forecasts
- reducing manufacturing uncertainty
- reducing communication delays between plants and suppliers
- improving coordination of engineering changes
- reducing product complexity

In 1981, Ford began to measure how actual production schedules varied from plan. It started with a firm, four-week assembly operation. Over a two- to three-week period, variability equaled 29%. The company has since reduced that to about 8%. One of Ford's techniques is to combine option packages rather than offering each feature individually. This improves demand predictability. The company's goal is to establish a two-week production schedule, right down to individual part numbers, with no changes during the two weeks. If something interrupts the schedule, the company stops production, solves the problem, and resumes production rather than diverting to products scheduled for other times.

In 1986, Chrysler adopted a fixed ten-day supplier at four assembly plants. The ten-day period exceeded the production cycle time of most Chrysler suppliers, which meant they could deliver just-in-time.

Ideal just-in-time linkages occur when the JIT producer firms up its schedules and communicates them well in advance—allowing suppliers to provide parts, components, and assemblies directly to the point-of-use and in the sequence in which they'll be used. Such linkage is happening as more and more just-in-time suppliers and OEM producers implement computer-based pull systems keyed to final demand.

QUALITY

We've all heard a lot about "quality" since the early 1980s. Increasingly, the focus on quality is more than just talk; U.S. firms serious about becoming world-class competitors are finally taking steps to boost their offerings' quality.

Quality guru Philip B. Crosby has contributed significantly to the U.S. quality movement, both by motivating companies to develop quality processes and by understanding how to proceed. His widely disseminated "Absolutes of Quality Management" form a sound base for quality improvement.[12] The four absolutes center on the *definition* of quality; the *system* that avoids defects; performance *standards;* and *measurement.*

• The first absolute is that "the definition of quality is conformance to requirements." Crosby's definition of conformance emphasizes the customer's point of view. This eliminates a tremendous number of engineering- and management-generated requirements that don't meet customers' needs—and the associated waste.

• Crosby's second absolute says, "The system of quality is prevention" of defects. Companies achieve this through proper product and process design and process control systems.

• His third absolute is uncompromising: "The performance standard is zero defects." This may sound unrealistic to the uninitiated, but it's the just-in-time producer's ideal. Companies with state-of-the-art systems are using the zero-defect approach.

• The last absolute says, "The measurement of quality is the price of nonconformance." That price factors in the cost of everything that wouldn't need doing if everything were done right the first time.

Three others who have preached the quality concept and provided great insights and implementation techniques are W. Edwards Deming and J. M. Juran of the United States, and Kaoru Ishikawa of Japan. Deming and Juran, who failed to get the attention of U.S. firms in the 1950s and 1960s, spent those years helping Japanese firms develop quality processes.

Ishikawa emphasizes *total quality control* to "develop, design, produce, and service a quality product which is most useful and always satisfactory to the consumer." With his approach, everyone in the company, from CEO to line worker, promotes and actively participates in the quality process.

Clearly, we cannot divorce quality from the just-in-time process. The two are interdependent. Just-in-time processes require quality input and they produce quality products and services. Each just-in-time process—product design, work center preparation, equipment maintenance, layout, model changeover, and demand scheduling—hinges on the total quality concept. And employees involved in and supporting these processes must hold that attitude.

In the last several years, technologies such as the Taguchi methods (see *Product Design,* earlier in this chapter) have emerged to make high quality levels practical. Additional quality technologies include "quality function deployment" (QFD) and "statistical process control" (SPC). Quality function deployment translates the "voice of the customer" into specific product characteristics. With this approach, the company deploys the quality function to the unit responsible for that phase of product or service quality (see Chapter 7).

Statistical process control monitors key product characteristics during processing to make sure the system is "under control." The goal is to keep the product measures within predetermined tolerances. If readings show quality declining, even within the specified limits, the company shuts down the process to avoid producing defective products. This approach is preventive rather than corrective.

The emphasis throughout the process is on doing the *right* thing *right* the *first time*. The JIT producer gets the right requirements from customers, using QFD; develops the right product design, per Taguchi; and processes it right, via QFD and SPC. A quality-at-the-source philosophy in which each processing unit views the next operation as its customer is the best way to implement this approach. Every processing unit must provide a quality product or service the first time. This eliminates the need for in-process inspectors, because the operators inspect their own work. They immediately detect defectives and stop processing until they can determine and correct the problem.

The following examples illustrate how the JIT/TQC process can improve quality.

General Electric's dishwasher operation, before implementing a major JIT/TQC program in the early 1980s, measured incoming materials' acceptable quality level on a scale that ranged from 0.5% (5,000 parts per million, or PPM) to 2.0% (20,000 PPM), depending on the component's importance in the product. The operation's new system focuses on defective parts per million and separates parts into three classes: "very critical," "critical," and "noncritical." The company rejects very critical parts if they exceed 100 PPM, and critical parts if they exceed 1,000 PPM. Noncritical parts continue under the AQL standard.

3M's Columbia, Missouri, plant started a JIT program in 1984. At that time, its average outgoing quality (AOQ) measure of critical defects, appearance defects, and packaging problems was 20,800 PPM. During 1985 and 1986, it dropped to 298 PPM—a 70:1 reduction.

There is certainly opportunity for improvement in product quality, as more U.S. firms are realizing. But unfortunately, many companies are doing very little to boost quality. *Purchasing* magazine's January 1988 survey of U.S. industrial buyers found that 40% had not yet implemented a formal quality program.

The just-in-time process requires total people involvement. As workers change from specialists to generalists, they must enthusiastically accept, and be trained for, their new role. All JIT activities hinge on teamwork. Management may need to organize formal teams for product design, equipment setup, production, and other activities. In other cases, the "team" is more informal, with cooperative and trusting relationships growing up between workers who depend on each other.

SUCCESS STORIES

Clearly, all the traditional manufacturing rules change with just-in-time. The myths of "economies of scale" and the "learning curve" explode as the company adopts one-touch setup processes that produce quality products, starting with the first unit. And the company starts to refine product designs to reflect customer needs and provide both the desired function and ease of manufacturing and service.

Lot sizes that are small enough to match the customer's requirements for daily or more frequent processing become feasible. Buffer inventories held "just-in-case" shrink, and eventually disappear, as the company uncovers and solves just-in-case problems. Quality problems are prevented, but if they do occur, the operation stops until they are corrected rather than generating scrap and rework. Workers operate as a team. Cross-trained to do one anothers' jobs, they constantly look for better ways of working.

Is this nirvana? It probably seems that way to those who have not started the journey to just-in-time. JIT pioneers who have committed to the JIT/TQC/TPI philosophy know otherwise. The journey is certainly not smooth. It's not easy to make everybody believe, "It can work here, too!"

The examples outlined earlier give a glimpse of just how successful JIT can be. The following presents the broader based results of just-in-time leaders:[13]

• *Omark Industries.* The Mesabi, Michigan, twist drill plant reduced large drill inventory 92%, increased productivity 30%, and reduced lead time from three weeks to three days. The company's Oroville, California, firearms reloading equipment operation reduced inventory 50%, lead time from six weeks to two days, and lot size from 500 to 30 units. Omark's Prentice, Wisconsin, log loader plan, a pilot operation, reduced total inventory 45% and cut lead time from 30 days to minutes. It also reduced the distance parts travel from 2,000 feet to 18 inches, and cut work-in-process from 60 pieces to one piece.

• *Harley-Davidson.* The company's York, Pennsylvania, operation reduced the manufacturing cycle for motorcycle frames from seventy-two days to two. It also increased final product quality from 50% to 99%.

- *Westinghouse Corporation,* Pittsburgh, Pennsylvania. The firm reduced the manufacturing cycle for automotive printed circuit boards by 70%, and for cabinets and cables by 75%. With JIT, gross inventory shrank 45% within fifteen months, quality improved 50%, and factory output increased 25%. And, the operation requires 20% less floor space. Westinghouse also cut the lot size for PC boards in half and now produces cabinets in lots of one unit. Westinghouse's electric propulsion operation increased shop capacity 500% and cut inventory and direct labor in half. It also reduced average cycle time by 90%.

- *Eaton Corporation,* Watertown, Wisconsin. In producing automation products, the company cut lead time in half, reduced material handling costs 35%, cut total inventory by 60%, reduced work-in-process inventory 75%, and reduced floor space requirements 40%.

- *Digital Equipment Corporation.* The company's Albuquerque, New Mexico, computer-workstation pilot program reduced overall inventory from sixteen weeks to three weeks, overall process cycle time from six weeks to three days, and the number of "defectives" manufactured from 17% to 3%.

- *Cincinnati Milacron,* Cincinnati, Ohio. Within the first two years of JIT production, the company's programmable controls operation cut inventory from $17 million to $7 million, and lead time from thirteen weeks to five weeks. It also reduced indirect labor requirements by 23%, and direct labor, 15%.

But the best example of state-of-art just-in-time production is probably on the eighth floor of Allen-Bradley Company's main plant in Milwaukee, Wisconsin. That operation is a focused "factory-within-a-factory." Allen-Bradley developed this focused factory because of sluggish growth in the U.S. market and increased international competition in two major segments it serves: the machine tool and automotive industries.[14]

Allen-Bradley's goal was to design a new electrical component, a world contactor, to meet international standards, using manufacturing as a strategic weapon. The company aimed to increase its global market share with a product costing 60% less than comparable, manually produced products. The finished product would sell anywhere in the world at a profit. The product was ready for market within twenty-four months.

The Milwaukee facility can produce 600 units per hour, in two sizes, and it accommodates up to 700 product design variations. The company achieved its JIT goals and immediately boosted market share. With the system, Allen-Bradley reduced lead time to twenty-four hours. The company receives orders one day, and it manufactures, tests, and ships the product the next day. It also achieves higher quality at lower cost. The company met its 60% cost-reduction goal. The JIT system includes 3,500 data collection points; this enables the company to detect defects at any point and analyze data immediately to identify the cause of a problem and correct it.

The system allows instant response to demand changes. Flexibility is another important benefit. Allen-Bradley can provide 700 different product configurations, versus the 125 originally planned for the system. Finally, the factory-within-a-factory holds only a five-day materials inventory.

Allen-Bradley illustrates the key characteristics of a world-class industrial marketer: extremely short *lead time,* which provides fast response; *flexibility; high quality;* and *low cost.* Individually, these characteristics are desirable. In combination, they provide a formidable competitive advantage in the global marketplace.

The importance of suppliers in successful just-in-time operations cannot be overstated. The following chapter shows how supplier-customer relationships are changing and suggests how to develop successful partnerships.

NOTES

1. Complete references for these sources include: Robert Hall, *Zero Inventories* (Homewood Ill: Dow Jones-Irwin, 1983); Richard Schonberger, *Japanese Manufacturing Techniques* (New York: The Free Press, 1986); Robert Hall, *Attaining Manufacturing Excellence* (Homewood, Ill: Dow Jones-Irwin, 1987); Richard J. Schonberger, *World Class Manufacturing* (New York: The Free Press, 1986).

2. "GE's Major Appliance Division," *Purchasing,* March 29, 1984, pp. 113–15.

3. Larry Sullivan, "The Power of Taguchi Methods to Impact Change in U.S. Companies," *Target,* Summer 1987, pp. 18–22.

4. Ibid., p. 20.

5. Gary Corvis, General Manager, NUMMI, presentation, "Toyota—General Motors: Lessons Learned," at 1986 Association for Manufacturing Excellence Conference, October, Chicago, Ill.

6. Russell J. Leo, Douglas Mocny, Frank Natoli, and Howard Stenglein, "JIT and Cellular Assembly," *Proceedings of the 1987 Annual Conference,* Association for Manufacturing Excellence (Wheeling, Ill: AME, 1987).

7. J. Kirk Olin and Paul Denmark, "Total Circuit Board Assembly: Changing the People, Plant and Systems," *Proceedings of the 1987 Annual Conference,* Association for Manufacturing Excellence (Wheeling, Ill: AME, 1987).

8. Shigeo Shingo, *A Revolution in Manufacturing: The SMED System* (Stamford, Conn.: Productivity Press, 1985).

9. John McElroy, "The Best Damn Die Change Team in America," *Automotive Industries,* August 1986, pp. 46–51.

10. John McElroy, "Die-Change Challenge!", *Automotive Industries,* November, 1987, pp. 32–38.

11. Joseph M. Callahan, "Stabilizing Production Schedules," *Automotive Industries,* September 1984, pp. 32–35.

12. Philip B. Crosby, *Quality Without Tears* (New York: McGraw-Hill, 1984).

13. The examples are taken from reports of AME Workshops conducted at these firms.

14. Robert L. Stasey, "Allen-Bradley Achieves World-Class Manufacturing," *Target,* Winter 1987, pp. 28–30.

PART II: ADDITIONAL SUGGESTED READINGS

Allan Ayers, "JIT—One Well-thought-out Step at a Time," *Transportation and Distribution,* January 1988, p. 53.

"American Industry Goes Ape Over Just-in-Time Strategy," *Purchasing,* September 12, 1985, pp. 21–23.

Bryan Berry, "Sagas of Success: Making Just-in-Time Work," *Automotive Industries,* February 1987, pp. 72–74.

Lindsay Brooke, "Buick City—GM's Gamble in Flint," *Automotive Industries,* December 1984, pp. 19–20.

"Controls Maker Trims Inventory by 60% in 18 Months with JIT," *Purchasing,* April 9, 1987, p. 28.

James Donohue, "It's Up to Systems Integrators to Implement Just-in-Time," *Mini-Micro Systems,* February 1987, pp. 46–47.

Steven Flax, "An Auto Man Tunes Up Warner-Lambert," *Fortune,* March 4, 1985, pp. 70–78.

Matt Gallagher, "Just-in-Time: Best Taken Straight," *Distribution,* November 1985, pp. 92–93.

Walter Goddard, *Just-in-Time: Surviving by Breaking Tradition* (Essex Junction, VT: Oliver Wight Limited Publications, June, 1986).

Roy Hayley and Bruce Piper, "New Inventory-Managment Approach Can Substantially Cut Inventory Costs," *The Practical Accountant,* February 1986, pp. 60–68.

Bruce Henderson, "The Logic of Kanban," *The Journal of Business Strategy,* Winter 1986, pp. 6–12.

Kaoru Ishikawa, *What is Total Quality Control? The Japanese Way* (Englewood Cliffs, NJ: Prentice Hall, 1985).

J. M. Juran, *Juran on Planning for Quality* (New York: The Free Press, 1988).

Darryl Landwater, "The Rise and Fall of Just-in-Time," *Infosystems,* November 1984, p. 62.

Neal Lorenzi, "Just-in-Time: Kanban Comes to Boah Printing," *American Printer,* February 1986, pp. 48–52.

Jeremy Main, "The Trouble with Managing Japanese Style," *Fortune,* April 2, 1984, pp. 50–56.

G. H. Manoochehri, "Improving Productivity with the Just-in-Time System," *Journal of Systems Management,* January 1985, pp. 23–26.

Raymond Mayer, "A Critical Look at Kanban, Japan's Just-in-Time Inventory System," *Management Review,* December 1984, pp. 48–51.

John McElroy, "Back to Basics at Nummi: Quality Through Teamwork," *Automotive Industries,* November 1985, pp. 63–64.

———, "No Business as Usual: Ford's Production Philosophy," *Automotive Industries,* April 1985, pp. 42–44.

Robert McIlhattan, "How Cost Management Systems Can Support the JIT Philosophy," *Management Accounting,* September 1987, pp. 20–25.

Russell Miller, "Buick City: Hope for Flint," *Management Review,* March 1985, pp. 34–37.

Christopher Mullelwhite, "The Just-in-Time Production Challenge," *Training and Development Journal,* February 1987, pp. 27–29.

Bruce Neumann and Pauline Jaouen, "Focus on Industry: Kanban, ZIPS, and Cost Accounting," *Journal of Accountancy,* August 1986, pp. 132–41.

"Quality, Why Is It so Important?" *Purchasing,* January 28, 1988, pp. 66–69.

Arjon Sadhwani, M. H. Darhan, and Doyal Kiringode, "Just-in-Time: An Inventory System Whose Time Has Come," *Management Accounting,* December 1985, pp. 36–44.

Roger Schreffler, "Nissan's Electronic Kanban," *Automotive Industries,* November 1986, pp. 93–95.

Richard Walleigh, "What's Your Excuse for not Using JIT?" *Harvard Business Review,* March–April 1986, pp. 38–54.

Craig Waters, "Why Everybody's Talking About Just-in-Time," *Inc.,* March 1984, pp. 77–90.

All the Relationships Change

Chapter 3

Just-in-Time Purchasing Requirements

INTRODUCTION

The industrial supplier plays a double role in the just-in-time purchasing scenario. In the first role, which we will discuss in greater depth in Chapter 4 and Part IV, it acts as industrial marketer to the just-in-time industrial customer. To become an effective just-in-time marketer, the supplier must thoroughly understand the JIT purchasing process and how the rules change as new, very different customer requirements and relationships emerge.

In its second role, the supplier is a producer: a customer of second-tier suppliers. The successful just-in-time industrial supplier must at the same time be a just-in-time marketer, producer, and purchaser. It must feel comfortable with all changes in the purchasing process—from *both* sides of the desk.

Figure 3-1 illustrates this set of relationships and establishes the framework for Chapters 3, 4, and 5.

As Fig. 3-1 shows, the industrial supplier practices just-in-time marketing with OEM customers and requires just-in-time service from its own suppliers. And those linking points aren't the only ones character-

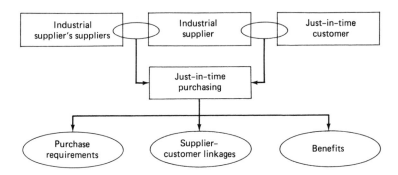

Figure 3-1 Just-in-time purchasing.

ized by the JIT philosophy. As we move upstream to basic materials processing, additional value-added levels may also depend on the just-in-time approach to meet *their* customers' needs. As the OEM shifts to JIT manufacturing, it is critical that each member in the value-added chain act quickly, but carefully, to adopt the just-in-time philosophy. Each supplier strongly affects the performance of its common customer—the final-product OEM—via cost, quality, and response time.

The importance of an effective just-in-time purchasing system cannot be overstated. It can significantly reduce waste and shorten lead times, leading to the triple-threat competitive advantage of flexibility, cost leadership, and benchmark quality. Top managers of leading U.S. firms are starting to recognize this untapped potential.

SUPPLIER IMPORTANCE

Although U.S. managers have worked hard to reduce their products' direct-labor cost content, they haven't paid as much attention to reducing purchased materials cost. The irony is that direct-labor costs now represent about 5% to 10% of the OEM's total product cost, while purchased materials represent 30% to 80% and average about 50%.

Xerox's product cost analysis, displayed in Fig. 3-2, is quite revealing. It separates Xerox's internal value-added from the value external suppliers add at various stages of the manufacturing process.[1]

Clearly, the value contributed by suppliers of parts, subassemblies, and assemblies far outweighs the value Xerox adds. Although this may be a rather extreme example of supplier–producer value contribution, it is broadly applicable, particularly as OEMs move to greater external sourcing of materials requirements. This kind of analysis would certainly benefit most manufacturers.

XEROX PRODUCTION STAGES:

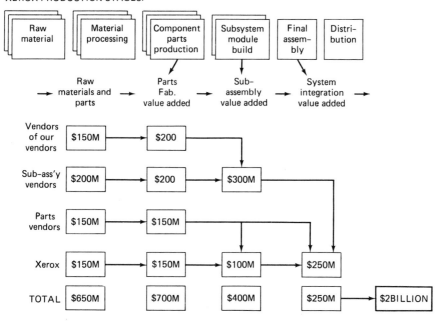

Figure 3-2 Xerox: Comparison of internal and external value added. Source: Reprinted by permission of the Xerox Corporation.

POTENTIAL PAYOFF

Table 3-1 illustrates how reducing direct-labor and purchased materials waste may improve profitability.

Table 3-1 evaluates three kinds of manufacturing processes: high, moderate, and low value-added. Example A, in which the producer adds quite a bit of value, includes a fairly high level of fabrication as well as assembly. Consequently, the direct-labor content is high—20%—while purchased materials cost is relatively low.

Example B has only a modest proportion of basic fabrication and a higher share of assembly. Purchased materials become a substantially higher cost factor in this case, accounting for 50% of the finished product's sales value. This is about average for U.S. producers.

Example C is essentially an assembly process, with purchased components and subassemblies representing most of the finished product's cost.

Table 3-1 contrasts the effect of a 10% direct-labor cost reduction with a 10% reduction in cost of purchased materials. The improvement

TABLE 3-1   The Profit Impact of Purchased Materials Cost Reduction

	A High Value-Added Process	B Moderate Value-Added Process	C Low Value-Added Process
Selling price	$1,000	$1,000	$1,000
Direct labor	200	100	50
Purchased materials	300	500	750
Overhead	400	300	100
Profit (before taxes)	$100	$100	$100
As % of sales	10%	10%	10%
Assume:			
(1) 10% reduction in Direct labor	(20)	(10)	(5)
New profit	120	110	105
As % of sales	12%	11%	10.5%
(2) 10% reduction in cost of purchased materials	(30)	(50)	(75)
New profit	130	150	175
As % of sales	13%	15%	17.5%
Improvement ratio (1):(2)	3:2	5:1	7.5:1

ratio at the bottom is based on the percentage point increase in before-tax profit-to-sales.

Method of Calculation (using example A)

1. Original profit-to-sales ratio = 10%
2. New ratio as direct labor cost is reduced = 12%
3. Difference: (2) − (1) = 2%
4. New ratio as purchased materials cost is reduced = 13%
5. Difference: (4) − (1) = 3%
6. Improvement ratio = (5)/(3) = 3:2

Interpretation: Purchased materials cost reductions have a significantly greater impact on profit-to-sales ratios than do proportionate direct-labor cost reductions. In Example A, the effect is a *50%* greater improvement (3% *vs* 2%); in Example B, a *400%* greater improvement (5% *vs* 1%); and in Example C, a *650%* greater improvement (7.5 *vs* 1). The improvement percentage is calculated as follows:

$$[DP \text{ (materials)} - DP \text{ (labor)}]/DP \text{ (labor)} \times 100 = \text{improvement percentage}$$

where DP (materials) is the percentage increase in profit-to-sales resulting from purchased materials cost reduction. DP(labor) is the percentage increase in profit-to-sales resulting from direct-labor cost reduction.

Thus, in Example A:

Improvement percentage = [(3% − 2%)/2%] × 100 = 50%

In Example B:

Improvement percentage = [(5% − 1%)/1%] × 100 = 400%

In Example C:

Improvement percentage = [(7.5% − 1%)/1%] × 100 = 650%

The improvement ratios range from 3:2, for Example A, to 7.5:1, for Example C. This example emphasizes how important it is for the industrial producer to analyze suppliers' contributions to total cost and focus on eliminating waste in procurement.

Although suppliers may interpret purchased materials' cost reductions as price reductions to them, particularly in light of traditional purchasing practice, this may not be the case with just-in-time purchasing. Major cost reductions may be achieved by the OEM customer without affecting the unit price, by examining the entire range of waste elimination opportunities.

Although we're focusing on purchases from external suppliers in this chapter, many of these concepts and techniques are equally applicable to *internal* suppliers—frequent offenders in the waste-generation process.

CUSTOMER REQUIREMENTS

Just-in-time systems cause many changes in purchasing requirements; Fig. 3-3 displays the more significant ones. Let's examine each.

Small Lot Sizes

Traditionally, OEMs purchased in large quantities and produced in long runs of single models. The economies of scale and learning curve myths discussed in Chapter 2 supported those approaches.

The long-trusted economic order quantity (EOQ) model also supported larger purchase quantities. The EOQ model's goal is to minimize the total cost of ordering and carrying inventory, based on traditional assumptions and manufacturing practices.

Manufacturers have historically treated individual ordering costs as fixed and constant, much like setup costs in manufacturing. But that's

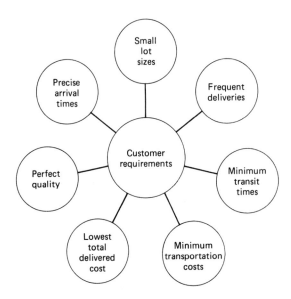

Figure 3-3. Just-in-time customer requirements.

erroneous. Leading OEMs have learned that ordering costs are *not* fixed. They may be substantially reduced with just-in-time processes, which make much smaller orders—purchased lot sizes—economically desirable. The basic ordering costs include those associated with:

1. Negotiating
2. Scheduling
3. Order receiving and preparation
4. Transportation

By using just-in-time and total quality control techniques, the manufacturer may reduce or totally eliminate each of these costs.

Frequent Deliveries

Delivery frequency relates directly to the lot size a customer orders. If the buyer's usage rate is constant, smaller individual lots correlate with more frequent deliveries. The reorder point, or inventory level at which the buyer places an order, depends on its usage rate, replenishment lead time, and the safety stock level. The replenishment lead time depends on whether the supplier delivers product from stock or produces it to order. The latter includes a period to produce and/or process the order, as well as transportation time.

Because the just-in-time philosophy aims at eliminating inventory, the approach, at least for significant production materials, is to purchase them as needed rather than stocking them. Suppliers' reductions in lead time to delivery—based on improvements in their processing cycles—can help them increase delivery frequency. The objective is to synchronize the supplier's and customer's processing operations. As the customer reduces its own lot sizes, it reduces purchased materials lot sizes accordingly.

Exact Quantities

It is crucial that the quantity delivered match the quantity needed. Variation in either direction is wasteful. In the past, suppliers typically shipped against open orders that varied modestly from the customer's production schedule. The supplier usually adjusted this with the final shipment against the order.

This practice conflicts with the just-in-time philosophy. The delivery of more units than required wastes resources. It brings the customer material not needed to produce the lot for which it was designated, and it forces an adjustment in subsequent production and delivery schedules.

Deliveries of fewer units than needed are also wasteful. Short deliveries can be particularly damaging to up-and-running JIT operations, because those systems don't incorporate buffer inventories. Such inventory has historically cushioned shortages and headed off production interruptions.

Precise Arrival Time

Traditionally, suppliers have scheduled orders to be shipped at a certain time: on a particular week or day. In contrast, just-in-time orders are scheduled to be *delivered* at precise times: on certain days or at a particular hour of the day. The delivery time window has shrunk from days to hours.

Deliveries arriving before the time window opens play havoc with just-in-time efficiency. There's usually no receiving dock open for early deliveries. If, by some fluke, they can be unloaded upon arrival, there may not be a place to store them because storage space is at such a premium in the JIT system.

Late deliveries present some of the same problems, including the dock space issue. Although customers place a high priority on unloading late deliveries, this interrupts the scheduled delivery flow. Even more damaging are the processing interruptions that late deliveries may cause, and the effect on subsequent schedules.

Transit Time and Transportation Costs

Under the JIT philosophy, any time or cost expended to transport products from supplier to customer that exceeds the minimum for meeting the customer's service requirements is considered wasteful.

If the supplier quotes an order FOB (free on board) destination, assuming responsibility for transportation costs as well as routing and carrier selection, it must develop creative approaches to minimize both time-in-transit and transportation costs.

This is a particular challenge for remote suppliers, because distance from customers influences not only transit time and cost but increases the chance that a shipment may not arrive as scheduled.

Perfect Quality

Just-in-time customers require near-perfect quality and deal with suppliers whose quality processes incorporate a continuous improvement philosophy.

Experts estimate that purchased materials cause 30% to 50% of manufacturing quality problems.[2] Such statistics prove that a just-in-time system can't tolerate defective materials.

Defective materials cause several kinds of waste. The first is that associated with figuring out what caused the quality problem. Because advanced just-in-time systems rely on supplier quality assurance and waive incoming inspection for certified suppliers, many incoming materials, parts, or components move immediately into production. The customer may not even know they are defective until they are well into production.

A second source of waste is scrap or rework to recover processed units containing the defective materials. Yet another source of waste is the production interruption that keeps the OEM from meeting customer commitments without extra expediting and processing time.

Defective materials also waste the supplier's time. The supplier must give the customer extra service to make up for the defective material; that racks up hours in technical service and application assistance. Defectives also interrupt the supplier's schedule as it scurries to replace bad units with good ones. This forces unscheduled production, which in turn causes overtime and the need to expedite materials from lower tier suppliers. A first-tier supplier's quality breakdown can multiply *all* suppliers' costs, as adjustments ripple through the system.

Lowest Total Delivered Cost

Lowest total delivered cost is the bottom line. It measures the supplier's effectiveness and efficiency in meeting each of the customer requirements discussed above.

   Just-in-time customers are using total cost as the ultimate measure
of suppliers. This is their yardstick in choosing long-term partners. And
the suppliers who can provide the lowest total delivered cost are those
who have done the best job of wringing waste out of their processes.
   These new, more demanding, purchasing requirements present a major challenge to industrial marketers—a challenge they will not meet by
following traditional marketing practices. Chapter 4 examines the new
linkages between customers and suppliers under just-in-time conditions—
the new player–team relationships.

NOTES

1. Stephen L. Tierney, "Strategic Planning and Just-in-Time," *Strategies for
   World Class Manufacturing Excellence.* Proceedings of the 1986 Annual Conference, Association for Manufacturing Excellence, Chicago, Ill., October
   1986.
2. S. M. Groocock, *The Chain of Quality: Market Dominance through Product
   Superiority* (New York: John Wiley & Sons, 1986), pp. 58–64.

Chapter 4

Supplier–Customer Linkages

Purchasing magazine, in its 1983 Chief Executive Survey, reported fundamental changes in purchaser–supplier relationships. Buyers increasingly preferred to deal with *fewer* suppliers. Those they would buy from were likely to be:[1]

- More reliable on quality and delivery.
- More helpful on technical assistance and product standardization.
- More versatile in lot sizing.
- Demonstrably committed to their specialties or core business.
- Choosier in selecting their customers and aware that a better "fit" between buyer and seller benefits both parties.
- Equipped to take full advantage of computers and telecommunications.

The purchasing executives did not view the trend toward close, long-term relationships with suppliers as a fad; they speculated that in five to ten years, or less, almost all mass manufacturers of discrete products—and a lot of others—would operate this way.

The magazine's 1987 Chief Executive Survey indicated that CEOs were relatively pleased with their purchasing units' progress.[2] Helping the purchasing departments select sources and determine costs more accurately were: stocking programs, just-in-time delivery agreements, world-sourcing programs for major raw materials, suppliers' quality-improvement programs, earlier supplier involvement, and more talented purchasing and materials-management personnel.

However, the purchasing executives said supplier relations could still bear improvement. To foster better relations, management is pushing purchasing to enlist suppliers with similar philosophies. F. James McDonald, president of General Motors Corporation (GM), pointed out that in some industries, companies supplying GM have not yet committed to the changes needed to become globally competitive. Others are moving too slowly for the competitive situation.[3]

In some cases, all the supplier lacks is a sense of the situation's urgency. In his address before the Association for Manufacturing Excellence in September 1986, William J. Weisz, Motorola's chief executive officer, said, "Not enough of our current suppliers appear to recognize the seriousness of the competitive realities they face with their major competitors."[4] Weisz said Motorola was consolidating purchases to form a world-class supplier base.

He explained that world-class marketers, like Motorola, are "aggressively striving for perfect quality, leading edge technology, just-in-time manufacturing, and cost-competitive servicing." Weisz emphasized the need for suppliers to not only develop a sense of urgency, but successful methods for meeting customers' high expectations as well.

Weisz's comments reflect the attitudes and intentions of major industrial firms' managers, who are currently mapping strategies to become stronger global competitors. A critical issue underlying such strategies is linkage between industrial marketers and the final product manufacturers, or OEMs, they serve.

Figure 4-1 contrasts the traditional supplier–OEM relationship with that required for effective just-in-time operations. Some key differences between the two relationships are shown in Table 4-1.

TABLE 4-1 Key Differences Between Traditional and Just-in-Time Linkages

Characteristic	Traditional Linkages	Just-in-time Linkages
1. Number of suppliers	Multiple sources	Single source
2. Goals	Independent	Mutual
3. Relationship	Adversarial	Partnership
4. Agreement length	Short-term	Long-term
5. Functional interdependence	Limited to moderate	Very high

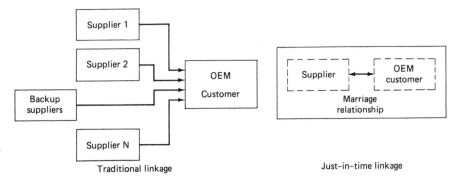

Figure 4-1   Traditional vs just-in-time supplier–OEM linkage.

NUMBER OF SUPPLIERS

Many have debated whether a manufacturer should choose several sources for identical supplies or commit to a single source for that item. Until relatively recently in U.S. history, industrial firms generally used single sources, primarily to simplify logistics. The country's limited transportation infrastructure demanded nearby suppliers.

As rail transportation became more efficient and as motor freight emerged, the supplier-selection decision shifted to price, performance, and quality factors. Rather than choose one local supplier, manufacturers began to select several qualified sources. Through multiple suppliers, the customer gained substantial leverage in negotiating favorable terms. Firms favoring multiple sourcing say it reduces supply disruptions and holds down prices through competitive bidding.

In many cases, manufacturers base multiple-source analysis on price rather than the total long-term cost of using the suppliers. They don't realize that low-bidding suppliers may provide marginal products as well as minimal service, making them the *highest cost* suppliers. Costs also suffer because multiple sourcing keeps all the suppliers from achieving economies of scale. Multiple sourcing is generally a "just-in-case" approach that manufacturers use to reduce risk.

Japanese manufacturers have shown that single sourcing is preferable for just-in-time producers. The chosen supplier operates much like an internal supply department. JIT producers choose single sourcing because of the openness required between buyers and sellers, the sensitivity of information they share, the number of people and functions involved on both sides, and the frequency of interaction in just-in-time operations.

Single sourcing also reduces the number of suppliers in the new-product development cycle and the number of quality-monitoring programs. And it helps the producer track, pinpoint, and assign responsibility for problems.

Numerous U.S. just-in-time producers are switching to single sourcing. A vivid example is General Motors' Chevrolet-Pontiac-Canada Group (CPC); more than 90% of the 80,000 production parts it buys daily are single-sourced—compared with fewer than 2% a decade ago.[5]

The natural result of single sourcing is supplier-base reduction. Rank Xerox, a British Xerox affiliate, reduced the number of suppliers for its Model 1025 photocopier, produced in Venray, Netherlands, from 3,000 to 430 during the early 1980s as it implemented a just-in-time system.[6] Xerox's corporate goal is to reduce its base of 5,000 suppliers to 300 worldwide.[7]

Similarly, Hewlett-Packard Company has reduced its aluminum sheet-stock supplier base from twenty-two to three, and its printed-circuit laminate supplier base from thirteen to two.[8]

AMP Inc., which controls 15% to 20% of the worldwide electrical-connector market, placed several hundred suppliers on inactive status in the mid 1980s as part of its just-in-time program.[9] Chrysler buys from more than 15,000 suppliers, with 500 vendors supplying 80% of all materials; 90% of the company's suppliers are single sources.[10]

A 1985 survey of automotive industry final-product assemblers conducted by Dr. O'Neal showed that, although 70% of the respondents had traditionally used multiple or dual sources, only 45% were then doing so, because of just-in-time programs. The results showed that only 25% of the respondents expected to rely on multiple sourcing through 1990. This will lead to major reductions in the supplier base.[11]

GOALS, RELATIONSHIPS, AND AGREEMENT LENGTH

The goals of industrial marketers and OEM customers have often clashed in the past. The marketer's major objective was to negotiate the highest price and the best quality and delivery requirements—for itself. Its goal in negotiating each of those issues was to enhance its own bottom line.

The OEM customer, in contrast, negotiated for the lowest unit price and, secondarily, acceptable quality levels and logistical and support service. These goals are obviously incompatible, and the two firms viewed negotiating as a win–lose struggle. Negotiations were adversarial, with the OEM customer often pitting alternative suppliers against one another to maximize its advantage.

Short-term agreements were another problem in the traditional relationship. Contracts were often less than one year long and frequently included limited-notice termination clauses. The latter allowed the buyer to back out if a competing supplier presented a more attractive package.

In stark contrast, just-in-time partners work toward a common goal; satisfying their mutual customer at a reasonable profit for each. Mutual trust, confidence, and loyalty are critical as the two firms establish a longer term, single-source relationship.

Xerox emphasizes the importance of early supplier involvement (ESI) in the new-product development process. Steve Tierney, vice-president of materials management with Xerox's Reprographics Division, emphasizes, "If we are really going to get at quality, lead time, and weight per function, we must get our suppliers 'way up front' for them to have an understanding of the architecture selection, the technology, and what their capabilities are."[12] The chosen supplier stays involved throughout the product's life cycle. Competitive bidding is certainly inconsistent with the Xerox approach.

The automotive industry presents a good example of how OEMs' sourcing philosophy is changing. In 1980, each of the domestic auto makers signed only a few contracts of more than a year's duration. In 1985, more than half of Ford's North American Operations contracts were for five years or more; that could increase to 85% by 1990. For suppliers, especially those enjoying a larger share of business as dual or single sources, longer term contracts are an incentive to invest in quality- and productivity-improvement programs, joint design, and joint value analysis.

The sweeping significance of the changes occurring in supplier–customer relationships is reflected in the comments of Donald Pais, GM's materials management director. He says, "The supply industry is going through a real structural change, and the relationships formed now will last through the turn of the century." He also emphasizes the need to deal with world-class suppliers. The effect, Pais says, "will not be confined to the automotive industry."[13]

FUNCTIONAL INTERDEPENDENCE AND COMMUNICATIONS

Although the industrial marketer's various functional units have always been somewhat interdependent, the just-in-time system—with its call for perfect quality and logistical precision—greatly accentuates this interdependence. The customer's functional units also depend more on each other than in the past. In addition, complementary functional units of the marketer and customer organization must interact to develop and implement just-in-time processes.

Traditionally, the OEM–supplier relationship has not required extensive intercompany communications. The customer typically invited known, qualified suppliers to bid, or it requested proposals. The suppliers provided information on design specifications, quantities, and delivery dates. After winning the contract, a supplier would arrange operational and logistical schedules to meet the customer's requirements. The supplier and customer usually communicated only to discuss problems or schedule changes, and most interactions transpired between the marketer's sales or customer-service representative and the OEM's purchasing representative. Both parties guarded confidential information on costs, product plans, and the like, because they were afraid the other would break the confidence.

The just-in-time system introduces a dramatic shift in communications flow. More and different participants are involved, and the exchange is much more open. These are essential characteristics of successful just-in-time partnerships.

PLAYERS INVOLVED IN THE CONVENTIONAL RELATIONSHIP

In conventional industrial marketer-customer relationships, just a few representatives from each organization interact. Figure 4-2 shows how OEMs interact with multiple sources of similar materials or components.

OEMs often rely on multiple sources to reduce the risk of supply interruption and gain "pricing leverage." They realize it would be prohibitively expensive to establish extensive communications networks with all suppliers. Fortunately, elaborate networks are not required.

The customer typically provides quality specifications in terms of acceptable quality levels; specifies the shipment date within a particular week; and requires a "unit price" to determine cost. Primary players include the supplier's sales representative, who interacts with the customer's purchasing representative; and the supplier's customer service representative, who provides order-status information as required. The two design-engineering departments interact limitedly, generally to clarify and modify product specifications.

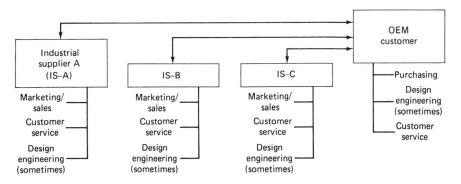

Figure 4-2 Traditional supplier-customer interaction.

To understand how customer and supplier representatives interact in a successful just-in-time/total-quality relationship, let us examine the expectations, requirements, and activities of a few JIT users.

M. F. Rose, Brunswick Corporation's director of purchasing, says, "The supplier will be able to provide and, in fact, be required to provide advice to the customer based on its particular technical skills—to help him design parts better for lower price and better productivity within his plant."[14]

Vincent Gregg, manager of General Electric's materials resource and traffic operation, says, "The single biggest change we expect in supplier relationships is in the area of quality. Suppliers are going to have to take 'ownership' of quality requirements of jobs they quote on—each supplier is going to have to be state-of-the-art in his specialty so that he can be an equal partner."[15]

Kenneth Borsch, Brunswick's purchasing director, echoes the supplier quality theme. He says, "Quality is the chief contribution the supplier can make to improving productivity." He adds that "total quality (includes) service, value, and the physical quality" of the product.[16]

Ken Stork, Motorola's corporate materials director, says, "Our 'partnership for growth' program has the objective of eliminating adversarial roles, emphasizing that the two organizations (Motorola and its suppliers) have mutual objectives. (It) lays the groundwork for just-in-time delivery plans."[17]

According to Chrysler's vice-president for procurement, David Platt, 70% of Chrysler's parts and materials come from suppliers. Because the company is "more highly outsourced than GM or Ford . . . outside suppliers play a bigger role in our success or failure as a company," Platt says.[18] He adds, "The corporation's procurement strategy is to continue to find sources of supply capable of doing the research and development into quality components that are on the leading edge of technology."

Chrysler rates its suppliers using the Supplier Defective Material Report Card program. They must have statistical process control certification for the parts they supply, and they must have new product research and development capabilities. Platt explains the justification for such high-level quality and technology requirements: "By 1988, all of Chrysler's plants in the United States and Canada will have 100% 'in-line sequence' manufacturing systems. That makes 100% zero-defect parts and just-in-time delivery capabilities imperative."[19]

Hughes Aircraft Company expects suppliers to play a key role in its own value analysis (VA) and value engineering (VE) programs. Hughes wants to augment the suppliers' existing expertise with VA and VE capabilities.[20]

Northern Telecom Company trains all its purchasing personnel in value analysis. The company's value seminars always include suppliers.

The supplier attendees then train their own people. As an incentive to use value analysis, Northern offers innovative suppliers a share of the savings it incurs through value analysis. The arrangement is contractual with selected suppliers.[21]

General Electric's Major Appliance Business Group also meets with vendors to create a new attitude. The meetings focus on achieving zero defects with products, components, and materials. Together with suppliers, the company:

- sets mutually agreed upon quality levels, measured in parts per million, and a stiff penalty for failure to comply;
- measures how well all participants meet the quality standard;
- resolves problems and establishes controls in the supplier plants.

The Material Resources Operation (MRO) of GE's Major Appliance Group promotes quality as a continuing and cooperative goal. MRO employees participate in multidisciplinary product teams that also include individuals from the group's purchasing, engineering, quality control, manufacturing, marketing, and finance functions. These teams form at the new-product concept stage.[22]

The teams analyze vendor capabilities to find the few best suited to the job; their mission is to procure materials based on quality, technology, delivery, and price. According to Joseph H. Kehlbeck, MRO's manager, "No parts are going to be designed that are not producible in PPM (parts per million defective measurement)." Court Clayton, MRO program administrator, adds, "Smart people in the industry have spoken of vendors as being an extension of their manufacturing. Now we're making the vendor an extension of our engineering."[23]

Caterpillar is also turning increasingly to the team sourcing concept—using cross-disciplinary teams to search out world-class sources with better quality, lower costs, and consistent delivery. According to Ronald E. Temple, purchasing manager, a team might consist of twelve people—from purchasing, engineering, parts service, marketing, and other departments. He says, "Our buyers usually head up the teams, but we're working hand in glove. When you put a lot of experience together, you get better decisions."[24]

Robert Stone, General Motors' corporate materials manager, advises JIT manufacturers to integrate suppliers into their processes. He recommends full supplier participation in the product's early design stage; family-of-parts sourcing (sourcing similar parts from a single supplier); long-term, cooperative relationships; capital investment by suppliers; price negotiations based on cost analysis; and reduction or elimination of routine paperwork. Suppliers that cooperate in the customer's total process approach and extend it to include internal just-in-time systems are most likely to succeed, according to Stone.[25]

Lance Dixon, Bose Corporation's director of purchasing and logistics, emphasizes the importance of the purchasing and engineering interface *within* the OEM organization, particularly in the product design stage. At Bose, "From day one, purchasing is running with design engineering," he says. This means weekly meetings with project leaders. The meetings include a purchasing staff member. Buyers are encouraged to question engineering plans and to suggest alternatives early in product development. It's much easier and less costly to make changes at the start of the design cycle than to make engineering design changes later.[26]

Managers from other OEM firms that are successfully reaching positions of global competitiveness agree wholeheartedly. They also say the OEM's first step in selecting suppliers with such capabilities is to know what it needs from the supplier. Manufacturers aspiring to world-class status need suppliers with total quality programs, state-of-the-art technology, JIT manufacturing and logistics, and cost-competitive service.

Ideally, potential suppliers provide these capabilities in an atmosphere of mutual sharing, understanding that their goals and rewards will merge with the customer's as they work together. Global competitors need world-class suppliers, and their suppliers need to be just-in-time industrial marketers.

According to representatives from leading OEMs, successful partnerships include a greater number of active players from both organizations and many new, more intense relationships.

PLAYERS AND TEAMS IN THE JIT MARKETING RELATIONSHIP

The industrial marketer's relationship with its customer is just one link in a much longer chain of similar relationships. Figure 4-3 illustrates the chain.

The vertical marketing network in Fig. 4-3 extends from the raw

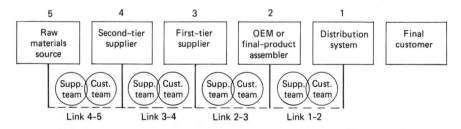

Figure 4-3 The vertical marketing system supplier–customer team relationships.

materials source to the final industrial user or reseller. Each company in the chain has a team that represents it as a customer to suppliers, and as a marketer to customers. At some companies, the customer team (the "buying center," which sources from suppliers) and supplier team (the "marketing center," which sells to customers) includes the same members. That's the case with Xerox's commodity teams, which follow a product from development through marketing.

The final-product manufacturer—an OEM—has typically initiated just-in-time systems, developing its own team of functional members to evaluate current and potential suppliers and establish ongoing supply relationships.

The teams, team members, and relationships linking OEMs with first-tier suppliers (Fig. 4-3, Link 2-3) are currently the most developed. This link also tends to set the standard for any preceding linkages vis-a-vis product quality, logistical requirements, and total-value specifications.

Of course, both organizations must also build relationships beyond those immediate linkages for just-in-time success. Other relationships occur at different supply levels—with second-tier suppliers, for example—and with subsequent organizations' design and development units, based on the ultimate customer's requirements. These interorganizational relationships continue through the production, delivery, and post-sale service of the product.

Both organizations have extensive team rosters, and the individual players' activities vary with their company's role in the supply chain. Most important, JIT teams do not play against each other. Instead, they combine capabilities to boost their mutual world-class status.

It helps to examine the value the OEM and its suppliers add to that manufacturer's product, because this determines which team members are active at different stages of the relationship. Table 4-2 illustrates the industrial marketer's and the OEM customer's value-adding activities and the sequence in which they usually occur.

TABLE 4-2   Value-added Phases of Industrial Marketer–OEM Customer
Partnership

Industrial Marketer	Phase	OEM Customer
Evaluative	1. Partner evaluation	Evaluative
Commercial	2. Identifying needs	Commercial
Technical	3. Product design	Technical
Logistical (inbound)	4. Procurement	Logistical (inbound)
Operational	5. Processing	Operational
Logistical (outbound)	6. Delivery	Logistical (outbound)
Evaluative	1–6. Monitoring	Evaluative

The partners' activities in these phases—commercial, technical, operational, logistical, and evaluative—determine which functional areas are paramount in each phase.

Of course, the value-added activities are not necessarily sequential nor strictly forward-flowing. For example, partner evaluation may follow the need-identification phase: if the buyer decides it needs a certain commodity, it alerts potential suppliers and then evaluates those interested.

Similarly, engineering changes caused by product- or process-design modifications cause a looping effect. Looping occurs when the supplier or customer moves backward to an earlier value-added activity and repeats one or more steps. There are many possible reasons for looping: product design changes before, or after, production begins; discovering new customer needs that affect the product or delivery process; deciding to reevaluate the customer/supplier as a long-term exchange partner.

SUPPLIER EVALUATION

Clearly, OEMs striving for world-class status must join with suppliers that have, or can readily develop, world-class marketing capabilities. Such companies couple as *equal* partners.

JIT industrial marketers also select OEM customers that will most likely become world-class competitors in their markets. Both the buyer and supplier evaluate potential partners extensively before entering into the JIT "marriage." We hear more about OEMs evaluating suppliers, but it is equally important for industrial marketers to evaluate their potential partners before signing long-term supply contracts.

Historically, many OEMs have evaluated prospective suppliers rather superficially. This may have been because supply agreements were short term—as short as a single transaction. Multiple sourcing also influenced the buyers' approach: Because the customer used several sources, no one supplier posed a significant risk.

Customers' primary selection criteria were: availability, low unit price, and quality conforming to acceptable quality level specifications. Suppliers often qualified by submitting a few samples of their product to the customer's quality-control department for testing. The vendor may have selected the samples carefully, meaning they would not typify its manufacturing capabilities. A few months after becoming qualified, suppliers commonly raised their prices and/or requested looser product tolerances.

With just-in-time, the old vendor-selection process is no longer feasible. As manufacturers reduce the supplier base and increasingly favor single sourcing, chosen vendors represent the best fit with the customer.

Customer personnel who evaluate suppliers must understand and be able to judge candidates' relevant performance capabilities—both current and potential. Some of the aspects they consider are:

• **Product Quality.** Suppliers' ability to provide products measurable in defective parts per million is an essential consideration. This approach replaces the old AQL specification. In evaluating the vendor's quality capabilities, the customer analyzes product design, production, and quality assurance. The OEM approaches the evaluation with a philosophy of defect prevention rather than detection after the fact. The quality objectives moves beyond just conforming to specifications to focus on continuous reduction in variability from the target.

• **Financial Strength and Stability.** Because the JIT relationship focuses on long-term success for both partners, suppliers need the financial resources and management commitment to remain competitive even during turbulent economic periods. The customer evaluates the vendor's ability to sustain major investments in employee education and training, productivity-improvement processes, capital facilities, and quality programs.

• **Location.** Geographic proximity is a very important consideration. The closer the better. Remote suppliers may offer outstanding characteristics that overcome their location disadvantage, but JIT's demand for logistical precision and constant interaction generally favors local suppliers.

• **Supplier Size and Production Capacity.** Customers also consider how important they would be to a supplier. The customer wants to represent an important part of the supplier's business but not so crucial that the OEM's natural demand fluctuations will wreak chaos on the supplier. The supplier should also be equipped to meet the customer's future requirements. Further, all appropriate levels of supplier management should be easily accessible to the customer.

• **Technology Capability.** The supplier must be committed to state-of-the-art technology—in the present and for the future—for a successful long-term relationship. Suppliers demonstrate their commitment through research and development and capital expenditures. The former ensures leading-edge product technology; the latter guarantees continuous improvement of operational- and logistical-process technology.

• **Delivery Capability.** The logistical precision associated with JIT mandates a system centered on timely deliveries of exact quantities, provided damage-free.

• **Service Responsiveness.** Customer service is a critical element of the system. Suppliers must respond promptly to the OEM's and the final customer's service needs and help solve any customer problems.

• **Management Attitude and Philosophy.** This characteristic is integral in the foregoing factors but is also important apart from them. Supplier management must wholeheartedly endorse aggressive just-in-time/total quality control programs and commit resources for their implementation. In addition, management must foster a similar commitment among employees at all levels and grant them the creative freedom to create a world-class organization.

• **Lowest Total Cost.** This characteristic contrasts with the "unit price" issue that traditionally influenced supplier selection. "Lowest total cost" is a composite characteristic based on the customer's total acquisition cost. Among suppliers offering lowest total cost, quality levels preclude return or rejection of materials and rework on the customer's product. Delivery performance is not marred by delays, overages, shortages, or damage. Through the customer service function, the supplier makes key personnel accessible and cooperates to solve service problems.

It is in the JIT industrial marketer's own best interest to understand what the OEM considers an "ideal supplier." Beyond that understanding, the supplier can streamline the evaluation process by preparing select individuals for interviews with their functional counterparts on the customer's evaluation team. Both teams should be open, honest, cooperative, and willing to participate in a continuous-improvement program.

Clearly, the buyer cannot conduct such an in-depth evaluation through a single evaluator or auditor. Supplier evaluation requires a team of individuals to judge various factors.

Evaluation teams may resemble the commodity teams Xerox formed in 1985 to evaluate, select, and manage its suppliers. A team leader, preferably chosen from the purchasing area, coordinates the effort. Other team members provide expertise in technical, operational, logistical, and support functions. These include research and development, design engineering, production, process engineering, quality control, distribution, materials management, finance, and information management.

The team need not include representatives from every area under evaluation, but if a team member wears more than one hat, he or she must be qualified to judge the supplier in those areas.

The evaluation includes on-site visits with the team members' functional counterparts on the supplier side. The customer's evaluation team gathers objective performance data to compare with its benchmarks for incoming material. This would include data such as incoming product quality measured in defective parts per million; on-time deliveries in exact quantities specified; and total acquisition cost of material received.

CUSTOMER EVALUATION

Traditionally, industrial marketers have not seriously evaluated potential customers. Customer evaluation and selection has been even more superficial than the supplier evaluation, with suppliers primarily concerned about whether the customer's demand requirements justified the sales effort and whether the buyer represented a serious credit risk.

The customer's overall financial soundness has generally not been a major concern because contracts have often been short-term or single transactions with limited investment in the customer. Customer delinquency or default in payment would not have a catastrophic effect. The supplier could rationalize the loss as just the direct cost of the product sold.

Marketing products to the just-in-time/total quality customer presents a totally different challenge. Rather than negotiating a series of single transactions, each based on price, the OEM and supplier establish a relationship that may last the product's entire life cycle.

Because the relationship links the destinies of the two companies, JIT marketers must select customers carefully: The customer's marketplace performance directly affects the supplier's overall success. The marketer's objective is to *choose a winner*.

Selecting sound customers is particularly important if the OEM's competitors are also implementing just-in-time programs. The parallel trend toward single sourcing severely limits the JIT marketer's pool of alternative customers; the JIT marketer should team up with the most appropriate ones.

The customer-evaluation process is quite similar to supplier evaluation. The supplier examines the following aspects of the customer's setup:

• **Sourcing Philosophy.** OEMs always face the make-or-buy decision when considering production materials. They usually prefer making the part, when business is slow and they have unused plant capacity, rather than buying it. A long-time commitment to external sourcing is very important to suppliers.

Customers that rely on their suppliers to add value are particularly attractive to suppliers. General Motors relies on Davidson Panel Instrument Division of Davidson Rubber Company to provide complete panel-instrument *assemblies* rather than basic panel instruments. Similarly, Ford is starting to buy "dressed" axle assemblies from Eaton Axle Division of Eaton Corporation for its medium-duty trucks.

In both cases, the supplier adds substantial value to the sourced part—and significantly lowers the OEM customer's total cost.

• **Geographic Location.** Suppliers prefer nearby customers for the same reasons cited in the supplier-evaluation section: Proximity gives the JIT supplier a strategic advantage. The supplier should evaluate distant customers very carefully; they must have other needs that put the supplier in a position of strategic advantage. If not, the supplier will be hard pressed to provide a net advantage to the customer over the long term.

• **Financial Strength and Performance.** Again echoing the supplier-evaluation process, suppliers check potential customers' financial and market track records. They also look for a prospectus that points to vigorous performance in the long term. Such historic and potential stability is much more critical in the just-in-time environment, because each customer is more important to the supplier.

• **Communications Capability.** Just-in-time demands a greater exchange of information between the JIT marketer and customer. Much of the data is sensitive or proprietary—research and development results, new-product plans, demand forecasts, cost information, quality levels, and more. For the system to work properly, both parties must be willing to share such information openly. With the customer's cooperation, the JIT marketer can work much more efficiently to plan and implement customer projects.

• **Market Responsiveness.** OEM customers must respond to their own customers. They must stay close to their market to determine customer needs and quickly meet those needs. All of the OEM's operations—from marketing, which identifies needs, through product design, production, delivery, and post-sale service—must focus on the customer.

• **Compatibility with the Supplier.** This is probably the most elusive criterion. The customer and marketer should share the same goals and objectives, have similar operational philosophies, and be committed to the just-in-time/total quality concept. Tension in the relationship should be constructive, and the general tone should be cooperative and trusting.

Successful customer evaluation requires teamwork, much like supplier evaluation. The OEM may instinctively recoil from the supplier's probing, but it should try to cooperate. Because the goal is to establish a long-term relationship, each party must know its potential partner intimately. Any reluctance or resistance from the customer during an evaluation should raise a flag for the supplier regarding the potential for a long-term relationship.

Because the customer assessment is comprehensive, it should rest with a supplier team that includes all the functions that would interact under a long-term agreement.

Marketing, represented by the salesperson and possibly the product manager, should lead and/or coordinate the customer–evaluation team. Other members include individuals from design engineering, for technical input; production, quality assurance, and process engineering, from operations; materials management and distribution, for logistical representation; and finance and information management.

The team members should translate each evaluation criterion into operational terms and measure it objectively against established benchmarks. For example, the supplier may gauge the customer's financial strength and performance using a five-year history of sales and profit growth and an analysis of competitive market position.

In both customer and supplier evaluations, the candidate may be an organization with which the evaluator has a long-standing positive relationship. This can streamline the evaluation, but neither party can let existing relationships bias the results. The characteristics required for future success are quite different from those required in the past.

It is important to realize that both supplier and customer evaluations are *processes,* not events. Each comprises several stages; they may begin with a preliminary survey of basic capabilities, followed by a more intense analysis of processes and systems capabilities. If the results are positive, the parties may initiate a trial program to test their joint performance. If the trial is successful, a series of more substantial agreements usually follows.

VALUE-ADDED ACTIVITIES

As the evaluation process suggests, the ways in which supplies and customers interact—and the way their own people cooperate internally—change greatly with just-in-time. In comparing the JIT value-added process to that of conventional operations, just-in-time may be described as integrative versus functional, team-based versus individually driven, parallel versus sequential, and focused on continuous improvement rather than conformance to specifications. Figure 4-4 illustrates these differences.

The OEM initiates the value-adding process by determining its customers' needs and translating them into new-product requirements. This marketing activity focuses on the product's features and the customer's expectations.

The manufacturer's product design group converts these requirements into detailed specifications, and its materials management/

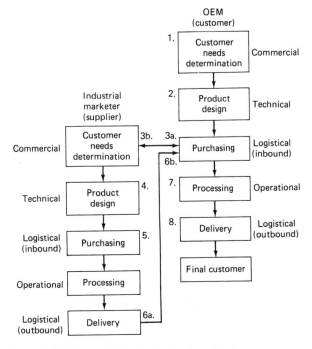

Figure 4-4   Conventional value-added process.

purchasing unit determines materials requirements. This triggers supplier contact. The OEM sends a copy of materials specifications and a request for quotation to qualified suppliers.

The supplier designs the part or component per specification, produces it, and delivers it to the OEM. Prototype models come first, then pilot products, and finally, production units.

The OEM manufactures its product using the supplier's materials, plus goods producted in-house and by other suppliers, and delivers the final product to the customers. This is a simplified explanation; the OEM customer actually goes through several product refinement cycles before releasing a product in production quantities.

The boxes in Fig. 4-4 broadly represent the functional units responsible for each stage. Marketing generally determines customer needs; design engineering develops the product and specifications; materials management and purchasing source components; production manufactures the product, and so on.

This process is subject to numerous problems. For example:

• A sales rep's technical limitations or limited application knowledge may cause miscommunication. The rep may transfer inadequate or incorrect customer-requirement information.

• OEM design engineering may provide detailed product specifications that limit the supplier's designers.

• The customer's or supplier's various functions may not interact with other internal functions. If, say, product design acts independently from quality assurance, pruchasing, and manufacturing, its designs may not provide highest quality, lowest cost, or manufacturing ease.

• The process sequence minimizes multifunctional information sharing and blocks continuous improvement.

• Suppliers are basically passive. They simply provide parts or materials to meet OEM specifications.

• The process requires lengthy lead times, both because it is sequential and because supplier input is delayed. The customer and supplier must execute each functional step before starting the next. Additional supplier tiers aggravate this problem: First-tier suppliers lose time waiting for their suppliers to research, design, produce, and deliver products; the suppliers' suppliers must wait for their suppliers, and so on.

All of these problems disappear when the OEM and supplier shift to just-in-time operations. Figure 4-5 illustrates the JIT value-added process.

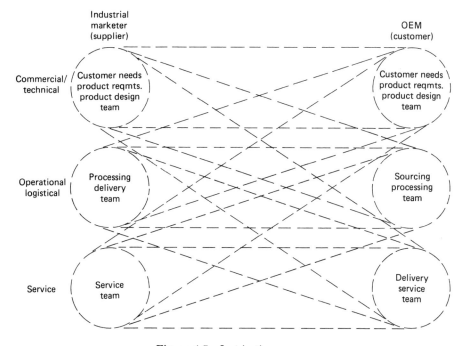

Figure 4-5   Just-in-time process.

With just-in-time, the buyer's and supplier's internal functional unit are not compartmentalized. This approach fosters cross-company integration. To build internal and external networking, Xerox, General Electric, and Hewlett-Packard have used the team approach.

In addition, leading OEMs such as General Motors (Pontiac Division), Pitney Bowes, AT&T, BOSE, and Xerox involve suppliers early in the product-design process. The JIT value-added process minimizes sequence and emphasizes the constantly looping interactions of continuous improvement.

As Fig. 4-5 indicates, JIT OEMs assess customer needs and develop preliminary new-product specifications. This process doesn't just happen. It requires a "catalyst" or "product champion."

The individual in the OEM company primarily responsible for the new product, the team leader or product champion, may be a new-project manager, chief engineer, or project manager. To make sure the product meets customer requirements and expectations and can be produced within acceptable price and delivery constraints, the product champion fashions a team knowledgeable in:

- **Marketing:** to determine product features and performance expectations.
- **Design engineering:** to convert the features and expectations into specifications.
- **Process engineering:** to make sure the design can be manufactured and assess production requirements.
- **Purchasing:** to set procurement requirements.
- **Logistics:** to assess materials-management and distribution requirements.
- **Accounting/finance:** to make sure the product's price is realistic.

Each of these functional areas should participate in product development, because each can contribute greatly to a lowest cost/total quality product.

Because purchased materials represent about 50% of new-product costs, suppliers contribute significantly in reducing costs and increasing product quality. The supplier interacts with the customer's new-product team through a team of its own, headed by marketing—sales and product management. Others on the supplier team assess the customer's needs and product requirements and participate in product design. Team members on the customer and supplier side each have a counterpart on the other team, whether in design engineering, process engineering, quality control, production, distribution, or finance.

The supplier and OEM absolutely must break down any barriers that inhibit cooperation internally or with members of the opposite team. Communication must flow freely within each company and between the two organizations. The supplier's salesperson and the customer's purchasing representative should facilitate and coordinate the cross-company flow.

The advantages of internal and interorganizational teams are obvious. The supplier team's early involvement in new-product development brings to the OEM additional design engineering, process engineering, and purchasing expertise. Cross-functional involvement in the early design stages can sharply reduce the design cycle's lead time and produce easily manufactured, lowest cost designs.

The personal interactions involved help the supplier team understand the OEM's *real* needs—and those of the final customer—well beyond the data on printed specifications. These interactions also stimulate personal relationships, which grow invaluable as the companies sequentially modify the design to improve its performance and cost.

The internal interactions required also help the various team members understand and appreciate other functional areas in their own company and the importance of working together. In addition, the exercise focuses each organization more intensely on its customer.

As the OEM's product moves from design and development into production, the teams are reoriented. As the focus becomes production and delivery, the OEM's and supplier's purchasing, production, process engineering, and quality units take the most active roles. The OEM new-product manager may continue as "product champion," with design engineering and research and development moving into the background until engineering changes demand their involvement.

Team membership essentially stays the same during the design and development, processing, and delivery stages, providing continuity and tremendous time and cost savings. Throughout the process, the OEM's purchasing unit is the key coordinator. OEM materials-control specialists responsible for materials schedules and supplier releases take charge of most routine interactions.

As the value-added process unfolds, supplier team members' roles also shift. The research and development and technical members' input becomes less important than that of the materials management, process engineering, quality, and distribution representatives.

The marketing or sales representative continues to coordinate the team, but that role is reduced to solving problems and executing product changes. The supplier's customer service or order entry personnel are responsible for routine interactions.

In general, the switch to just-in-time substantially reduces the technical and logistical trouble-shooting service needed by the OEM. This is because the system is based on a mutual understanding of each partner's responsibilities.

The supplier is obsessed with meeting its customer's expectations *every time,* and that means doing things right the *first* time. But when problems arise, as they inevitably do, the solutions are simpler. The customer and supplier representatives concerned with the problem already have a personal relationship, are familiar with the process or product causing the problem, and are committed to solving the problem together. This isn't nirvana. It's world-class marketers working with world-class producers!

Even as the customer and supplier teams shift to accommodate the value-added process, the companies continually monitor the system. Monitoring begins during the trial stage, before the companies strike a formal agreement, and extends throughout the value-added process to include post-sale service. Each team continuously assesses its own and its partner's performance. And because each team has line-function members as well as support staff members, the goal setters are also responsible for the company's actual performance. The functions leading the monitoring effort change with the phase of the value-added cycle.

The supplier and customer teams also evaluate their partner's performance continuously. Because each provides its partner with in-depth performance expectations regarding product, quality, delivery, service, and more, the two firms usually develop a two-way communication network. With such a tool, the partners can exchange performance data continuously.

NOTES

1. "How Tomorrow's Suppliers Shape Up: Vendor Profile Forecast," *Purchasing,* January 27, 1983, pp. 80–85.
2. Somerby Dowst, "CEO Report: Turning the Corner in Purchasing— Teamwork is the Vital Key," *Purchasing,* January 29, 1987, pp. 58–62.
3. Jack Gallagher, "Quality From the Top," *Purchasing,* January 28, 1988, pp. 70–77.
4. William J. Weisz, Keynote Presentation at the 1986 Association for Manufacturing Excellence Conference, *Proceedings of the Annual Conference,* October 1986, Chicago, Ill.
5. Douglas Williams, "CPC Supergroups' Single-Source Strategy," *Automotive Industries,* March 1985, pp. 55–56.
6. Joseph Barks, "Strategies for International Distribution," *Distribution,* May 1985, pp. 64–72.
7. Stephen Tierney, "Strategic Planning and Just-in-time," *Proceedings of the Annual Conference, Association for Manufacturing Excellence,* October 1986, Chicago, Ill.

8. Ernest Raia, "JIT USA: Journey to World Class," *Purchasing,* September 24, 1987, p. 51.

9. Ibid., p. 51.

10. Tom Stundza, "Chrysler: The Purchasing Story That Hasn't Been Told," *Purchasing,* July 25, 1985, pp. 42–49.

11. Charles O'Neal, "The Buyer-Seller Linkage in a Just-in-Time Environment: An Empirical Assessment," *Journal of Purchasing and Materials Management,* April 1987, pp. 7–13.

12. Stephen Tierney, "Strategic Planning and Just-in-Time," p. 24.

13. Douglas Williams, "CPC Supergroups Single-Source Strategy," p. 56.

14. "How Tomorrow's Suppliers Shape Up," p. 81.

15. Ibid., p. 81.

16. Somerby Dowst, "Wanted: Compleat Vendors," *Purchasing,* January 26, 1984, pp. 97–101.

17. Ibid., p. 98.

18. Tom Stundza, "Chrysler: The Purchasing Story That Hasn't Been Told," pp. 42–49.

19. Ibid., p. 49.

20. "How Value-Trained Vendors Put the Focus on Function," *Purchasing,* March 28, 1985, pp. 120–22.

21. Ibid., p. 121

22. "In Search of Logistical Excellence," *Purchasing,* September 15, 1983, pp. 30–39.

23. Ibid., p. 39.

24. Somerby Dowst, "CEO Report," p. 61.

25. Somerby Dowst, "Design Report: The Purchasing Connection," *Purchasing,* June 13, 1985, pp. 81–111.

26. "Early Purchasing Involvement: Purchasing and Engineering Together," *Purchasing,* June 13, 1985, pp. 148A17–A21.

Chapter 5

The Benefits of Just-in-Time Purchasing

The preceding chapter on just-in-time customer requirements and buyer–seller linkages hinted at the benefits of just-in-time purchasing. In fact, a customer's just-in-time purchasing can help both the buyer and seller, *if* they both have JIT systems in place.

If the marketer doesn't yet have an in-house just-in-time system up and running, it won't benefit as much from the customer's JIT purchasing. The lagging just-in-time marketer may suffer from higher inventory levels, more rigorous final product inspection requirements, and the like.

Figure 5-1 illustrates the point.

REDUCING THE SUPPLIER BASE

As Fig. 5-1 indicates, narrowing the supplier base is an essential strategy of just-in-time purchasers.

A major OEM has hundreds, or more commonly thousands, of purchased-materials suppliers. Xerox had 5,000 suppliers before paring its supplier base. Such levels place a great administrative burden on the

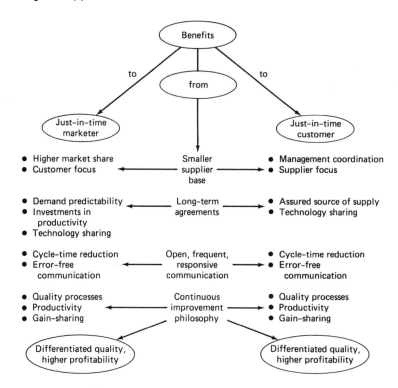

Figure 5-1   Benefits of just-in-time purchasing.

buying organization. It must plan purchases, assign responsibilities to buyers in the purchasing unit, establish communication networks with suppliers, and monitor each supplier's performance against the plan. That's a tremendous coordination problem, with mountains of waste.

Consider the normal paperwork flow between buyer and seller. Thousands of documents, including inquiries, requisitions, acknowledgments, order changes, shipping notices, invoices and payments, flow both ways. That necessitates elaborate processing, storage, and retrieval systems. And expediting is often necessary because of the number of transactions, probability of miscommunication, and lack of supplier commitment. Suppliers' past experience with customers that held backup stock to cover late deliveries and quality problems aggravates the problem. In the end, a large supplier base is an administrative nightmare.

To solve the problem, just-in-time adopters systematically analyze and weed out their suppliers, as discussed in Chapter 4. The JIT purchaser can often cut its supplier base in half within a year and reduce it still further in three to five years. Xerox reduced its supplier base by more than 90% between 1980 and 1985.

The buyer's payoff is a streamlined purchasing system that requires less coordination and fewer administrative and clerical people and lowers administrative costs. The purchasing unit can focus on those suppliers that furnish the lion's share of required materials.

Obviously, all suppliers won't benefit from the just-in-time single-source philosophy. Marginal suppliers are already being displaced. But stronger suppliers that don't make the cut with a particular customer may have locational or technological advantages that other buyers value enough to reward with single-source status.

Successful suppliers gain by focusing on fewer customers and winning all their business for particular items. That ultimately increases the supplier's market share.

Consider the following example in which, for simplicity's sake, four suppliers serve four major producers (see Table 5-1). The producers are all the same size—each represents $1 million in purchasing power—and each starts a just-in-time program to move to single-source suppliers within two years.

Supplier A is the dominant supplier at Customer X, with a 40% share. But A holds only 20% of Customer Y's business and 10% of Z's. Meanwhile, Supplier B is dominant with Customer Y, and Supplier C is dominant with Z.

In moving to single sourcing, the three customers give their dominant suppliers even more business and eliminate one of their other suppliers. In the first phase, Customer Y eliminates Supplier D, and Customer Z reduces share with that supplier. In the second phase, each customer moves to a single supplier, choosing the supplier that controlled most of its business previously. This eliminates Supplier D from the industry.

The analysis shows Supplier D is a pure loser in the customer's move to single sourcing. But all three of the other suppliers gain market share. Supplier A moves from $700,000 in the current year (70% of $1 million) to $800,000 in the first transition year and $1 million in the second year.

TABLE 5-1   The Effect of Single Sourcing on Market Share

	Suppliers' Share of Customer Business								
	Current Year			First Year			Second Year		
	(%)			(%)			(%)		
Supplier	X	Y	Z	X	Y	Z	X	Y	Z
A	40	20	10	60	20	–	100	–	–
B	20	40	30	–	60	30	–	100	–
C	20	30	40	20	20	60	–	–	100
D	20	10	20	20	–	10	–	–	–

Supplier B, with $900,000 in the current year, holds that level the following year and moves to $1 million in the second year. Supplier C, with $900,000 in the current year, moves to $1 million in the first year and holds that level in the second year.

Although the illustration is oversimplified, it demonstrates the potential for market share growth among firms selected as single-source suppliers. Attrition is inevitable. But firms that move aggressively to meet the new requirements can win big. Consider the payoff for Supplier A if it replaced B at Customer Y.

LONG-TERM AGREEMENTS

Negotiating long-term agreements positively influences both the JIT customer and its suppliers, as illustrated in Fig. 5-1.

Short-term transactions cause uncertainty for both parties. There is the question of how long the arrangement will last and whether an order is one of a kind or the first of several. Such uncertainty does not encourage either party to invest in the relationship via improved productivity or quality processes.

Long-term agreements remove the uncertainty. They free the customer and supplier to rise above negotiations, which are often adversarial, and concentrate on reducing the waste inherent in short-term transactional relationships. The customer benefits from sharing its technology with a supplier that holds specific expertise in its own field. The customer's and supplier's design and process engineers can develop creative ways to integrate the two companies' technical expertise. Both organizations are motivated to invest in productivity and quality improvements because they know the partnership will last long enough for them to enjoy the rewards.

The supplier organization reaps another benefit: demand predictability. The supplier's planning horizon can extend beyond the next quarter or the next year without the question of who the customer will be—at least for the customers with whom long-term agreements have been negotiated. Suppliers can focus on long-term customers' specific needs.

COMMUNICATIONS—OPEN, FREQUENT, RESPONSIVE

Communication is a crucial issue in just-in-time purchasing. Interactions between just-in-time customers and their suppliers must be open, frequent, and responsive. Purchasing communication is usually *high-tech,* incorporating electronic data interchange technology, but it is also *high-touch,* nurturing amiable personal relationships.

The high-tech, high-touch approach leads to error-free cycle-time reduction. With the theme "Do it right the first time" in mind, the supplier finds ways to determine precisely what the customer wants before designing and developing it. This compresses the design cycle by removing false starts. The supplier compresses its production cycle by adopting the processes discussed in Chapter 2. And the customer compresses the order cycle by communicating a series of schedules to the supplier. Those start with a long-term rough-cut schedule that gives the supplier a basis for capacity planning; they end with a fixed line set, that is, a firm production schedule of products to be delivered, which remains firm for a period of perhaps ten to fifteen days—long enough to cover the supplier's cycle time.

Even as it works to improve communications with its just-in-time customers, the supplier establishes similar communications with upstream suppliers. The goal is to achieve the same kinds of results with those suppliers.

Because much of the time consumed in the order cycle represents waste—as in the production and design cycles—the final lead time or cycle time proves how successful the just-in-time customer and suppliers have been in removing waste from the purchasing system.

CONTINUOUS IMPROVEMENT PHILOSOPHY

The continuous improvement philosophy becomes standard for both the customer and supplier as they adopt just-in-time purchasing techniques.

Rather than setting a goal, achieving it, and patting themselves on the back—which doesn't help anyone make the world-class cut—successful just-in-time practitioners target "the best of the best" as the standard in every part of their business. It's a benchmarking system that provides constantly changing, ever more challenging goals.

The results speak for themselves: The partners' combined efforts yield much greater results than those of either organization alone. The synergy shows up in quality levels, where "quality at the source," as far back as original materials processing, is each partner's watchword. The supplier and customer measure quality not only as conformance to requirements, but as continuous reduction in variation from the target or the customer's ideal value.

The waste the partners cooperatively eliminate as they implement just-in-time purchasing reduces costs for both organizations. In a healthy partnership, the customer and supplier share cost savings and jointly reinvest in further waste elimination processes.

THE BOTTOM LINE

Clearly, just-in-time/total quality purchasing processes are extremely important in JIT marketing, to both the customer and JIT supplier. Because the just-in-time relationship is equitable, both partners win by implementing purchasing processes and in-house operational techniques effectively. The reward is a highly differentiated product. *Customer-perceived quality* is the differentiator.

What is the value of customer-perceived quality? Extensive research has shown that it provides the supplier with higher market share *and* reduces the industrial customer's costs.[1] Both of these characteristics—higher market share and lower costs—influence profitability. Market share is an indirect determinant, and lower cost is a direct determinant. So, the bottom line of an effective just-in-time purchasing process is that it contributes to both partners' profitability.

IT'S NOT ALL ROSES

Although the experience of practitioners proves the benefits of just-in-time purchasing, this approach isn't problem-free. Research among firms contemplating, developing, or implementing just-in-time processes shows some are reluctant to engage in just-in-time purchasing or that they have had problems implementing it. Prime reasons include a lack of support from suppliers, transportation providers (carriers), or internal units; supplier quality levels; and employee resistance.[2]

Each of these reasons could stem from a common root: failure to instill a sense of commitment in all players. This usually happens when organizations try to move too fast, mixing traditional attitudes with just-in-time practices. That's analogous to using last week's game plan on this week's opponent.

The preparation phase is critical. It requires educating and training everyone—employees at all levels in the customer, supplier, and carrier organizations—to believe in the new philosophy and implement the new processes.

NOTES

1. For example, see Lynn Phillips, Dae Chang, and Robert Buzzell, "Product Quality, Cost Position, and Business Performance: A Test of Some Key Hypotheses," *Journal of Marketing,* Spring 1982, pp. 26–43; and Robert Buzzell and Bradley Gale, *The PIMS Principles: Linking Strategy to Performance,* New York: The Free Press, 1987.

2. See Larry Guinipero and Charles O'Neal, "Obstacles to JIT Procurement," *Industrial Marketing Management,* February 1988; and A. Ansari and Batoul Modarress, "Just-in-Time Purchasing: Problems and Solutions," *Journal of Purchasing and Materials Management,* August 1986.

PART III: ADDITIONAL SUGGESTED READINGS

Susan Avery, "CEO Report: Turning the Corner Takes Purchasing Muscle," *Purchasing,* January 29, 1987, pp. 50–54.

——, "JIT Delivery Demands a Purchasing/Traffic Linkup," *Purchasing,* July 24, 1986, p. 35.

——, "Single Sourcing: The Risks Aren't as Bad as They Seem," *Purchasing,* July 16, 1987, p. 33.

Shirley Cayer, "Buyers in the Appliance Industry Thrive in the New Global Market," *Purchasing,* April 14, 1988, pp. 46–55.

——, "Special Report: Major Household Appliance Makers . . . ," *Purchasing,* January 15, 1987, pp. 42–50.

"CEO's to Purchasing: Buy Quality, Staying Power," *Purchasing,* January 27, 1983, pp. 57–63.

Philip Crosby, "Have a Buyer Day, and Let Suppliers Talk Back to You," *Purchasing,* April 11, 1985, p. 88A37.

Somerby Dowst, "Knowing Your Customers Is a Must," *Purchasing,* March 28, 1985, p. 99.

——, "Quality Suppliers: the Search Goes On," *Purchasing,* January 28, 1988, pp. 94A4–94A12.

——, "What Makes a 'Medal of Excellence' Winner," *Purchasing,* June 21, 1984, pp. 62–71.

Paul Farrell, "The Challenge Is To Run Purchasing as a Business," *Purchasing World,* February 1985, pp. 30–31.

——, "Expect More, Get More from Suppliers," *Purchasing World,* May 1982, pp. 30–33.

Gary Frazier, Robert Spekman, and Charles O'Neal, "Just-in-Time Relationships in Industrial Markets," *Journal of Marketing,* October 1988.

Chan Hahn, Peter Pinto, and Daniel Bragg, " 'Just-in-Time' Production and Purchasing," *Journal of Purchasing and Materials Management,* Fall 1983, pp. 2–10.

William Hampton and David Cook, "Detroit Raises the Ante for Parts Suppliers," *Business Week,* October 14, 1985, pp. 95–97.

"How Pitney Bowes Avoids 'Undeliverable Designs'," *Purchasing,* March 27, 1986, pp. 87–90.

Maryann Keller, "Suppliers Facing New Frontiers," *Automotive Industries,* August 1987, p. 13.

Robert Lee, "Teamwork Is Buying's Backbone at Siemens-Allis," *Purchasing,* June 13, 1985, pp. 120–23.

Michiel Leenders and David Blenkhorn, *Reverse Marketing: The New Buyer-Seller Relationship* (New York: The Free Press, 1988).

Donald Lehmann and John O'Shaughnessy, "Decision Criteria Used in Buying Different Categories of Products," *Journal of Purchasing and Materials Management,* Spring 1982, pp. 9–15.

Theodore Levitt, *The Marketing Imagination* (New York: The Free Press, 1986).

G. H. Manoochehri, "Suppliers and the Just-in-Time Concept," *Journal of Purchasing and Materials Management,* Winter 1984, pp. 16–21.

John McElroy, "1988 Man of the Year: Ford's Harold A. Poling," *Automotive Industries,* February 1988, pp. 36–39.

———, "Outsourcing: The Double-edged Sword," *Automotive Industries,* March 1988, pp. 44–46.

Hannah Miller, "Just-in-Time: Some Textile Industries Call It 'Linkage'," *Purchasing,* April 1987, pp. 58–61.

Jennifer Mintzer, "Supplier-Side Economics: The Silent Majorities Speak," *Automotive Industries,* December 1986, pp. 56–59.

John O'Connor, "Is Your Company Ready for the Ultimate Seller's Market?" *Purchasing,* August 7, 1986, p. 37.

———, "Just-in-Time USA," *Purchasing,* February 13, 1986, pp. 48–62.

Michael Robinson and John Timmerman, "How Vendor Analysis Supports JIT Manufacturing," *Management Accounting,* December 1987, pp. 20–24.

Amy Rogers, "Buyers Looking to Trucking Services to Make JIT Work," *Purchasing,* April 24, 1986, pp. 36–55.

———, "Out of Restructuring, a New Purchasing," *Purchasing,* July 11, 1985, pp. 73–76.

Richard Schonberger and Abdolhossein Ansari, " 'Just-in-Time' Purchasing Can Improve Quality," *Journal of Purchasing* and *Materials Management,* Spring 1984, pp. 2–7.

John Schorr and Thomas Wallace, *High Performance Purchasing* (Essex Junction, Vt.: Oliver Wight Limited Publications, 1986).

Tom Stundza, "Alcoa: Taking the Next Step to Computerized Purchasing," *Purchasing,* March 27, 1986, pp. 124B3–B5.

Peter Walters, "Transportation-Purchasing Interface," *Distribution,* January 1988, pp. 56–60.

"When Your Customer is Operating Personnel," *Purchasing,* March 28, 1985, pp. 108–13.

"When Your Customer is the Supplier," *Purchasing,* March 28, 1985, pp. 115–19.

David Wilson and Jack Hayyo, "Implications of the Just-in-Time Purchasing Philosophy to Intercompany Bonding," Proceedings of the *3rd International I.M.P. Research Seminar on International Marketing,* Lyon, France, September 1986.

Chapter 6

Developing a Winning JIT Marketing Strategy

INTRODUCTION

With the playing arena taking on global proportions, and marketing's game rules and player relationships changing, industrial marketers are rewriting their playbook. They need guidelines to design game plans that will let them outdistance the competition in serving individual customers. Those game plans—marketing strategies—include long-term partnerships with key customers and prospects.

In the just-in-time environment, marketing strategy development takes on a new significance. Strategy development hinges on the marketer's determination of product markets' and individual accounts' long-term potential. Such evaluations require careful market assessment, including customer and competitor analyses. Those reveal the marketer's key accounts—current and potential—and suggest how the firm should "position" itself with them. This provides the basis for the just-in-time marketing program.

These concepts are the heart of JIT industrial marketing. This chapter explains how marketers design effective strategies to serve key just-in-time accounts. The four subsequent chapters build on this framework, focusing on various elements of marketing strategy. Chapter 7 considers product strategy; Chapter 8, pricing strategy; Chapter 9, distribution strategy; and Chapter 10, communications strategy.

These dimensions are intimately related, and the industrial marketer must combine them carefully to create a winning marketing program positioning strategy.

Developing successful strategies isn't easy. It takes lots of information, based on sound research, and good judgement grounded in experience.

We will not document in detail the strategic marketing planning process. Several other authors have already done that very capably.[1] Instead, we will sketch out the basic approach, stressing aspects that are more critical to just-in-time industrial marketers. The schematic in Fig. 6-1 lays the groundwork for this discussion.

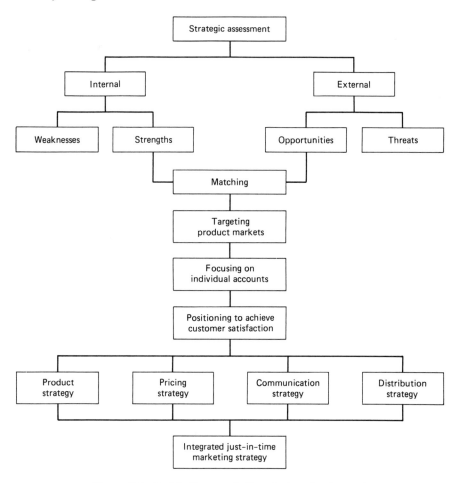

Figure 6-1   Just-in-time marketing-strategy development.

STRATEGIC ASSESSMENT—INTERNAL

Strategic assessment is a process that examines the organization to determine its strengths and weaknesses. It also examines the external environment to uncover opportunities and threats facing the organization.

The internal assessment is an objective analysis of the firm's own shop. It answers the question, "What do we have, or what do we do that makes us distinctive . . . or could do so if properly focused?" It looks at all critical areas: the company's organization; location; human resources; financial, technical, operational, logistical, and marketing capabilities; and more. Above all, the internal assessment must be *objective*. This may pose problems as the firm tries to identify weaknesses or the absence of critical skills or resources.

The search is for "distinctive competencies." These are areas in which the company excels, versus competition, and that are important to key customers. This is where competitive advantage starts. The internal analysis should be conducted through the *eyes of the customer*—from the customer's point of view.

The firm should conduct a strategic assessment for each product-market offering. The organization with a narrow product-market focus, such as a supplier marketing heavy-duty truck axles to auto makers, probably has only one product-market offering to analyze. The analysis is much more complex for the circuit chip or microprocessor marketer that serves OEMs in the automotive, appliance, computer, and instrumentation industries. The product-market analysis is extremely important for those multiple-application product makers.

EXTERNAL ASSESSMENT

The external assessment analyzes what's happening in the marketplace—how it affects the marketer today and how it will tomorrow. It evaluates demand for customer's products, and consequently, for the marketer's. This assessment looks at customer's buying behavior, industry practices and trends, and the state of present technology and direction of technological developments. It also includes an intensive competitor analysis.

The goal of this analysis is to uncover strategic opportunities in the marketplace, and current and potential threats. The latter may emerge from the shift to new technologies, entry of new competitors, and political or regulatory issues.

THE MATCHING PROCESS

A careful analysis of internal strengths and weaknesses, coupled with a systematic assessment of the market's characteristics, needs, and trends, allows the marketer to match its strengths and with market opportunities. But distinctive competencies are a competitive advantage only when potential customers perceive them as such. This means a capability that differentiates a supplier in the eyes of one customer or customer group may not do the same with another. Consequently, the marketer may have several strengths of varying importance, depending on the customer.

It's critical that the marketer understand how its strengths relate to market needs. This is the first step in product-market targeting.

A way to systematically display the results of this cross-analysis and establish a *product-market* focus is to use strategic marketing display grids. Two are particularly appropriate.

The Boston Consulting Group (BCG) market-share grid is a two-dimensional matrix that positions the product-market offering by market growth rate and relative market share (see Fig. 6-2).[2]

The marketer positions each product-market offering on the grid based on the rate of market growth and the offering's relative market share. The market growth rate generally reflects the maturity of the product in its life cycle or market-application phase, with young products and applications enjoying a faster growth rate. Relative market share is computed by comparison with the largest competitor's share.

Research shows that offerings in quadrants I and II are the most profitable, based on cash flow generation. Products positioned in quadrants III and IV tend to be marginal or negative profit generators. The recommended strategy for quadrant-I products is investment, to maintain their preferred position. In that way, the marketer eases the "stars'" transition to quadrant II while continuing to generate cash.

The marketer should also maintain products in quadrant II to keep generating the cash promised by high market share in a mature market. Careful analysis of quadrant-III offerings shows the feasibility of moving

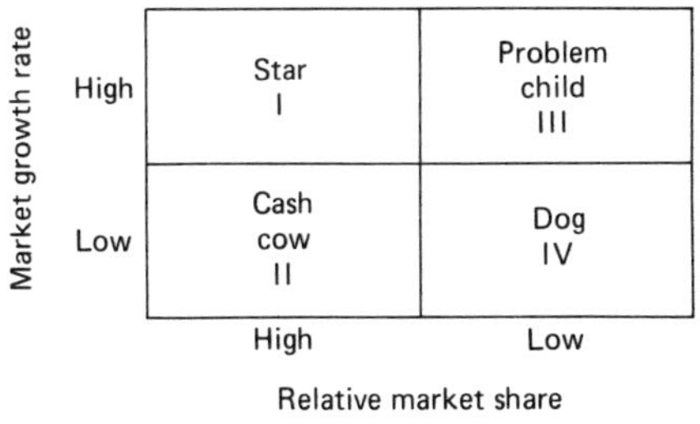

	High	Star I	Problem child III
Market growth rate	Low	Cash cow II	Dog IV
		High	Low

Figure 6-2 BCG product-market growth share matrix.

Relative market share

them to quadrant I. If this isn't feasible, the company should drop these offerings.

Products in quadrant IV are in real trouble. The probability of gaining market share in a mature market isn't great. Unless the marketer can redefine the market with a niche strategy, to serve a desirable and achievable subsegment of quadrant IV, the best strategy is to divest these products.

This is a much simplified presentation of BCG's approach, but it gives the just-in-time industrial marketer a feel for how to analyze its product-market offerings.

A similar approach comes from General Electric. The firm's "Company Position-Industry Attractiveness (Stoplight) Matrix" is illustrated in Fig. 6-3.[3]

The GE Stoplight Matrix extends the BCG approach in both dimensions, making it more complex and meaningful. The vertical dimension, "business strengths," comprises several factors besides relative market share. These include the marketer's size, growth, profitability, margins, technological position, and image. The horizontal dimension includes, in addition to market growth rate, the market's size, diversity, competitive structure, industry profitability, technology position, and the like.

Each offering is positioned in one of the matrix's nine cells. Three basic strategies are suggested based on the cell position. For the promising products in green cells (1, 2, and 4), the marketer's strategy is "invest to grow." And because the products in red cells (6, 8, and 9) are generally unprofitable, the strategy is to either harvest or divest them. Meanwhile, the products in yellow cells (3, 5, and 7) are in a caution zone because of their marginal profitability. Rather than harvesting or divesting those products, the marketer carefully maintains them while trying to move them into green cells.

The value of General Electric's and BCG's approaches springs from the matrix user's willingness and ability to conduct a careful, objective assessment. The assessment, in both techniques, forces the marketer to

Industry attractiveness

		High	Medium	Low
Business strengths	High	1 Green	2 Green	3 Green
	Medium	4 Green	5 Yellow	6 Red
	Low	7 Yellow	8 Red	9 Red

Figure 6-3   GE product-market stoplight matrix.

review its organizational strengths and weakness *and* industry opportunities and threats. This produces a more focused set of product markets and is a move away from what Tom Bonoma, in *The Marketing Edge,* calls "global mediocrity,"[4] By that he means trying to be good at all things—developing many products and serving numerous markets—but excelling at none.

INDIVIDUAL ACCOUNT FOCUS

The above analyses reveal specific product markets that the marketer serves well or could serve well. But suppliers don't serve product markets, they serve individual customers. How can they target their marketing efforts to focus on individual accounts? An extension of the GE Stoplight Matrix can help.

In Chapter 4, we discussed partner evaluation and looked at specific criteria the supplier and customer could use to evaluate partners. These evaluations provide data for individual account analysis. Figure 6-4 illustrates the results of such an analysis.

This matrix is much like that in Fig. 6-3. The marketer positions

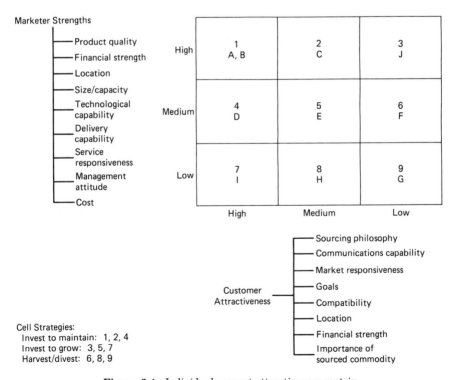

Figure 6-4   Individual account attractiveness matrix.

current and potential customers on the matrix individually, based on their attractiveness as measured in the customer evaluation. Positioning is also based on the marketer's own strengths, evaluated as much as possible *from the perspective of the customer or prospect* being positioned.

Customers A and B are in the most desirable position. They are the most attractive clients or prospects and they perceive the marketer, according to its own evaluation, as having strengths desirable in a supplier. It clearly has one or more distinctive competencies to offer A and B. The same is true, to a lesser extent, of customers C and D. With an appropriate marketing strategy, the supplier will receive a large share of their business. Clients F, G, and H represent the opposite extreme. They are unattractive customers or prospects that don't perceive the marketer as having strengths desirable in a partner.

The goal of this analysis is to identify customers and prospects that rank high on the attractiveness dimension and also value the marketer's self-identified strengths. These customers, in cells 1, 2, and 4, become high-priority accounts.

In conducting the analysis, the marketer must carefully assign accounts to cells. Its approach to cells 3, 5, and 7 is particularly important. It shouldn't put accounts in those cells based on an improper customer assessment or faulty understanding of customer-perceived strengths.

Although the marketer should focus initially on the "green light" customers in cells 1, 2, and 4, it also needs to develop the strengths needed to move cell-7 accounts to cell 4 and cell-4 accounts to cell 1. In this continuous process, the marketer's strengths change over time, as does their importance to individual accounts.

This account analysis yields a select set of individual accounts that the marketer can focus on and work to serve more effectively than does the competition. It also reveals customers and prospects the marketer doesn't really match up with—those it should not pursue. Such accounts may be marginally attractive and unlikely to become more desirable. Or the marketer may not have the features, or the short-term ability to develop the features, those customers desire in a supplier.

Backing off from existing customers is painful but essential. The key to success in the just-in-time environment is focus. The individual account, not the market segment or customer group, is the ultimate target. Resources devoted to marginal accounts that are unlikely to develop must be diverted to key accounts, even if those customers aren't currently active or give the marketer only a modest share of their business. This is where the marketer must apply its resources, investing in these key accounts to transform them into major customers.

The investments are crucial to keep the industrial marketer from being just a little better than its competitors. William Davidow, in *Marketing High Technology,* warns, "Slightly better is dangerous."[5] He emphasizes that truly successful marketers are significantly better than their competitors in one or more ways that customers value.

DETERMINING CUSTOMER REQUIREMENTS

Choosing which individual accounts to serve is a critical step in strategy development. But it's just as important to determine these individual accounts' needs. This may be easy, especially for accounts with whom the marketer already enjoys the dominant share of available business and a satisfying relationship. It's much more challenging with firms that are still prospects or with whom the supplier doesn't enjoy preferred status.

The key to success in identifying key accounts' needs is to generate an atmosphere of trust, confidence, and openness. They must believe the marketer sincerely wants to become a partner and needs complete information about their requirements from *their point of view.* Such rapport takes time to develop and requires teamwork.

The marketer may set the stage with a meeting that includes top managers from both companies. On the customer side, this reinforces the supplier's seriousness about becoming a partner. And internally, it brings the marketer's senior managers onto the marketing team, showing them what it takes to be a successful supplier to key individual accounts.

The quality function deployment concept discussed in Chapter 2 is an excellent tool for determining customer needs. It can also help translate them into technical requirements for the various stages of product and process development. Mitsubishi Heavy Industries introduced QFD in Japan in 1972. Toyota adopted it in 1977, after four years of preparation, with impressive results. Larry Sullivan, chairman of the American Supplier Institute, reported in the June 1986 issue of *Quality Progress* that all Toyota suppliers were then using QFD.[6] Xerox's U.S. operations "imported" the process in 1984, based on the experience of Fuji Xerox, the company's Japanese arm.

QFD, sometimes called the "voice of the customer," should pervade the *entire* organization, starting with initial product and process design and concluding with post-sale service. By determining customer needs, the marketer validates or nullifies the opportunities/strengths matches it made earlier. It's entirely possible that some customers' requirements won't match the industrial marketer's current or even its potential strengths. Rather than wasting resources on such accounts, the marketer should divert them to more productive prospects.

It is quite common for certain groups of accounts—those in the same product-market industry or with similar technologies or competitive environments, for example—to have similar requirements. These groups become customer clusters or market segments, simplifying marketing-strategy development.

POSITIONING

The concept of "positioning" has become popular since the late 1970s.[7] Positioning, a psychological concept referring to the placement or position of a product, company, service, or other offering in the minds of household consumers or organizational buyers, can be extremely useful in marketing-strategy planning. Organizations considered marketers of particular products or services are positioned on the basis of product/service attributes or characteristics important to customers.

The industrial marketer's goal is to achieve the most favorable position possible in the minds of customers and prospects. To make this happen, the marketer must identify that position. After doing so, it must *develop* products and processes to achieve that position and *communicate* information about these products and processes to appropriate individuals in the customer or prospect organization. This communication is called the marketing-program positioning strategy.

It's important to remember that the industrial marketer's positioning is much more than window dressing. It's the marketer's *raison d'etre*. Positioning is designed into each product and process and requires the proper infrastructure and attitude to succeed.

JUST-IN-TIME MARKETING STRATEGY DEVELOPMENT

In developing a marketing strategy, the just-in-time marketer relies heavily on its knowledge of customer requirements. Table 6-1 summarizes just-in-time customers' needs and shows the marketing strategy components the marketer positions to meet each.

TABLE 6-1   Matching Marketing-Strategy Components and Just-in-Time Customers' Needs

	Marketing-Strategy Components *that Satsify the Need*			
Customer Needs	Product	Price	Communication	Distribution
Quality products . . .	x		x	
Every time, etc. . . .	x		x	x
Lowest total cost.	x	x	x	x
Frequent deliveries in . . .			x	x
Small lots, and . . .			x	x
Exact quantities, . . .			x	x
Precisely as needed.			x	x

The just-in-time customer requires quality above all else. The marketer's offering must conform to the customer's requirements in all important dimensions: product performance, delivery, and service. This means quality must be designed into the product, into the manufacturing process, and into maintenance and service. These aren't independent; they must be integrated, with very close coordination from the start of the design cycle.

Smaller lot sizes demand more frequent deliveries, of exact quantities, with shipments arriving precisely as needed—and no mistakes. The marketer must meet the customer's logistical requirements with quality, just as it meets product and service requirements. The supplier carefully assesses each requirement in the first stage of quality function deployment. The final requirement, lowest total cost, is the bottom line measurement of how efficiently it meets all the requirements.

THE ROLE OF MARKETING

Marketing plays a key role in determining and satisfying just-in-time customers' needs. The marketing unit is the primary link to the customer, initiating, coordinating, and integrating activities that promote customer satisfaction. To call this a challenge is a vast understatement. Fortunately, marketing has all the organization's resources to draw from in meeting the challenge. It's imperative that it use them, and effectively.

In carrying the "voice of the customer" to its organization, marketing relies heavily on a team comprising the firm's best available technical, operational, and logistical personnel. These individuals, together with their facilities and processes, form the infrastructure. A characteristic crucial to the team's success is attitude: a customer-oriented attitude toward external *and* internal customers.

"Customer orientation" usually relates to external customers, and that is critical. Market-driven firms are intensely committed to their external customer. All teams and individuals working with customers, whether in product design, development, manufacturing, delivery, service, or on the support staff, need strong positive relationships with their customer counterparts. But that's not enough.

There must also be an *internal customer* orientation—an application of the customer-satisfaction marketing concept *inside* the organization.[8] Every unit in the organization usually supplies another unit with some services or items. At the same time, it's a user or customer of a different internal processing unit. Too often, the relationships between these internal suppliers/customers are adversarial. Their win-lose goals are often departmental and compartmented and often conflict with those of internal suppliers and/or customers.

For example, consider the typical objectives of engineering, manufacturing, and marketing managers. Engineering produces state-of-the-art designs that may be costly and tough to manufacture and service, while manufacturing plans for long runs, stable designs, and few models. Meanwhile, marketing lobbies for many models, short runs, flexibility, and responsiveness.

What's the answer? An internal-customer orientation led by the marketing unit can do much to solve the problem. The first task is to pinpoint external customers' requirements. The process flows backward from there, with each prior unit determining what it must do to meet its internal customers' needs. From there the supplier can develop specifications for each internal unit.

This approach deviates from traditional operations in several ways. Internal supplier and user units must talk to each other *before* the supplier unit finalizes its product or process. Both interdepartment communication and clearly specified timetables are extremely important.

The internal process works like the external-customer process. The internal supplier and user units form teams to assess each others' needs and capabilities. They focus on the next process and ultimately on the final customer. Properly implemented, this approach reduces costs and improves quality. It lets the supplier unit know what the user unit needs before processing, which reduces or eliminates defective incoming products or processes. Quality input is available when it's needed.

All internal processes focus on doing the right thing—based on user needs—and doing it right, in consultation with internal users and suppliers. This sounds idealistic. In fact, it's very logical and practical. Several leading-edge organizations have well-established internal-customer programs, and their results have been quite positive.

POSITIONING THE MARKETING STRATEGY

Determining the customer's exact requirements, a process explained more fully in the next four chapters, is only half the battle. The other half is meeting the requirements to the customer's satisfaction. The marketer does so by positioning its marketing program according to the requirements it identified (see Fig. 6-5).

A simple example will illustrate the positioning concept (see Fig. 6-5). Let's assume that a prospective customer is a just-in-time producer that values incoming product quality and timely delivery and has set high standards for both. Currently, the company has five potential suppliers: A, B, D, E, and U.

When the customer evaluated these five suppliers several months ago, it selected A and B. The customer perceived (positioned) these suppli-

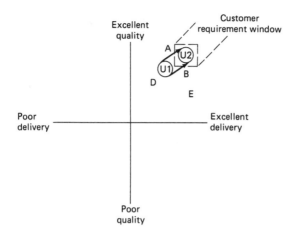

Figure 6-5   Positioning the marketing program.

ers as being better able to meet its requirements than D, E, or U. But neither A nor B completely meets its needs. The customer positioned A as consistently meeting product quality requirements but falling short on delivery requirements. In contrast, B meets the delivery requirements but does not consistently meet product quality expectations. The customer isn't currently considering either D or E because of their much less desirable positions.

Our company, U, is also an outsupplier. The customer positioned us at U1 based on its initial evaluation. At that time we were just starting to implement our JIT/TQC plan. Since then we've demonstrated to several companies in the customer's industry that we can meet delivery and quality requirements equal to those of this customer.

The fact that we can do so doesn't change our position with this prospect. The customer must change its perception of us, and that requires a combination of communication and demonstration. We must let the company know about our new capabilities and persuade it to let us demonstrate them. A successful demonstration should move us to a favored position, U2. That would let us displace A, B, or even both suppliers, in time.

To expand this simple illustration of positioning, consider the key customer needs presented in Table 6-1. Recapping, they are:

1. Delivering quality products every time is critical, because JIT reduces and ultimately eliminates the customer's backup or buffer inventories. Defective components interrupt production. They cause waste, whether detected early in the manufacturing process or in the final product. If the latter, the amount of waste and associated costs may be an order of magnitude higher—or more.

2. Lowest total cost shifts the customer's emphasis from the lowest initial price to the cumulative cost of all elements contributing to its product. In choosing suppliers, the OEM considers how defective materials, untimely deliveries, order processing delays, rework, and backup inventories boost its product cost.

3. Frequent deliveries of small lots are the heart of the system. They let the producer reduce or eliminate inventories at all levels, from raw materials through work-in-process to final product. This is quite different from traditional large-batch processing.

4. Exact quantities, delivered precisely as needed, reduce waste from over- and underproduction and let the supplier and customer synchronize materials inflow with production. The JIT customer may not need to stage or store incoming materials, if they flow directly to the production-line point of use.

It's important to note that the customer or prospect positions suppliers and potential suppliers. It does so based on the perceptions of those organizations held by its key buying influences in research and development, purchasing, quality assurance, and manufacturing. The customer positions suppliers using dimensions these buying influences value most. The just-in-time industrial marketer faces a challenging assignment. It must determine:

1. Key buying influences in the customer/prospect organization;
2. What supplier characteristics each buying influence considers important;
3. What level of each characteristic the customer requires;
4. How it, as a supplier, is positioned vis-a-vis these characteristics; and
5. Its chief competitors' positions.

These data give the marketer the needed ammunition to develop a marketing-positioning strategy. This development is a "gap-closing" process with two goals. The marketer's first is to *match* its capabilities with the customers' requirements. The second is to *communicate* these capabilities to the customer and ask for a chance to demonstrate them.

The successful just-in-time marketer carefully develops and closely coordinates the strategy components of product, price, communication, and distribution to develop the unique competitive advantages that position it most favorably with key accounts. (The next four chapters explore marketing positioning strategy more fully, focusing on those strategy components.)

THE MODEL SUPPLIER

The integrated marketing strategy's goal is to transform the marketer into the "model supplier" that world-class just-in-time manufacturers seek. Xerox's specifications for the model supplier reflect the desires of an increasing number of leading-edge producers. In a nutshell, these specifications focus on the supplier's:[9]

1. Management attitude. Senior managers:
   - view customer satisfaction as a driving principle;
   - have a "vision of the future" and want their firm to be the "best of the best;"
   - are willing to change the company;
   - employ progressive and involved employees;
   - are committed to state-of-the art technologies;
   - use benchmarking for self-evaluation;
   - support and implement the just-in-time philosophy;
   - have an investment plan for success; and
   - participate in product design process (ESI).
2. Company history, including its:
   - organizational stability; and
   - demonstrated experience and expertise.
3. Financial status. Xerox considers the supplier's:
   - financial stability and growth ability;
   - demonstrated productivity;
   - resources invested in its vision of the future; and whether
   - Xerox is a significant customer to the supplier.
4. Product and service quality.
   - Is the supplier's quality measurable in parts per million defective?
   - Does it meet or exceed Xerox's quality benchmark?
   - Does the supplier embrace total quality control?
   - What about statistical process control?
   - Is it certified as a subtier supplier?
   - Does it use closed-loop systems?
   - Does it have functional/reliability test capability?
5. Cost orientation. The supplier should:
   - know and control cost elements;
   - price on cost, not on market;

- be willing to engage in cooperative costing; and
- avoid hidden markups.
6. Service. Does the supplier:
- provide spares support?
- follow up on problems?
7. Delivery capabilities and location. The supplier should have:
- demonstrated flexibility;
- ability to reduce lead times;
- no major import restrictions or cultural impediments;
- an established subtier of its own suppliers, or vertical integration;
- appropriate material, process control, and configuration systems.
8. Technical capabilities. Is the supplier:
- using state-of-the-art production technologies?
- capable of "black box" designs?
- able to process technical changes efficiently?
- Does it have process and tool engineering capability?
- What about prototype capability?
9. Work force.
- Do the supplier's wage rates and skills balance at the benchmark?
- Are its skills inventories in balance?
- Does it have supportive training programs and productive, involved people?

These specifications are quite challenging and will stretch just-in-time marketers to the limit. The industrial marketer must recognize that becoming a model supplier takes time—and a philosophy of continuous improvement. A vision of the future is essential, as is a committed attitude and the resources to back up those intangibles.

Other suppliers are quickly becoming formidable competitors. They are training their teams rigorously, to become world class. Players reluctant to match this quantum leap may be forfeiting the game.

NOTES

1. Examples of excellent sources include: D. F. Abell and J. S. Hammond, *Strategic Marketing Planning* (Englewood Cliffs, N.J.: Prentice Hall, 1979); David Cravens, *Strategic Marketing* (Homewood, Ill.: Richard D. Irwin, 1982); Philip Kotler, *Marketing Management: Analysis, Planning and Control,* 4th edition, (Englewood Cliffs, NJ: Prentice Hall, 1987).
2. George Day, "Diagnosing the Product Portfolio," *Journal of Marketing,* April 1977, pp. 29–38.
3. Abell and Hammond, *Strategic Marketing,* pp. 272–78.

4. Thomas V. Bonoma, *The Marketing Edge* (New York: The Free Press, 1985), pp. 27–28.

5. William H. Davidow, *Marketing High Technology* (New York: The Free Press, 1986), pp. 37–52.

6. L. P. Sullivan, "Quality Function Deployment," *Quality Progress,* June 1986, pp. 39–50.

7. Refer to: Al Ries and Jack Trout, *Positioning: the Battle for Your Mind* (New York: McGraw-Hill, 1981); David A. Aaker and J. Gary Shansby, "Positioning Your Product," *Business Horizons,* May/June 1982, pp. 56–62.

8. Refer to: Kaoru Ishikawa, *What is Total Quality Control?* (Englewood Cliffs, NJ: Prentice Hall, 1985), pp. 105–06; Charles R. O'Neal, "Applying the Marketing Concept to Satisfy Internal Customers," *Marketing News,* March 14, 1988, p. 18.

9. Xerox model supplier characteristics provided in personal communications to the authors from Tony Pollock, Manager Materials Operations, Xerox Corporation, Webster, N.Y. Used by permission of Xerox Corporation, 800 Long Ridge, Stamford, Connecticut.

Chapter 7

Product Strategy

John Warne, CEO of Omark Industries, in addressing the 1986 AME annual conference, defined a world-class manufacturer as "a company that provides products of such high value that they can compete effectively in any market in the world."[1] This also describes the just-in-time marketer with a world-class industrial marketing capability.

THE VALUE CONCEPT

The key words in Warne's description are "products" and "value." This chapter focuses on the product. But first, let's deal with the issue of value.

Value, the relationship between quality and price, may be expressed as follows:

$$\text{Value} = \frac{\text{Quality}}{\text{Price}}$$

A customer who gets higher quality at the same or lower price receives better value. It's important for the marketer to evaluate quality from the *customer's* point of view. Quality is whatever the customer believes or *perceives* it is. Customers usually base their perception of quality on comparisons with competitive offerings. Consequently, it is the customer's perceived relative value of the marketer's *total offering* that influences purchase behavior, and not coincidentally, market share and profitability.

Figure 7-1, from *PIMS Principles*, by Robert D. Buzzell and Bradley T. Gale, summarizes this thinking.[2] The data that fed their conclusions included the comprehensive Profit Impact of Marketing Strategy (PIMS) data base.

An industrial marketer may choose one of the value positions shown in Fig. 7-1, after comparing the marketer's offering to competitive packages. The comparisons yield one of the following five positions:

1. Premium value = Superior quality at a premium price
2. Average value = Comparable value at a comparable price
3. Economy value = Inferior quality at a low price
4. Better value = Superior quality at a comparable or lower price
5. Worse value = Inferior quality at the same or higher price

It is important to recognize that the relationship between quality and price is dynamic. It changes when the industrial marketer changes what it's doing, when competitors change what they're doing, and/or when customers' needs change.

The just-in-time marketer strives for the "better value" position.

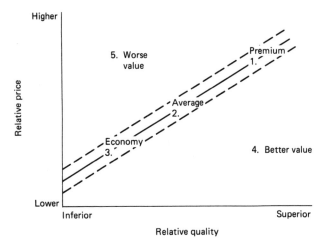

Figure 7-1 Alternative value positions. Source: Robert D. Buzzell and Bradley T. Gale, *The PIMS Principles* (New York: The Free Press, 1987), p. 112.

This requires focusing on the offering's quality and on price, or the cost of providing the offering. An "offering" includes all benefits or elements the customer buys. These are the physical product, supporting technical and logistical services, personal business relationships, and the marketer's reputation.

To provide total customer satisfaction, the marketer delivers those elements of the offering that the customer considers important—and does it according to the customer's requirements. Success mandates total quality orientation for the industrial marketer. Its organization must develop products and processes that allow complete, effective control over all elements that provide customer satisfaction.

The just-in-time marketer aspiring to world-class status embarks on a continuous journey toward a perfect quality offering. It's a journey in which each step begins and ends with the customer.

Figure 7-2 illustrates the just-in-time industrial marketer's quality journey. But before going into detail, an overview is in order.

The journey begins with a careful customer-needs assessment that translates the "voice of the customer" into meaningful product and process design characteristics. This is the quality function deployment process's basic task and is a crucial step. Roughly 40% of all quality problems, as the customer views them, spring from designs that don't satisfy its requirements.[3]

Value engineering tackles design problems and takes advantage of

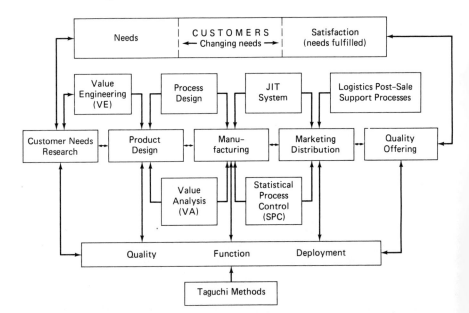

Figure 7-2 The JIT industrial marketer's journey to a perfect quality offering.

opportunities to add value to the product before it is placed into production. The Taguchi Methods may be used with QFD to identify and resolve design conflicts. They are also helpful in evaluating, improving, and maintaining quality. Value analysis continues this process in the product's manufacturing cycle. Manufacturing process design can also significantly improve quality—fully 30% of quality problems spring from manufacturing and processing problems.[4]

In-house just-in-time systems boost the offering's value by continually improving all processes related to it. Quality improvement and cost reduction are the JIT manufacturer's two major emphases. QFD ensures that the proper functions throughout the organization accept their quality responsibility. Statistical process control monitors the progress of critical manufacturing and logistical processes to make sure they stay within control limits. Post-sale support, including logistical and technical service and application engineering, completes the quality assurance loop.

By listening to customers, the JIT supplier satisfies their needs. But these needs change, and that launches another cycle of continuous improvement. The constant goal is to maximize the offering's value in the customer's eyes.

THE NEEDS: TRANSLATING THE VOICE OF THE CUSTOMER

The first and most important step in developing a high-value offering is to determine the customer's exact needs—from the customer's point of view. This is not simple. Unlike consumer sales, which often hinge on meeting the needs of a single person, business-to-business sales pivot on the needs of many individuals in the buying organization. All the participants influence the purchase decision in their own way.

There are three main categories of influences:

1. The *technical* buying influences include research and development, design engineering, and quality assurance. These functional groups evaluate the product's or service's ability to meet objective specifications. While technical influences don't usually have final-approval authority, they can veto a supplier's product.

2. The *user* buying influences include process engineering, manufacturing, and quality assurance. They are the groups that use the product in manufacturing and are directly affected by the product's quality.

3. The *economic* buying influences, such as top management, purchasing, or finance, have the financial authority to approve the purchase.[5]

Just meeting customer's needs may not be enough to get the business. Competition may also be able to meet those needs. The marketer's goal is to provide a *better value* than competitors. Because each customer has unique needs, each requires a unique offering.

To develop that offering, the marketer assigns a customer needs assessment team that includes those best qualified to determine the customer's needs. The individuals on the team are often the supply-side counterparts of the customer's buying influences. This process of marketer-customer communication came up in Chapter 4 and will be covered in more depth in Chapter 9.

Whatever other needs the customer may have, it shares one basic need with the just-in-time marketer: *low cost.* For the marketer, this poses the challenge of minimizing both the cost of providing the offering *and* the customer's cost of using it.

THE PROCESS: QUALITY FUNCTION DEPLOYMENT

Quality Function Deployment (QFD) is a planning tool used to translate and diffuse customer requirements throughout the marketing organization. As in weaving fabric, the offering's quality depends equally on the vertical dimension, or warp, and the horizontal dimension, or woof. American firms have historically emphasized the vertical communication flow while neglecting the horizontal. This has resulted from the compartmentalization of the various functions of the organization. For example, design engineering may have very limited contact with process engineering or manufacturing, or even with the customer, prior to the design of a particular product. As a result, the product, perceived by the design engineering unit as a "quality" design, may be very difficult and expensive to make and/or to service. QFD corrects this deficiency by bringing each of the relevant functional units into the product development process at the very beginning and allowing them to work as a team in developing a quality product from the "customer's" point of view. The "customer" is defined as the next link in the process.

Although the complete QFD process is rather complex, its potential for reducing product development lead time, improving quality, and lowering costs—as proven by the American frontrunners using it—illustrates the technique's merit. An outline of how the technique works follows, and more complete information is available from other sources, such as the American Supplier Institute.[6]

The voice of the final customer is critical to the success of the process. The final product OEM—Ford or Chrysler, for example—translates this and diffuses it throughout the appropriate units of its organization. The industrial supplier assumes the OEM customer organization can accurately assess and communicate these requirements. Upon receiving them, the supplier must continue to preserve their integrity as it translates them into materials, parts, and process characteristics. To ensure accuracy, the supplier must help the OEM customer identify its own, and the final customers' needs.

Figure 7-3 shows an extremely simplified version of the QFD planning matrix, which is the heart of the process. We will identify and briefly discuss each of the steps involved in developing the matrix. Each step is designated on the matrix. The following description is drawn from the work of Lawrence Sullivan, of the American Supplier Institute;[7] John Hauser and Don Clausing, of MIT;[8] John McElroy, of *Automotive Industries*;[9] and Chris Fosse, of Omark Industries.[10]

Step 1 establishes the customer's quality requirements—what it is the customer wants in the product, in the language of the customer. This

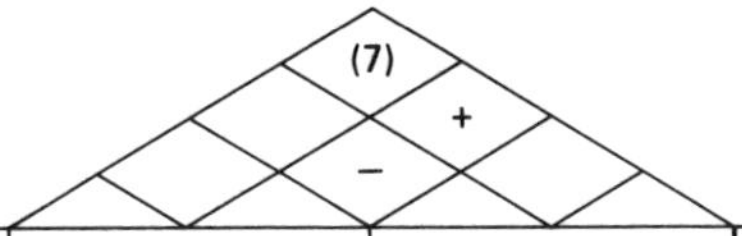

(1) Cust. reqmts. (Whats)	Engineering characteristics (Hows) (4)				Important to customers (2)	(3) Evaluating competitive evaluations 7 8 9	(8) Selling points
	Material		Design				
	Specific weight	Tensile strength	Magnet position	Terminal protection			
Light weight	S	W (5)	DK	S	10	B A C	X
Ease of warning recognition	DK	DK	M	M	6	A C B	
Durability (Thermally stable)	W	S	W	S	9	A B C	X
Serviceability (removal)	W	W	M	M	5	A C B	
Significance (6)	104	142	64	226			
Competitive A evaluations *B (9) C	85 95 103	etc. etc. etc.					
(10) Targets	105	etc.					
(11) Engineering characteristics to be deployed	X	X		X			

*Competitor Key
A = competitor A
B = competitor B
C = supplier C

Relationship Symbols
S = strong
M = moderate
W = weak
DK = don't know

Roof Matrix Key
+ = positive correlation
− = negative correlation

Figure 7-3 Quality function deployment planning matrix.

is the most critical and probably the most difficult step in the whole QFD process. It requires determining and expressing what the customer really wants—not what the marketer thinks it wants. The marketer determines customer requirements in the customer-needs assessment discussed earlier. It should examine not only product requirements, but delivery, service, procedures, relationships, and other aspects of the sale. It can fine-tune each area while developing the offering.

Consider the following oversimplified example: An automotive supplier is assessing the needs of a major customer for a coolant-level indicator on a new car model. The customer requirements may be separated into three categories: functional, performance/ durability, and serviceability.

Under functional requirements, the automotive customer needs an indicator that provides the driver with an easily recognized warning when the coolant level drops too low. It also requires a lightweight indicator. The durability checklist requires that the indicator be thermally stable. Serviceability centers on the item's ease of removal after it's installed in a car. We will consider the single quality of light weight in the rest of the illustration.

Step 2 answers the question "How important is each of the customer's requirements *to the customer?*" Recognizing the potential problem of not being able to satisfy all the customer's needs, this provides a relative ranking of the significance of each attribute to the customer. This may be determined by the team members in their discussions with the OEM customer who, in turn, will be reflecting the needs of the final user.

Step 3 adds the market evaluation. This includes the customer-expressed evaluations of competitive products for each customer quality requirement. Such an evaluation provides insights into relative strength of competition on each of the important customer-desired features, and also identifies opportunities for improvements that will result in a competitive advantage.

Step 4 answers the question *"How* can these customer requirements be delivered?" This takes each requirement identified by the marketing-oriented assessment, and asks the technical and processing functions to determine *how* it can be provided—converting from customer language into internal technical language. In our example, the engineering (product) characteristics identified as controlling the customer-desired attributes include the *material* characteristics of specific weight and brittleness (tensile strength), and the *design* characteristics of magnet position and terminal protection.

Step 5 develops the relationship matrix. It describes the degree to which each engineering characteristic influences the customer-desired requirements. The strength of these relationships is described by placing an appropriate symbol in each cell of the matrix. The symbols used in our example are S, M, and W, denoting a strong, moderate, or weak relationship, and a DK (don't know) for relationships that have yet to be tested. The firm needs to identify engineering characteristics that have a strong relationship with each important customer requirement, so that the desired level of that requirement may be developed in subsequent processing. Absence of such engineering characteristics generally means there has been an oversight by the technical analysis team.

In the example, there's a strong relationship between the customer quality of light weight and an engineering characteristic, specific weight of the material. We have also identified a weak relationship between the light weight requirement and the design characteristic of terminal protection, and a moderate relationship between it and the tensile strength of the material. We have not tested for the relationship between the magnet position and weight of the unit. This is indicated by DK (don't know). We will need to determine this relationship by experimentation.

Step 6 develops a weighted score for each of the engineering characteristics to determine its significance in delivering the required customer-desired attributes and thereby influencing customer satisfaction. The method can be quite simple. Each customer requirement was given an importance rating in Step 2; this becomes the weighting factor. Each relationship between the customer requirement (what) and engineering characteristic (how) can be assigned a value based on the strength of the relationship. For example, strong = 9, moderate = 5, and weak = 1. The weighted score for each engineering characteristic is computed by multiplying the importance of each of the customer requirements it influences by the value representing the strength of that relationship. For example, the "significance score" of the specific weight characteristic would be computed as follows in Table 7-1:

TABLE 7-1

Customer Requirement	Relative Importance		Strength of Relationship	Weighted Value
Light weight	10	×	(S) 9	= 90
Ease of warning recognition	6	×	(DK)–	= –
Durability	9	×	(W) 1	= 9
Serviceability	5	×	(W) 1	= 5
			Significance Score	104

Note: The ease of warning recognition relationship will need to be determined before a final score can be computed.

Using the same approach for the other three engineering characteristics, the significance scores are as follows: tensile strength = 142; magnet position = 64; terminal protection = 226.

Step 7 builds the roof matrix, which identifies how changes in one engineering characteristic impact other characteristics. This effect may be negative, resulting in design conflicts, or positive, enhancing total performance. In our example, there is a positive correlation between material tensile strength and terminal protection, and a negative correlation between tensile strength and magnet position. Near-optimal designs that consider these potential design conflicts may be developed by using experimental design approaches such as Taguchi Methods.

Step 8 establishes the key selling points. These are the "best-in-class" customer quality requirements, such as light weight, that the marketer uses to promote the product to individual customers. These key selling points are based on customer needs, the marketer's past performance on the quality requirement, and the cost to incorporate the feature into the product or process.

Step 9 provides in-house competitive benchmark evaluations of the engineering characteristics. The marketer translates these into quantitative performance ratings for its product and equivalent products of key competitors. It then compares these ratings with the customers' evaluations from Step 3 to spot inconsistencies.

Step 10 sets the target values for each engineering characteristic. These are based on the key selling points, the customer importance rating, and the current product's strengths and weaknesses. These targets form the basis for performance measurement at each subsequent stage of product and process development.

Step 11 selects the engineering characteristics that will be emphasized through the balance of the QFD process. In choosing, the marketer looks at the characteristic's importance to the customer, the selling points, competitive evaluations, and how hard it will be to meet target values. The significance score is a major factor in determining which engineering characteristics will be emphasized in further deployment.

A marketer must translate characteristics that are strong selling points, are important to the customer, that do not match favorably with competition, and/or have challenging target values, into the language of each function involved in product and process development and delivery. It establishes requirements and controls for the responsible functions to assure that the voice of the customer resonates from initial product development through processing, delivery, and post-sale service.

The marketer can use the QFD planning matrix to screen for parts and characteristics that need intensive quality deployment. After identifying characteristics that need the most attention, it develops a process plan and control system to bridge the planning and execution phases of the process. It also develops a relationship matrix to match the process used to produce the component with critical characteristics for the component. If the marketer needs to monitor certain process parameters to optimize the component's characteristics, these parameters become the basis for process control strategy and specific operating instructions. This takes the customer quality requirement all the way to the specific machine or process operator. By the same token, problems occurring at the individual process or operator level can be traced back to the impact they have on specific customer requirements.

The process is complex. To execute it properly takes extensive training and experience. The Pareto principle—the idea of focusing on the vital few rather than the trivial many—is crucial. The marketer uses this principle in choosing customer requirements to focus on, identifying essential product control characteristics, choosing competitors to evaluate, and so forth. By determining the vital few in each instance, the marketer streamlines the QFD process.

On the other hand, the process is not as awesome as it first appears. A rough cut of a relationship matrix matching customer requirements and engineering characteristics for a typical product can be made by a team of knowledgeable technical specialists in a day or so. Cells in which no data have been developed (DK) must be tested and other relationships confirmed. Also, once a specific product is analyzed using QFD, the results can be used for other products in the same family or class. Naturally, some modifications will be required, but the basic analysis will be usable.

The beauty of the process lies in its goal of *systematically* taking the *voice of the customer* and translating it into internal technical characteristics that will assure that the voice is not only heard but accurately represented in the resulting product and service.

Some critical points relating to QFD include the following:

- QFD is a cross-functional *team* process.
- The *customer's point of view* must be heard and followed.
- Focus is on the *few important* characteristics
- Emphasis is on *superior performance* for the important requirements—not just filling the competitive gap.
- A systematic approach can provide for *individual creativity*.
- Time spent in the *early steps* of the process is rewarded in lower cost and higher quality.

Marketing professionals may wonder why they should even be concerned with such a detailed and technical quality tool. In fact, marketing and product managers, sales managers and reps, marketing researchers and customer service reps desperately need to understand these basic concepts and how to apply them.

QFD requires the cooperation of all the industrial supplier's prime internal functions. Those are marketing, including physical distribution, for market and delivery information; engineering for technical input; and manufacturing for operational feedback. Marketing, often the product manager, takes the lead role in certain steps. The marketing department identifies customers, or "market quality" requirements; provides a market evaluation from the customer's viewpoint; and develops key selling points and target values for product control characteristics. In the other QFD steps, marketing professionals participate as interdisciplinary team members.

The QFD process is as applicable to product logistics and service as it is to the offering's physical properties. The quality of the entire marketing process is crucial to provide offerings that satisfy customers. The just-in-time marketer striving for world-class status must be on speaking terms with QFD.

Japanese firms that have adopted QFD have reported outstanding results:[11]

- Toyota reports a one-third reduction in its design cycle time.
- Toyota reduced its start-up costs on one product line by 61% over seven years.
- Aisin Warner halved its design cycle time and the number of engineering changes.
- Tokyo Juki Kogyo used QFD to redesign its sewing machines and increased sales so much it became the market leader.

Some U.S. firms currently using QFD include: Ford Motor Company, Budd Company, Kelsey-Hayes, Sheller-Globe, Xerox, Digital Equipment, Procter & Gamble, and Omark Industries.

Omark began its first QFD pilot projects in 1984 and established a company policy that all major new products would follow QFD. In 1986, Omark set a goal to review current product lines using QFD. By early 1988, products representing 59% of sales had been completed or were being reviewed. Every project has resulted in significant and important discoveries about customers and product performance.

VALUE ENHANCEMENT THROUGH DESIGN

Industrial firms commonly try to enhance their offerings' quality by inspecting or testing after production and by establishing process controls during the production stage. There are two problems with these approaches. They are wasteful, and therefore costly, and they don't assure the quality level modern customers demand.

Quality must be designed into the product, the processes used to produce the product, and the marketing infrastructure. Product design and process design must be concurrent. This approach, called "simultaneous engineering," is used by world-class marketers such as Ford and Hewlett-Packard.[12]

The team approach to design and development described in Chapter 4 is extremely important. It encourages open communication between key functions—product and process engineers, operational and logistical specialists, and marketing representatives—from the start. This can significantly reduce the lead time to production and delivery and helps the marketer organization develop an offering that not only meets the customer's function and performance requirements but is manufacturable, testable, serviceable, and cost competitive.

Product design has a major impact on the offering's quality. It affects not only the industrial marketer's organization but that firm's suppliers and customers. Douglas Daetz, a member of Hewlett-Packard's technical staff, points out the many ways in which design can enhance quality and reduce costs in his "Design Guidelines for Quality Improvement." These are summarized in Fig. 7-4.[13]

The word that best describes the design objective is "simplicity." The product should contain the minimum number of parts, standardized as much as possible. And the parts should be on the list of those already approved and available from qualified suppliers. This approach is vastly different from that used to design many new products. Too often complexity, not low cost, ease of production, or after-sale service, seems to be the designer's main goal.

Similarly, the marketer should keep the processes used to produce and deliver the product simple and understand those processes well. Figure 7-4 provides guidelines for simplifying and sequencing the process flow. Introducing a product that requires new and unfamiliar processing techniques is extremely hazardous. It greatly increases the complexity of product and process development. New-product designs should, as much as possible, allow processing with established techniques. It's best to introduce new processing technology gradually, in the processing of well-established products.

Just as it's important to develop simple designs, it's important that they be robust, easy to produce, and continually improving. Since the mid 1980s, more producers have concerned themselves with these design characteristics, developing new techniques and revitalizing more traditional methods to meet these goals. Four of the most popular methodologies are: Design for Assembly, Taguchi Methods, Value Engineering, and Value Analysis.

Minimize Number of Parts

- Fewer part and assembly drawings → Less volume of drawings instructions to control
- Less complicated assemblies → Lower assembly error rate
- Fewer parts to hold to required quality characteristics → Higher consistency of part quality
- Fewer parts to fail → Higher reliability

Minimize Number of Part Numbers

- Fewer variations of like parts → Lower assembly error rate

Design for Robustness (Taguchi Method)

- Low sensitivity to component variability → Higher first-pass yield
  → Less degradation of performance with time

Eliminate Adjustments

- No assembly adjustment errors → Higher first-pass yield
- Eliminates adjustable components with high failure rates → Lower failure rate

Make Assembly Easy and Foolproof

- Parts cannot be assembled incorrectly → Lower assembly error rate
- Obvious when parts are missing → Lower assembly error rate
- Assy. tooling designed into part → Lower assembly error rate
- Parts are self-securing → Lower assembly error rate
- No "force fitting" of parts → Less damage to parts better serviceability

Use Repeatable, Well-Understood Processes

- Part quality easy to control → Higher part yield
- Assembly quality easy to control → Higher assembly yield

Choose Parts that Can Survive Process Operations

- Less damage to parts → Higher yield
- Less degradation of parts → Higher reliability

Figure 7-4   Design guidelines for quality improvement. Copyright © 1987 Hewlett-Packard Company. All rights reserved. Reprinted with permission.

Design for Efficient and Adequate Testing

- Less mistaking "good" for   → Truer assessment of quality,
  "bad" product and vice versa   less unneccessary rework

Lay Out Parts for Reliable Process Completion

- Less damage to parts during   → Higher yield, higher reliability
  handling and assembly

Eliminate Engineering Changing on Released Products

- Fewer errors due to change-   → Lower assembly error rate
  overs & multiple revisions/
  versions

Figure 7-4   (continued)

DESIGN FOR ASSEMBLY—INCREASING PRODUCIBILITY

Design for assembly (DFA) is a design technique that Geoffrey Boothroyd pioneered with a 1980 report published at the University of Rhode Island. At about the same time, Hitachi was developing an "Assemblability Evaluation Method" in Japan. GE gained a license to use the Hitachi methodology, improved it, and developed English language training materials. Several U.S. firms now use the two methods.[14]

Gerald Hock, a GE corporate engineering staff member, defines DFA as a means of evaluating a product against standard production criteria and quantifying the results. DFA lets the producer evaluate each part in a product design according to part insertion motions, fixturing needs, joining operations, and parts forming during assembly. The evaluation yields an "assemblability" score that shows how difficult the product will be to produce in the factory. It also provides an estimate of how long it would take to assemble the product versus alternative designs.[15]

DFA produces simpler designs that can be assembled with less operator skill and less chance of error. Other important benefits include higher product quality and reliability and a closer working relationship between the engineering and manufacturing representatives critical to the success of JIT marketers.[16]

TAGUCHI METHODS: MAKING DESIGNS ROBUST

As discussed in Chapter 2, Taguchi Methods allow producers to develop designs and manufacturing processes that are relatively insensitive to factors outside the manufacturer's direct control, such as customer misuse and environmental conditions. This approach produces product designs that are easier to build and manufacturing processes that are more capable, which in turn produce higher yields from the beginning of production. Taguchi Methods are a natural extension of QFD. Once the producer establishes target values to meet each important characteristic identified in the "voice of the customer" analysis, Taguchi Methods become the tool for developing product designs that meet the target values. This happens early in the product development process. TM's secondary goal is to reduce variability, but its main objective is to create robust product designs that perform satisfactorily on critical parameters, despite variability.

VALUE ENGINEERING AND ANALYSIS FOR CONTINUOUS IMPROVMEENT

Value engineering (VE) and value analysis (VA) are companion techniques designed to enhance value. The two are quite similar, but they are used in different parts of the product development sequence. VE is a preproduction technique used to enhance function and minimize costs while the product or process is still in development. It may be used independently or with Taguchi Methods. VA is used after the product is in production or the process is in use. Like VE, VA strives to reduce costs while maintaining or improving the product's or process's function.

In contrast to QFD, DFA, and Taguchi Methods, VA goes back many years. Larry Miles, of General Electric, is credited with developing VA shortly after World War II. Starting in the late 1970s, his technique became the focus of renewed attention.

A *Purchasing* survey conducted in the mid 1980s revealed a 50% increase in corporate VA programs between 1975 and 1986.[17] Respondents said their primary reasons for using VA, in order of importance, were to reduce costs, improve quality, encourage supplier involvement, encourage creative teamwork within their own company, better satisfy users' needs, and meet new marketing objectives. The survey revealed VA's growing significance; 88% of the respondents considered it more important than they had previously, and 71% said they were increasing their VA efforts.

Many authors have documented the VA process.[18] J. M. Juran's description covers its fundamentals.[19] VA's basic goal is to help supply product or process functions that the customer needs, at minimal cost. To do this requires certain inputs: customer needs and their importance to customers, product features and the cost of providing them, and information on competing products' features and costs.

Using these inputs, the process: precisely defines product functions; breaks the primary functions into subfunctions; estimates the cost of executing each subfunction; and, based on the cost estimates, judges the merits of other product development possibilities. The estimated cost of development options can be compared to the *value* of the product features they engender. The manufacturer makes decisions based on these comparisons.

VA's typical return on investment should convert even the most skeptical nonusers. During the four years following General Electric's adoption of VA techniques, in the 1940s, the company accumulated $10 million in benefits. And according to Art Mudge, who served for more than twenty years as Joy Manufacturing Company's vice-president of value planning, Joy had a 24:1 return on investment (ROI) ratio for every dollar it invested in VA.[20] Other investments of the same magnitude would be hard pressed to match the results.

Although VA provides significant benefits for users with traditional design approaches, there is one disadvantage. The technique enhances function and reduces costs *after* the product is in production. This can cause engineering changes that affect both the product and processing methods—and that promotes waste. In contrast, QFD, combined with Taguchi Methods, tends to optimize preproduction designs. Japanese companies that combine QFD and TM process about 90% of their engineering changes before starting production. That reduces lead time and cost and provides higher first-time quality.

We believe VA and VE will gradually give way to the more complex, but also more effective, QFD/TM design approach. Driving this will be the increasing number of companies that train their employees to execute the techniques, encourage a quality attitude, and develop an infrastructure to support these technologies.

MAINTAINING VALUE THROUGH CAPABLE PROCESSING

Like product design, process technology is crucial in producing high-value offerings. John Groocock reflects on the importance of process capability in *The Chain of Quality,* pointing out that manufacturing processes are inherently variable.[21]

If a manufacturer performs a process once and then repeats it, it will be somewhat different the second time—and so will the product. If the difference between the products is greater than the tolerance allowed in the design specification, or if the design requires tolerances that are tighter than the manufacturing process's variability, the process will produce defective products.

The product design engineer, or preferably the team responsible for designing superior products, must understand what the available manufacturing processes can do and make sure the product designs and processes are compatible.

A detailed discussion of process technology is beyond the scope of this book. But we will discuss the process concepts of just-in-time manufacturing and statistical process control and the closely related concept of early supplier involvement, all from the industrial marketer's point of view.

THE INDUSTRIAL MARKETER'S IN-HOUSE JIT SYSTEM

In Chapter 2 we considered the just-in-time operations philosophy from the OEM's, or JIT customer's, viewpoint. The OEM customer's decision to become a JIT producer signals its suppliers—industrial marketers—that the traditional rules no longer apply. The marketer trying to serve JIT customers with traditional processing methods will drown in quality and delivery problems.

The marketer's solution is an in-house JIT system designed like the OEM's. It may emerge in response to the JIT OEM customer's needs. Even better, the industrial marketer may develop a JIT system *in anticipation* of those needs. The latter lets the marketer develop process capabilities before its competition does and promotes a close working relationship with the JIT customer or prospect. As the marketer's JIT system develops, with production and delivery schedules geared to the JIT customer's demand, the industrial marketer starts to serve the same role as an internal supplier department.

The basic manufacturing technology changes required for JIT—workplace preparation, setup time reduction, lot size reduction, buffer inventory elimination, quality improvement—were covered in Chapter 2, and we will consider the logistical changes in Chapter 10.

Leading industrial marketers are fairly well along in developing in-house JIT systems. For example, the Davidson Instrument Panel Division of Davidson Rubber Company is the largest producer of automotive instrument panels in the United States, selling about one half of the total units marketed domestically. In 1987, three of the division's automotive assembly-plant customers were on a four-shipment daily JIT schedule with targets of eighteen-hour transit time in summer and twenty-four hours in winter. Davidson served those customers from a distance of 900 miles.

In two years of implementing this schedule, Davidson did not miss a delivery. The division's total annual inventory turns reached twenty-nine, with three days' inventory of raw materials, four days' inventory of finished goods, and only two hours' inventory of work-in-process. Start-up quality increased from 50% in 1980 to more than 80% in 1987. Ford and GM awarded Davidson their top quality ratings.

Davidson's own suppliers—the second tier—now participate in the process as well. The division reduced its supplier base from 100 to 35 and communicates with remaining suppliers using an on-line interactive system. The second-tier suppliers release materials directly against a previously agreed upon bill of material.[22]

Presmet Corporation, an inner-city producer and supplier of structural metal parts for several *Fortune* 500 customers, turned itself around using a JIT program that included a lot of employee involvement. In 1984, the company's future looked bleak. John Healy, Presmet's president, saw little reason to continue operations. The company controlled no capital, it had been forced to lay off many employees, and it was serving a market with little growth potential.

But Presmet did not close its doors. By spring 1988, thanks to an in-house JIT system, the firm was producing at a substantially higher level and at less cost than in 1984. With little or no capital investment, the company had reduced its inspection force by 30%, its supervisory staff by 36%, and its work-in-process inventory by 40%. Meanwhile, it increased production 38% and halved the number of inspection-item rejects. Xerox, Ford, and Mercury Marine, all Presmet customers, have awarded the firm the highest quality awards.[23]

A third example is Hutchinson Technology Incorporated (HTI), a leading supplier of suspension assemblies for computer disk drives.[24] In the early 1980s, Japanese competition in that market became very intense. Hutchinson's president, Wayne Fortun, traveled to Japan in 1983 to study the JIT approach; in 1985, HTI started its own JIT/TQC program.

By the end of 1986, HTI had increased production yields by more than 25%. At the same time, it cut manufacturing lead times by 50% to 90% on six product lines. Finished goods inventory turns increased from seventy-one in 1985 to 165 in 1986, and HTI was able to lower the price of one of its major products by 30%—while increasing per-unit profit by a third. By late 1987, customers in the Far East represented 40% of HTI's business, and the firm started a program to bring its key suppliers into the JIT system.

Each of these examples illustrates the value and necessity of an in-house JIT system for the industrial marketer serving producers that have—or soon will have—JIT systems. And in-house JIT systems are just as important for second- and third-tier suppliers as for marketers that directly serve JIT OEMs.

STATISTICAL PROCESS CONTROL

The fundamental ideas on statistical process control (SPC) were the work of W. A. Shewhart, whose 1931 book, *Economic Control of Quality of Manufactured Products,* outlined the technique. For the next two decades, few manufacturers seriously applied his ideas. But after World War II, a group of Japanese engineers learned of Shewhart's work. In 1948, they began a vigorous campaign to develop and apply SPC. Since then, millions of Japanese managers, engineers, and workers have learned the SPC techniques. American manufacturers' use of SPC has lagged behind.[25]

As explained earlier, manufacturing processes are inherently variable. If there are many different causes of variability—material, operator, machine, environment—and each consistently causes about the same amount of variability, the process will be stable. Variations in the resulting products will be normally distributed and describe a bell-shaped curve.

If there are one or more causes of variation, such as operator fatigue or tool wear, that contribute more to the product variation than each of the ordinary causes, resulting products' characteristics probably won't be normally distributed. Such processes are unstable, and the manufacturer cannot determine their capabilities without identifying and removing the special causes of variability. As the manufacturer eliminates these special causes, the product being processed will display characteristics with random variation, within the process's limits.

One of SPC's goals is to stop adjusting the process, because the narrowest possible product variation comes from leaving the process alone. Adjustment increases variation. Another objective is to show when a special cause of process variation, such as fixture position, is starting to affect the variation of product characteristics. Such causes must be corrected.[26]

SPC can be used to monitor the status of a particular process based on small samples of the process's output. One of the key values used to evaluate the process is the *mean,* or average, value of the characteristic in question (inside diameter, for example). The mean is called the "X-bar." Another key value is the *range* of values around the mean, referred to as the "R value." The range estimates process variation, or deviation from the mean.

Control limits are calculated for both the mean and range. When either the sample mean or range extends beyond these control limits, it indicates a special cause of variation affecting the process. Corrective action must be taken to remove this cause.

Larry Sullivan, in an article called "The Seven Stages in Company-Wide Quality Control," points out that the most serious and common pitfall in SPC use is the idea that it is a technique or method to control process output. That thinking leads SPC users to adjust the process, to center it, when the product starts to trend toward the control limit.

Sullivan explains that this approach ignores the ability of control charts to identify causes of variation and separate special causes from ordinary causes. It is desirable to have some points outside the control limits, because these represent causes of variability that can be corrected.

They permit continuous improvement in both the process and the product it produces.[27]

Leading OEMs are phasing SPC into every aspect of their operations and giving preference to suppliers who adopt this technology. This approach lets the JIT customer move to a "quality at the source" system with certified suppliers that provide quality documentation via SPC-generated data. It also gives the OEM a way to maintain high quality in each of its manufacturing processes.

A PRESCRIPTION FOR MAJOR QUALITY IMPROVEMENT

U.S. producers led their Japanese counterparts in quality progress during the first two decades after World War II (see Fig. 7-5). U.S. firms relied primarily on the traditional inspection, or defect-correction, approach. They applied modest efforts to the SPC approach until 1980, when a flurry of activity started. Also about that time, they began experimenting with design techniques, particularly Taguchi Methods.

In contrast, the Japanese began taking the focus off the traditional approach in the 1960s. They placed their primary efforts first on SPC, then, in the 1970s, on experimental design combined with SPC. The re-

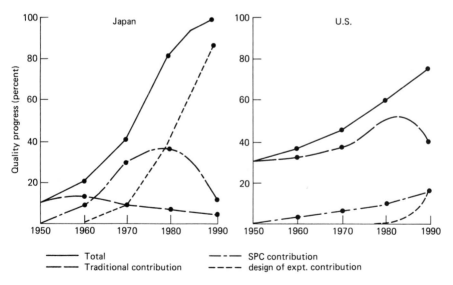

Figure 7-5 Contribution of traditional, SPC, and design of experiment tools to quality progress. Reprinted, by permission of the publisher, from *Supply Management: How to Make U.S. Suppliers Competitive,* by Keki R. Bhote © 1986, American Management Association Membership Publications Division, New York. All rights reserved.

sults are staggering. Japan's quality progress had overtaken America's by 1970, and it has taken a substantial lead since then.

Dr. Keki Bhote, corporate quality consultant for Motorola, provides valuable insights into Japan's quality superiority.[28] He says its secret weapon is extensive use of design of experiments (DOE). This approach can drastically reduce variability in product quality through improvements in product and process design prior to production. SPC doesn't provide the same benefit because it monitors quality levels during production. Taquchi Methods is a DOE approach.

EARLY SUPPLIER INVOLVEMENT

Regardless of the JIT industrial marketer's quality assurance approach, one thing is sure. The earlier *it* gets involved in customers' new-product and process development—and involves suppliers in its own product development cycle—the greater the payoff in lead time improvement, cost reduction, and quality enhancement.

The importance of the supplier in product and process development cannot be overemphasized. The JIT industrial marketer—the OEM's supplier—is a critical contributor to each OEM customer's quality, cost, and lead-time performance.

Early supplier involvement means early purchasing involvement. As Somerby Dowst, managing editor of *Purchasing,* explains, "Purchasing was perhaps the first to respond to the clarion call, recognizing the intrinsic value of suppliers as resource centers. A new role was emerging for purchasing: middleman in the exchange of technical knowledge between corporate inner sanctum and the outside world. Convincing the supplier that he was now on the design team was one of the many new assignments of purchasing."[29]

But as Patrick McMahon, manager of procurement quality engineering for IBM's General Product Division, points out, the real advantages of ESI do not come from a brief brain-picking session in which the customer's design engineer takes some drawings out to a supplier for a day or two. The benefits grow out of a *sustained technical partnership.*[30] NCR and Carrier Corporation provide excellent examples of how such relationships develop.

Joseph Bookataub, director of manufacturing at NCR's San Jose, California, plant, says purchasing is "an integral part of selecting a supplier base that will work with us in the early stages of new-product development to help us design to optimal quality and cost." He emphasizes that this is critical in meeting NCR's development-cycle goal of less than a year from product concept to customer hardware. NCR's new supplier contract specifies parts-per-million quality targets and supplier commitment to ESI, JIT, lead-time managment, and joint VA efforts.[31]

Meanwhile, Carrier has reduced its supplier base from 300 to 120. Allen Alexander, vice-president of corporate purchasing and logistics, says the firm has also adopted a multidisciplinary approach to sourcing. The firm's key expectations of suppliers include: improved business relationships, design integration and ESI, quality and reliability improvements, and transactional efficiencies.[32]

JIT industrial marketers such as Hurd Lock Company, Kelsey-Hayes, and Intel Corporation are moving the ESI concept back through the supply channel. Hurd Lock, a Ford Q1 supplier, guarantees defect-free products that can be used on the customer's production line without inspection. The company also works closely with its own suppliers to assure perfect quality in sourced materials. Through the customer-oriented procurement (COPE) program, as explained by Jack Kelly, director of materials, Hurd Lock's sourcing teams have selected twenty suppliers as key partners. These are equal partnerships in which Hurd Lock and the selected suppliers openly share information on product designs, logistics, and more.[33]

The need for ESI is clear. Leading JIT OEMs, aware of its importance, are involving their suppliers early in the product development cycle. For now, ESI further upstream is less apparent. But early supplier involvement between first- and second-tier suppliers—and even further up the supply chain—is critical. Design and quality integration must permeate the entire value-added quality chain.

PRODUCT FOCUS: ROAD TO PROFITABLE GROWTH

World-class JIT OEM customers consistently call for leading edge technology from suppliers. The JIT marketers serving these customers are the technology experts and may provide offerings that are differentiated in important ways from those of their competitors.

Industrial marketers that have not yet adopted JIT techniques and the accompanying focus on key customers suffer from global mediocrity, as discussed in Chapter 6. They try to serve too many different customers with too many different product lines or product variations. Unless the marketer has unlimited resources, which is rare, allocating its resources across many products and related marketing programs keeps the marketer from gaining any distinction.

Focusing on the vital few—industries, customers, and products—provides opportunities for technology leadership and growth. Becoming a state-of-the-art supplier and specializing in products that contribute significantly to the customer's offering leads to increased profit.

PRUNING THE PRODUCT LINE

Product proliferation is the industrial markter's natural tendency, particularly if the firm has no policy guarding against it. The inclination is to try, without analyzing the long-term effects of each new-product decision, to meet the needs of industrial customers and prospects producing a wide variety of products. To close individual transactions, the marketer may commit to low volume levels and short-term runs and to provide replacement spares for several years—a combination at odds with the goal of long-term profitability.

Product elimination can be painful, particularly if review-team members helped develop and launch the products under review. But intense, objective assessments are necessary. If previews are not already part of the product policy, the JIT marketer should initiate them—with follow-up reviews at least once per year.

To evaluate a product, the marketer needs to know the product's recent and projected sales volume and contribution to profit; what customers buy that product and how eliminating it would affect those customer relationships; the product's impact on the marketer's other offerings, especially their sales and profitability; and what role the product plays in the marketer's core product strategy.

The marketer rates each product on each of these dimensions, which have been previously weighted. Products falling below a minimum cut-off score are candidates for deletion, either immediately or gradually. The JIT marketer may divert the resources it saves by eliminating them into strengthening its technological position.

DEVELOPING TECHNOLOGICAL LEADERSHIP

Leading edge technology and world-class marketing clearly go hand in hand. The question is, how does the industrial marketer achieve technological leadership? Product and process design, described above, are crucial. In addition, Michael Porter, in *Competitive Advantage,* says the marketer should:[34]

1. Identify all the distinct technologies in its own and its competitors' value chains—and the value chains of its suppliers and customers. The value chain is the set of value-adding activities. Frequently, the value chain of the marketer and its customers and suppliers are interdependent. Incremental improvements in technology usually come from sources *within* the industry served.

2. Identify potentially relevant technologies in other industries or under development in the scientific community. These are often the source of discontinuous innovations, or "breakthroughs." Information systems, new materials, and electronics are technology areas to watch because they are frequently sources of innovation, either separately or in combination.

3. Determine how key technologies may change in each of its value activities and in the supplier and customer value chains.

4. Determine which technologies and potential technological changes could contribute to a sustainable competitive advantage.

5. Objectively assess its relative capabilities in the technologies it identifies as important, and determine the cost to improve those capabilities.

6. Plot a technology strategy that leverages on those key technologies *and* reinforces its overall competitive strategy.

Using these guidelines, the marketer can prioritize development projects based on their potential for boosting its competitive advantage. And that points to technology areas where the firm should be taking a leadership role in research and development.

The successful JIT industrial marketer offers customers a substantially better value by focusing on product and process technologies in which it can excel. It distinguishes itself by providing these technologies to the customer for whom they provide a competitive advantage.

NOTES

1. John L. Warne, Keynote Address to AME Annual Conference, Chicago, Ill., September 1986.
2. Robert D. Buzzell and Bradley T. Gale, *The PIMS Pinciples* (New York: The Free Press, 1987), pp. 103–34.
3. John L. Warne, "Developing a Quality Orientation," *Target,* Summer 1987, pp. 11–13.
4. Ibid.
5. Robert B. Miller and Stephen E. Heiman, *Strategic Selling* (New York: Warner Books, 1985).
6. American Supplier Institute, Six Parklane Blvd., Suite 411, Dearborn, Michigan 48126, (313) 336-8877. Education and training topics: Statistical Methods, Standard Methods, Taguchi Methods, Special Methods—JIT, QFD, FMS, Benchmarking, etc.

7. L. P. Sullivan, "Quality Function Deployment," *Quality Progress*, June 1986, pp. 39–50.

8. John Hauser and Don Clausing, "The House of Quality," *Harvard Business Review*, May–June 1988, pp. 63–73.

9. John McElroy's "For Whom are We Building Cars?" *Automotive Industries*, June 1987, pp. 68–70.

10. Chris Fosse, "Quality Assurance through Strategic Product Development and QFD," *Proceedings of 1988 AME Annual Conference* (Wheeling, Ill.: Association for Manufacturing Excellence, 1988).

11. Ronald M. Fortuna, "Quality Function Deployment: Taking Quality Upstream." *Target*, Winter 1987, pp. 11–16.

12. Somerby Dowst and Ernest Raia, "Design 88: Teaming Up," *Purchasing*, March 10, 1988, pp. 80–91.

13. Douglas Daetz, "The Effect of Product Design on Product Quality and Product Cost," *Quality Progress*, June 1987, pp. 63–67.

14. Ibid., p. 65.

15. Gerald Hock, "Designing for Productivity," *Target*, Summer 1987, pp. 14–17.

16. Ibid., p. 16.

17. Somerby Dowst, "Buyers Say VA Is More Important than Ever," *Purchasing*, June 26, 1986, pp. 64–83.

18. Sources include: Vincent G. Reuter, "What Good are Value Analysis Programs?" *Business Horizons*, March–April 1986, pp. 73–79; Donald W. Dobler, Lamar Lee, Jr., and David N. Burt, *Purchasing and Materials Management* (New York: McGraw-Hill, 1984), pp. 310–34; J. M. Juran, *Juran on Planning for Quality* (New York: The Free Press, 1988), pp. 131–35.

19. Juran, *Planning*, p. 131.

20. Lea Tonkin, "Larry Miles and Value Analysis: Blast, Create, and then Refine," *Target*, Winter 1987, pp. 17–18.

21. John M. Groocock, *The Chain of Quality: Market Dominance Through Product Superiority* (New York: John Wiley and Sons, 1986), pp. 120–33.

22. Charlene Adair and Ed Dawkins, "Workshop Report: Davidson Instrument Panel Division—Textron," *Target*, Winter 1987, pp. 31–32.

23. James King, "Workship Report: Inner City Manufacturers Proving It Can Be Made Better in America"—for Less—Thanks to Its Workers," *Target*, Spring 1988, pp. 25–26.

24. Ernest Raia, "Hutchinson Technology: Selling it to the Japanese," *Purchasing*, September 24, 1987, p. 71.

25. Groocock, *The Chain of Quality*, pp. 233–40.

26. Ibid., pp. 235–36.

27. L. P. Sullivan, "The Seven Stages in Company-wide Quality Control," *Quality Progress*, May 1986, pp. 79–80.

28. Keki R. Bhote, *Supply Management: How to Make U.S. Suppliers Competitive* (New York: American Management Association, 1987), pp. 59–80.

29. Somerby Dowst, "Design Team Signals for More Early Supplier Involvement," *Purchasing,* January 28, 1988, p. 83.

30. H. J. Harrington, *The Improvement Process: How America's Leading Companies Improve Quality,* Chapter 10, "Supplier Involvement," authored by Patrick McMahon (New York: McGraw-Hill, 1987), pp. 155–74.

31. Somerby Dowst, "Quality Suppliers: The Search Goes On," *Purchasing,* January 28, 1988, p. 94A12.

32. Somerby Dowst, "Quality in Design Means Quality in Production," *Purchasing,* January 28, 1988.

33. Ibid., pp. 87; and Shirley Cayer, "When You Don't Know the Rules, You've Got To Be Agile," *Purchasing,* July 30, 1987, pp. 30–33.

34. Michael E. Porter, *Competitive Advantage* (New York: The Free Press, 1985) pp. 176–90.

Chapter 8

Pricing Strategy

Comments by corporate leaders of the big three U.S. auto companies set the tone for JIT industrial markters' pricing strategies.[1]

Robert Stone, a vice-president on General Motors' materials management staff, explains: "As we develop and put a part into the system for the lifetime of one of our products—roughly five years—we have to . . . find ways to reduce cost. All of our ingenuity, technology, innovativeness have to be put toward that principle. This fact frightens a lot of suppliers."

Chrysler's vice-president of procurement and supply, Davis Platt, concurs. "We'll be supervising suppliers directly and are on an aggressive campaign to reduce our parts and materials costs. The emphasis is on cost containment and the shipment of superb quality parts from suppliers," he says.

And in the words of Ford's vice-president of purchasing and supply, Lionel Chicone, "What we are trying to do is maximize the opportunity for the supplier to be able to offset cost increases through productivity improvements."

This emphasis is true in all major U.S. industries that compete globally. A primary characteristic JIT OEMs look for when selecting supplier partners is *world competitive pricing.*

PRICING: A KEY STRATEGY ELEMENT

We cannot overemphasize the importance of pricing strategy to the industrial marketer—and to its JIT OEM customers. The negotiated price of the marketer's offering is the basis for both the "top line" *and* the "bottom line" on the firm's income statement. Price strongly affects whether or not the marketer wins the contract. It also determines the contract's potential total revenue, or sales. This establishes the marketer's profit level, after expenses.

If the price is set too high, it deters sales and the marketer doesn't realize the product's full potential. This gives competitors the chance to strengthen their position. On the other hand, if the marketer sets its price too low, it gives away profit.

The JIT OEM customer considers the supplier's price a critical cost element because it represents a substantial share of product cost. On average, components and materials represent 50% of an OEM's product cost. But in some cases they represent as much as 80%. Modest changes in materials prices can significantly influence the customer's total costs and profit.

THE TRADITIONAL PRICING APPROACH

The industrial buyer and seller have traditionally tried to maximize short-term results by negotiating the "best" price (see Fig. 8-1).

The top of the negotiating range is the value the customer places on the product, or the price it would pay. Traditionally, customers derived this value subjectively, using historical prices and competitive price data. And their purchasing units often pitted multiple sources against each other to get the "best" price. The unit price was generally considered the cost of the material purchased.

The floor of the range is the marketer's cost. The firm would normally calculate this as its full cost to provide the product, including overhead costs, plus profit margin. If the marketer had unused capacity or was attempting to improve market position, it might set the price closer to the variable cost level—direct labor, material, and variable overhead only—with perhaps a modest increment to apply to overhead costs. This is called contribution pricing because it emphasizes contribution to overhead.

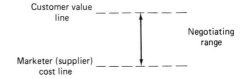

Figure 8-1 Traditional short-term pricing approach.

At both the top and bottom of the range, the marketer and OEM customer negotiated from their own win-lose viewpoints. Each wanted the outcome that would benefit it most. And each concealed its cost data from the other side to avoid giving the opponent a negotiating advantage. Contracts were typically short term—often less than a year's duration— and turned on the unit price negotiated.

Transactions were risky. For the marketer, winning one short-term contract didn't guarantee another in twelve months. In negotiations for subsequent transactions, the supplier generally had a higher cost base because of higher material and/or labor costs. This meant the transaction produced less profit for the supplier, or a higher price for the customer. During the 1960s and 1970s, the latter often prevailed, and the OEM customer passed its higher costs on to the final customer.

With the 1980s came global competition, which pushed down prices for final products. That trend brought the traditional cost-price push to a screeching halt. Final product OEMs could no longer pass on cost increases to the marketplace, and their profit margins wouldn't allow them to absorb the increases. The OEM mandate was for suppliers to hold the line on materials and components prices—or, in many cases, reduce them—while *increasing* their offerings' quality. It was a formidable challenge. The solution, as previously discussed, lay in JIT/TQC/TPI concepts and systems. A new approach to pricing complements those efforts.

JUST-IN-TIME PRICING STRATEGY

Final product OEMs developing just-in-time systems quickly recognized that short-term, transactional price negotiating was not the answer. It didn't give suppliers any incentives or resources to develop higher quality products, or higher productivity and quality in their design, production, delivery, and service processes. What did motivate those improvements were long-term contracts with single-source suppliers. By agreeing to contract solely with one supplier for certain materials over a relatively long period, the OEM gave the supplier some certainty, which it had never done before. Consequently, the just-in-time pricing approach began to take on a new profile.

Figure 8-2 contrasts the two approaches to pricing. It extends the traditional approach over subsequent time periods, with the assumption that the OEM gave at least some business to the supplier in each period. But because the supplier didn't know for sure it would be selected, the transactions were still risky.

With the traditional approach, supplier costs mounted as material and labor prices increased and the customer gave the supplier no incentive to overcome the increases. Value to the buyer diminished as the

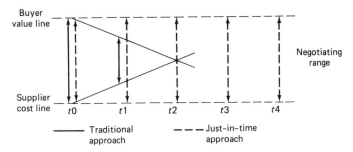

Figure 8-2   Traditional vs JIT pricing approach.

supplier, which did not invest in product and process quality improvements, became less competitive. Obviously, the customer would not continue to choose the supplier under such conditions.

The JIT approach paints a much different picture. The supplier reduces its costs, thanks to the efficiency of JIT/TQC processes. This helps it contain prices for JIT OEM customers, or even reduce them—which the OEM needs to be price competitive. Further, the supplier's focus on continuous product and process quality improvement adds significant value to the offering. That keeps the value line stable in the face of competitive offerings' increasing value. Rather than narrowing, the supplier cost line and the customer value line begin to spread modestly. This generates modestly higher total profit, which the two organizations share.

Let us look at how "supplier cost" and "buyer value" affect real-world JIT pricing.

COST-BASED PRICING

For industrial firms, cost has traditionally been an important factor in pricing. A major pricing study conducted jointly in 1980 by the National Association of Accountants of the United States and the Society of Management Accountants of Canada supports this.[2] The study revealed that both costs and market conditions were important factors in pricing product lines. Even in firms that priced their products mainly based on competitors' prices, cost considerations determined whether the firm could afford to sell the product at the established market price.

A 1987 study of *Fortune* 500 firms revealed they used cost-plus pricing (full cost plus a fixed percentage) 20% of the time. Respondents used the full cost-based approach, which considers the competitive environment, 70% of the time.[3]

Cost-based pricing is advantageous for certain kinds of industrial products. It's easy to understand, predictable, justifiable, generally accepted, and widely used. But it has some serious disadvantages, which are surfacing as firms adopt the new JIT/TQC technologies. The shortcomings include the technique's reliance on outdated cost systems, the prevalence of the 'standard cost' approach, treatment of overhead as a fixed cost, failure to look beyond manufacturing costs, and lack of customer orientation.

Because these problems and the cost system that spawn them are prevalent in many industrial firms, marketing representatives need to understand them. The following nontechnical explanations describe each of the shortcomings listed above.

Outdated Cost Systems

Contemporary accounting and control systems emerged at the beginning of the twentieth century and reflect extremely labor-intensive manufacturing practices. Labor content, at that time, represented nearly 80% of total product cost. Since then that proportion has dropped to 10%, or even into the single digits for highly automated manufacturers.

According to Robert Kaplan, a pioneer in the effort to revamp accounting systems to suit JIT/TQC processes, management (cost) accounting systems are not changing even though industry is making fundamental changes in the organization and technology of manufacturing processes.[4] Kaplan attributes the lag to the absence of good role models, even in leading U.S. firms; reliance on computers and the associated risk and complexity of modifying systems; the priority placed on stockholder interests and tax-reporting requirements; and senior management's failure to champion improved relevance and responsiveness in accounting systems.

A major problem with today's cost systems lies in how they allocate overhead costs. Traditionally, manufacturers have allocated overhead based on direct labor costs: Overhead equaled 100% to 200% of direct labor costs. Today the rate may be 1,000% or more. As Jeffrey Miller and Thomas Vollmann wrote in *The Harvard Business Review* in 1985, "We don't even know what that means."[5]

William Holbrook, vice-president of administration with Stanadyne Automotive Products Group, cited as a major problem of the firm's accounting system its inability to measure factors top managers had identified as critical in the profitability of their products, diesel systems. The system never did any of the following: measured the impact of lead time; revealed actual costs or quality costs; reflected service or quality levels; nor evaluated schedule performance, market share, market penetration, or employee attitude. It was machine oriented.[6]

Most U.S. manufacturing managers understand what drives direct labor and materials costs. They're much less aware of overhead-cost drivers. The problem with allocating overhead rates based on direct labor, materials, or machine hours—the traditional bases—is that they no longer drive overhead costs. *Transactions* do. These transactions, or activities, involve the materials and information exchanges that move production along but don't directly produce products. They include engineering change orders, material releases, purchasing, logistics, warranty clauses, and field service requests. The more complex the system, the more transactions and the higher the overhead.

Robert Kaplan vividly illustrates how a transaction-based overhead allocation system can influence the cost per unit and gross margin of a firm's product line.[7] In a study he conducted to compare the two approaches, cost per unit decreased 13% for a high-volume product line and increased 964% for a low-volume line with the transaction approach versus the traditional approach. Gross margins for the same products also changed radically, with several products slipping from acceptable positive margin positions to substantially negative margin positions.

The new and more realistic transactions-based approach significantly affected the cost and gross margins of each product he studied. A major reason JIT systems reduce costs so well is that they reduce the number of *transactions*.

Standard Costs

U.S. managers tend to associate 'standard costs' with product costing and may prefer that approach because it simplifies product and process design and operations. With a standard-cost system, management sets standards based on labor and materials input and compares them with actual costs to determine variances.

In a traditional manufacturing environment, the variances are usually substantial. However, with a well-developed JIT/TQC system, in which suppliers provide assured quality materials, materials variances are not very significant. In fact, they probably don't justify setting standards and performing variance analysis. The same is true with labor. As the direct labor portion of product cost falls below 10%, and as the manufacturer carefully controls production processes, absolute labor levels and variances against the standard are minimal.

An even more compelling argument against using standard costs is that they remove the incentive for continuous improvement. The standard becomes the goal, and the manufacturer is satisfied to meet it.[8]

Fixed Overhead Costs

Manufacturers have traditionally considered overhead costs "fixed" over a relevant range of production output. The idea is that even though output fluctuates within that range, overhead costs stay more or less the same.

Robert Kaplan has challenged the wisdom of fixed overhead costs based on his study of an electronic-instruments firm's twenty-five manufacturing plants.[8] The company's strategy was to reduce cost per unit by increasing the output of each plant. By spreading the fixed overhead costs across more units, the firm expected to reduce the cost per unit. But Kaplan made a surprising finding: Overhead costs went up with increases in purchases and use of labor, both variable costs.

To analyze this unexpected result, Kaplan separated overhead into three components: production overhead, procurement overhead, and support overhead. He found a positive linear relationship between: production overhead and changes in direct labor costs; procurement overhead and changes in direct materials costs; and support overhead and changes in labor and material costs.

Kaplan concluded that most "fixed" overhead costs are variable. They do *not* vary with production volume but with the increased number of transactions that higher volume generates, especially in traditional systems. And overhead costs don't increase when the manufacturer uses focused plants to simplify the network of transactions. The problem is the complexity and diversity a higher volume creates.

Japanese manufacturers, who enjoy less diversity, such as fewer product options, have learned to treat efficiently the diversity they have. By reducing the cost of each transaction, they can manufacture products with less than half the overhead a U.S. firm would need. Those overhead savings represent a significant cost advantage.

The major factors driving manufacturing costs include the following:[9]

- Average number of engineering change orders per month
- Total number of suppliers
- Number of parts representing 80% of usage (standardization)
- Number of parts in an average product
- Number of structural levels in an average product
- Number of products
- Number of production schedule changes per month
- Average number of options or accessories on products
- Average monthly rework or scrap dollars

Unfortunately, these are nonfinancial factors generally not incorporated into management cost systems. Clearly, fixed overhead costs are not all that fixed. Manufacturers may substantially reduce them by reducing the total number of transactions in the system and increasing the remaining transactions' efficiency. Two themes continue to emerge: Focus on the vital few, and keep it simple!

Looking Beyond Manufacturing Costs

Manufacturing is just one part of the industrial firm's value-creating process. For product costing, it's important to understand how costs cut across the entire chain of value-adding activities—from product design and design enhancement through post-sale service. To understand the true cost of creating and marketing different products, the manufacturer needs to consider all these costs and assign them to the appropriate products.

Customer Orientation

In product costing, as in all parts of a JIT/TQC system, the focus is on customers. The industrial marketer asks: "What is the *value* of my offering to the customer?" That's a question they often do not ask with traditional costing approaches. Further, the traditional approach can't accomodate JIT/TQC technologies, and that's crucial for both the JIT industrial marketer and its customers.

By matching product costing techniques to JIT technologies, the marketer is better equipped to measure its own costs as it enters negotiations with customers. But more important than that, it can evaluate costs that cross over into the customer's value chain and address the buyer's questions about *its* cost to purchase and use the product. Armed with this data, the JIT marketer can develop more effective pricing strategies.

JIT costing—and pricing—boils down to customer-perceived value.

PRICING REFLECTS VALUE TO THE CUSTOMER

Typically, commercial products are priced either as commodities or premium-priced offerings. The commodity price is the basic price for a generic product, subject to the forces of supply and demand. But certain marketers sell offerings in the same product category at a higher, or premium, price.

The price customers will pay is based on their perception of the offering's total relative value. This establishes the product's market price and the marketer from whom customers purchase the product.

The position a particular marketer's offering may hold is shown in Fig. 8-3.

The JIT industrial marketer's goal is to position its products in quadrant 4 as differentiated offerings. That sets the firm apart from competitors and lets it obtain a premium for the differential value it offers customers. The offering is differentiated in one or more ways the customer considers important, and the customer recognizes this differentiation.

An offering may be differentiated from competitors' without customers perceiving it. Such products are in quadrant 2. The reason for the gap

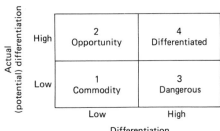

Figure 8-3   Customer perceived positioning of the offering.

is often communication. Marketers can reposition such offerings—move them into quadrant 4—by choosing an appropriate message and effective communications media.

Quadrant 3 represents a dangerous position. The customer or prospect perceives a differential that doesn't actually exist. This could happen if an overzealous product manager or sales representative told customers about features the offering didn't yet have. Those could be product characteristics, such as quality levels, or service features, such as lead time to delivery. The marketer must realign the offering quickly, bringing its performance up to customer's expectations, or the offering reverts to quadrant 1: commodity status.

This brings us back to the findings of researchers using the PIMS data base, mentioned in Chapter 7. To recap, product quality is a major differentiator for marketers of component products. Quality has a *direct* positive effect on return on investment and also influences ROI indirectly, by helping the marketer boost market share. Further, quality has a direct and beneficial effect on direct costs, and that significantly influences ROI.

Contrary to conventional wisdom, relative quality of the offering and cost position are *not* opposing goals requiring different strategies. High relative quality requires no significant trade-offs in terms of cost position. In fact, it aids low-cost positioning.

It is important that customers perceive the differentiation that permits premium pricing. The differentiated product must offer them more than competitive offerings in some important respects. The JIT industrial marketer's challenge is to develop pricing strategies based on the value contribution the marketer's offering makes to the customer's offering throughout the value chain, i.e., its "value in use."

VALUE-BASED PRICING

The value of the JIT marketer's offering to the customer is equal to customers' perceptions of the quality of the offering. That quality has several dimensions, which may each be important to the customer. Each

TABLE 8-1   JIT Marketer's Potential Contribution to Customer Value

JIT Marketer's Quality Differentiation Areas	Customer Value-Adding Activity Affected					
	Inbound Logistics	Operations: Design	Mfg.	Outbound Logistics	Marketing, Sales	Service
Basic product						
Performance	*				*	
Features	*	*			*	
Reliability	*	*			*	*
Durability					*	*
Serviceability					*	*
Conformance	*		*			
Augmented product						
Delivery	*		*	*		
Service	*		*			
Relationships	*	*	*	*	*	*

offers the marketer a chance to differentiate the offering. Michael Porter's pioneering research into the value chain, and David Garvin's research into the concept of quality, illustrate how this works.[10]

Table 8-1 is a convenient framework, showing the primary areas in which the JIT marketer's offering adds value to the customer's operations. These differentiating product and service attributes deserve careful analysis by the JIT industrial marketer. The table shows how the JIT marketer's offering affects various value-adding activities in the customer's value chain. It also shows how the offering's quality characteristics may add value to these customer activities—beyond what competitive offerings provide.

Clearly, value-based pricing requires a thorough knowledge of the customer's value chain. But the JIT marketer must also understand its own offering and its key competitors' offerings and how each could affect the customer's value-adding activities.

A brief discussion of each of the JIT marketer's quality differentiators will show how they may be used in value-based pricing.

Product Performance

This includes the product's primary operating characteristics, such as operating speed and quietness of operation. Whether the customer actually perceives performance differences as quality differences depends on its specific needs and preferences.

The JIT marketer may enhance the perceptions of the OEM customer's technical staff, including research and development teams and design engineers, by pointing out how the offering's performance level could enhance the OEM's product performance. As the OEM's own customers respond to those changes in the final product, its sales and marketing departments—perhaps even top managers—start to appreciate the value of the JIT marketer's differentiated product.

The OEM may quantify the differentiated component's value by looking at how much more its customers will pay for the improved final product based on their value perceptions. That produces objective revenue and profit projections to complement the engineers' improved product performance ratings.

Product Features

These are the secondary characteristics that supplement the product's basic functioning—the "bells and whistles." These features may simplify the customer's product design process, if they focus on design for assembly. Or they may add value to the customer's manufacturing process by reducing the number of processing operations. The features may reduce the cost of the customer's product even while enhancing it. The JIT marketer and customer can measure each of these value increments.

Product Reliability

The probability that a component may malfunction or fail within a specified period is important to OEM customers. Depending on the operation, a malfunction could seriously disrupt processing operations or boost maintenance costs. Design engineers commonly measure reliability by observing the "mean time between failure" (MTBF). Though valuable to engineering, the evaluation is subjective and difficult to measure. It is more important to manufacturing personnel who must deal with short-term failures, and the replacement and rework they prompt, minute to minute.

The customer activities to which product reliability adds the most value are marketing, sales, and post-sale service. The OEM may differentiate its own product based on improved components. And by promoting its new differentiation, the OEM may boost revenue. Reliable components also reduce the OEM's field failures, lowering service costs.

The last three value-adding areas can be objectively measured.

Product Durability

This measures the product's expected life, or the use the final customer gets from the product before it deteriorates. For firms marketing intermediate products—materials, components, assemblies—to OEMs, the value of durability depends on the expected life of the final equipment in which the component is placed. If the intermediate product strongly influences the final product's life, it could add a great deal of value to the OEM customer's offering.

Product Serviceability

This characteristic involves the ease and speed with which the product may be repaired or replaced. Again, the value of improved serviceability depends on the product's role in the OEM's product and on how that final product is used. Improved serviceability is almost always desirable but under certain conditions, such as the disruption of expensive processing operations, it is critical. The usual serviceability measure is "mean time to replace" (MTTR).

Product Conformance

Conformance represents how well the product's design/operating characteristics meet the customer's specifications. The latter usually comprise a "target": a centering dimension bounded by a range of acceptable tolerances. Traditionally, OEM customers ignored variations from the target as long as the component was within the specified range.

As discussed in Chapter 7, reducing variability around the target—a goal of more and more U.S. producers—improves the component's value. It reduces losses to customers from factors such as "tolerance stack up." This occurs when the manufacturer tries to mate parts from opposite ends of the acceptable range, such as a maximally acceptable diameter hinge pin and a minimally acceptable diameter opening in an automobile door-hinge assembly. Product conformance may directly affect durability and ease of use.

Each of these six characteristics relates to the physical product's quality. The characteristics of the total offering, referred to in Table 8-1 as the "augmented product," extend beyond physical features. Many factors affect customer perceived value, but the most important are delivery, service, and relationships.

Delivery

Just-in-time delivery may add significant value to the customer's value chain. Delivery may be separated into three separate dimensions: timing, quantity, and condition.

By delivering components precisely when the OEM customer needs them, the JIT marketer eliminates the waste associated with early and late deliveries. Early deliveries add the cost of storage space, inventory carrying, and rehandling. Late deliveries add the expense of expediting and processing interruptions. Delivery of the wrong size shipment causes similar kinds of waste. And so do logistical problems, such as improper materials handling, which can cause loss or damage or otherwise undermine the product's condition.

Each of these delivery dimensions affects the customer's inbound logistics, manufacturing, and outbound logistics. They may be objectively measured in terms of customer value-added potential. For example, delivery to the point-of-use precisely as needed, and in line sequence will substantially reduce the customer's logistics costs. Damage-free delivery will eliminate waste from scrap, fill-in requests, expediting, production disruption, and on.

Service

There are two separate aspects of service: logistical service, also called customer service; and technical service.

Customer service covers responsiveness and the efficiency with which reps handle transactions-related communications such as order placement, order status reporting, and expediting. This kind of service may add value to the customer's offering. A marketer's user-friendly electronic data interchange system, for example, may considerably reduce the customer's lead time and number of order processing errors.

Technical service, which includes product design help for the OEM customer and application assistance during manufacturing, may center on the proper use of the marketer's product. Or it may mean evaluating and correcting a quality problem. Technical service could also include post-sale service of the final product, if the JIT markter's product contributed to that field failure. The time and number of call-backs required to correct a problem are good measures of service quality.

Relationships

This characteristic, though extremely important, is undoubtedly the most subjective and the toughest to measure. And it's unique in that it affects all the customer's value-adding activities. The caliber of relationships comes through in the attitude of all the JIT marketer's representatives. Their openness, cooperation, responsiveness, and friendliness—or lack of same—reflect the strength of the marketer–customer relationship.

The marketer's goal is to develop a consistently positive tone and an ease of interaction. The global effect of high-quality relationships is a winning reputation for the JIT marketer. To evaluate its success in this area, the marketer may deploy its representatives in each value-adding activity to measure customer satisfaction.

PRICING: A JOINT EFFORT

Unlike traditional pricing practice, in which the marketer and customer independently develop an acceptable price range, JIT pricing requires the two to cooperate closely. Each firm must share information on its costs, values, processes, and plans. The goal is to optimize their mutual offering's value—something they can't do from arm's length.

The natural vehicle for value-based pricing is Quality Function Deployment, in which the JIT industrial marketer works closely with the customer or prospect to assess its physical-product quality needs and augmented product needs. Technical, operational, and logistical teams are perfectly positioned to evaluate the value to the customer of various product characteristics. The teams can provide data on the best ways to differentiate the markter's product—and the degree to which it will be differentiated.

ESTABLISHING THE PRICE

This approach is far removed from the traditional cost-plus approach to pricing. It truly reflects the JIT marketer's value contribution to the customer. Figure 8-4 contrasts the two approaches.

The customer value-based approach is built on the going rate of an undifferentiated offering, or commodity. Such a product has unexceptional quality levels on all product and service dimensions. To differenti-

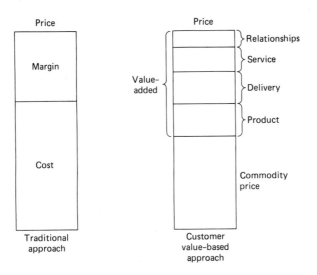

Figure 8-4 Contrasting the traditional and customer value-based pricing approaches.

ate the offering and increase its price beyond the commodity baseline, the marketer evaluates how quality improvements on each of the offering's characteristics would improve customer perceived value. As quality improves on each dimension, the offering's net value to the customer increases. Net value is the value-added characteristic's benefit to the customer, less cost to the customer.

Implementing a value-based pricing system isn't easy. But, for illustration's sake, consider a simple example. Assume the marketer enjoys a relatively well developed JIT/TQC system that allows it to exceed competitors' performance in several areas that customers value, including product conformance, reliability, and delivery. The prevailing competitive levels on those dimensions, on average, shape the commodity price of $10 per unit. Our marketer's higher quality levels add value to the undifferentiated product, in the customer's eye.

Consider how that differentiation helps the customer: Because our JIT marketer provides higher product conformance (PCv) levels, measured in defective parts per million, the customer can eliminate incoming inspection of these parts and reduce downtime and rework in assembly. That saves the customer that buys 100,000 units annually about $50,000 per year.

The value-added marketer's higher product reliability (PRv), measured in MTBF, reduces the number of "short-term" failures, which occur during the customer's manufacturing cycle. Higher quality also reduces the number of "long-term" failures, which occur after the final product is in the end user's hands. By reducing the number of short-term failures, the OEM cuts downtime, scrap, and rework. And fewer long-term failures mean lower field service and warranty costs. These cost savings add up to about $75,000 per year for the customer.

The customer also saves on inventory costs. The marketer's just-in-time schedule narrows the delivery time window (Dv) from four days to four hours and lets the OEM customer move the product directly to the production line. This saves the customer three and one-half days worth of inventory carrying costs plus material handling costs. This adds up to savings of about $75,000 per year.

Let's assume further that the customer and JIT marketer agree to share evenly in all these savings. The marketer would calculate its value-based price as follows:

$$Pv = \text{Commodity Price} + [(PCv + PRv + Dv)(.50)]/Q$$

where PCv = Product conformance differential value
         PRv = Product reliability differential value
         Dv = Delivery differential value
         Pv = Value-based price

The Pv = $10.00 + [(\$50,000 + 75,000 + 75,000)(.50)]/100,000$ units
= $10.00 + \$100,000/100,000$ units
= $10.00 + \$1.00$
= 11.00

This produces a 10%, $1 per unit, premium over the prevailing commodity price.

To use this pricing approach, the JIT marketer needs a transactions-based cost accounting system. With such a system it can determine the costs of its various offerings.

Cost-of-quality programs are extremely helpful in value-based pricing. According to Philip Crosby, a pioneer in developing the cost-of-quality concept, all costs created by nonconformance problems contribute to the cost of quality.[11]

Generally speaking, the cost of quality includes prevention, appraisal, and failure costs. *Prevention costs* reflect efforts—during design and development, purchasing, production, and other phases of creating an offering—to prevent defects. They include the cost of design reviews, product qualifications, supplier evaluations, and the like.

Appraisal costs are incurred while conducting inspections, tests, and other evaluations that determine conformance levels. Examples include supplier monitoring, receiving inspections, and status measurement.

Failure costs relate to nonconformance. They reflect the costs of redesign, engineering change orders, purchase change orders, rework, scrap, service, and product liability.

These three kinds of costs cut across the spectrum of value-adding activities of the JIT OEM customer. Many are directly related to the value added by the JIT industrial marketer.

The traditional cost system is virtually useless in accounting for the costs of quality incurred while enhancing the offering.

PRICE ADJUSTMENTS IN PRACTICE

After the customer value-based price is established, the JIT marketer will probably have to adjust it during the term of the agreement, based on how well it meets agreed-on quality levels. This gives the marketer a good incentive for continuous improvement—to make sure it always meets or exceeds quality levels.

A reasonable approach is to agree on certain baseline quality levels. The OEM customer pays the full negotiated price when the marketer consistently meets those levels.

But the marketer needs to adjust the price if its performance consistently falls below the baseline. If, for example, its deliveries miss the specified time window, its product's performance falls below the specified level, or its product doesn't conform to specifications, the price comes down. The price change should reflect the actual value reduction, or cost to the customer, that the failure produces. It shouldn't be a fixed percentage sliced off the negotiated price.

In some cases, performance outside the preset level may actually help the customer. If the supplier provides extra design or application engineering know-how or products that perform better than the specified level, the customer may reward the marketer with a bonus. Once again, the bonus should reflect the value of these contributions to the customer.

The bottom line for JIT industrial marketers and customers alike is that traditional cost-based approaches are no longer valid. They are based on outdated technologies and don't reflect the key element of *value to the customer*. JIT marketers may enhance the value of their offerings in many ways. Together with the customer, the marketer carefully evaluates its value-adding opportunities, selecting those that are important to the customer and feasible for the marketer.

The JIT industrial marketer must develop a transactions-based cost system that accurately and responsively reports the cost of performance. To function optimally, the reporting system must also collect and communicate nonfinancial data critical in the new operating environment, such as quality levels, lead time, delivery performance, and customer satisfaction levels.

NOTES

1. Somerby Dowst, "Auto Makers Asking for Price Cuts," *Purchasing,* February 1984, p. 49.
2. Lawrence Gordon, Robert Cooper, Haim Falk, and Danny Miller, *The Pricing Decision* (New York: NAA, and Hamilton, Ontario: SMAC, 1981).
3. Michael Cornick, William Cooper, and Susan Wilson, "How Do Companies Analyze Overhead?" *Management Accounting,* June 1988, pp. 41–43.
3. Robert Kaplan, "Accounting Lag: The Obsolescence of Cost Accounting Systems," *California Management Review,* Winter 1986, pp. 174–98.
5. Jeffrey Miller and Thomas Vollmann, "The Hidden Factory," *Harvard Business Review,* September–October 1985, pp. 142–50.
6. William Holbrook, "Accounting Experience in a JIT Environment," a presentation at the First Annual Management Accounting Symposium entitled Cost Accounting, Robotics and the New Manufacturing Environment, Vanderbilt University, February 26–28, 1987.
7. Robert Kaplan, "Regaining Relevance," a presentation at the conference cited in note 6.
8. Kaplan, "Regaining Relevance."

9. Ibid.
10. Michael Porter, *Competitive Advantage: Creating and Sustaining Competitive Performance* (New York: The Free Press, 1985); and David Garvin, *Managing Quality: The Strategic and Competitive Edge* (New York: The Free Press, 1988).
11. Philip Crosby, *Quality Is Free* (New York: McGraw-Hill, 1979).

Chapter 9

Physical Distribution Strategy

An excellent physical distribution strategy may be the one feature to differentiate world-class marketers from competitors.

After carefully assessing customer needs, the world-class supplier mixes the strategic marketing-mix elements of physical distribution, product, price and communications to serve each customer fully. These marketing elements combine to create customer satisfaction, with physical distribution as a major contributor because it provides *customer service*. (See Fig. 9-1.)

The JIT marketer and customer jointly determine a customer service level that will provide customer satisfaction, at least initially. The companies establish performance specifications for: the quality of products, as delivered; delivery frequency; lot sizes and quantity precision; delivery time windows; order-cycle length; and the total cost of meeting these requirements. The parties establish benchmarks in each of these areas, and in keeping with the JIT/TQC philosophy of ongoing improvement, they continuously upgrade the initial specification. The industrial marketer's goal is to be the "best of the best" in every area.

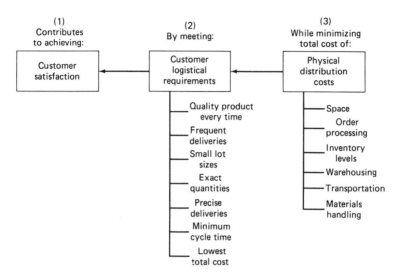

Figure 9-1   Physical distribution.

ESTABLISHING SERVICE LEVELS

Physical distribution specifications, like product specifications, are developed jointly by the marketer and customer. Each has a logistics team, which evolves from the initial design-processing team. The logistics teams have some members from the design teams, and they understand their partners' requirements and capabilities intimately. Distribution specifications flow out of the customer's operational, or processing, requirements. This means the customer cannot specify just-in-time deliveries until its own processing system can accommodate such deliveries.

The two organizations plan delivery logistics in tandem, just as they plan products. Rather than switching abruptly from "just-in-case" to just-in-time, the two smoothly shift to smaller quantities, delivered more frequently and at more precise time intervals. As the first step, the customer may reduce raw materials inventories by requesting weekly production shipments rather than monthly stocking shipments. Or, if the customer receives shipments weekly, it may shift to twice a week.

To minimize in-process inventories, the industrial marketer develops a shipping schedule based on the customer's demand schedule. Because the JIT customer's goal is continuous reduction of lot sizes, the suppliers' delivery frequency and lot size continue to change according to realistic, jointly planned schedules.

Physical distribution includes several factors that affect the mar-

TABLE 9-1   How Physical Distribution Influences Customer Service

Customer Service Elements	Marketer's Physical Distribution Activities				
	Location Plant/ Warehouse	Order Processing	Materials Handling	Transportation	Inventory
Quality product (every time)		x	x	x	
Frequent deliveries	x		x	x	x
Small lot sizes	x		x	x	
Exact quantity		x	x	x	x
Precise deliveries		x	x	x	
Minimum cycle time	x	x	x	x	x
Lowest total cost	x	x	x	x	x

keter's cost, JIT capabilities, and customer service. They include: location, order processing, inventory planning, transportation, and materials handling.

As Table 9-1 shows, each of the industrial marketer's physical distribution activities directly influences some or all customer service elements. Using the matrix, the marketer can develop a distribution strategy to achieve desired customer service levels and still provide the lowest total cost. Let us consider each distribution activity's role.

FACILITIES LOCATION

As previously discussed, plant location can give the marketer a competitive advantage in serving JIT customers. By shipping from a facility near the customer, the marketer can reduce transportation costs, inventory levels, average order-cycle time, and cycle-time variability. Proximity also aids the frequent intercompany communications vital to just-in-time operations.

The industrial marketer has many options in locating plants to serve OEM customers and prospects. These include: a remote location, a remote facility with flow-through warehouse, remote manufacturing with final processing near the OEM customer, and a focused plant near the customer. Let's consider each.

Remote plant, or no change from current location. Industrial marketers can be effective long-distance JIT suppliers under certain conditions, but it's increasingly difficult as more customers require line-sequenced, direct-to-assembly deliveries. (Long-distance here refers to 300 miles or more.) Marketers delivering daily or several times per day, in truckload quantities, are most able to meet such requirements.

These delivery schedules point to high-volume shipments of discrete parts, or moderate-volume shipments of bulky parts and assemblies. Davidson Rubber Company's panel instrument group provides an excellent example of the former. This group supplies about one half the panel instruments used in American-made automobiles. Davidson supplies several Detroit-area plants, roughly 800 miles away from its facility in New Hampshire, on a precise four-times-daily schedule.[1]

An example of moderate-volume assembly deliveries comes from Eaton Corporation's Axle and Brake Division. Daily, it ships medium-duty truck-axle assemblies to GM truck assembly plants more than 300 miles away.[2] The assemblies are line-sequenced, or shipped in the exact sequence in which they will be assembled on GM's production line.

This kind of marketer-customer coupling requires compatibility, open and frequent communications, and the supplier's commitment to meeting JIT requirements. Both Davidson and Eaton's Axle and Brake Division have their own just-in-time manufacturing systems with "quality-at-the-source" controls.

Lower volume suppliers that make daily or multiple-per-day shipments to remote OEM customers generally make "less than truckload" (LTL) or "less than carload" (LCL) shipments. That approach to motor and rail freight often boosts transit times and transportation costs prohibitively. Marketers and their carriers meet the challenge by creatively consolidating partial shipments into truckload (TL) or carload (CL) quantities.

The industrial marketer's success with remote customers depends on whether strong competitors are based nearer the customer. If so, the remote marketer will have trouble negotiating a single-source agreement with the customer. Even if it could become a single source, the remote marketer would be hard pressed to maintain the agreement, particularly if local competitors were evolving into world-class suppliers.

Nearby flow-through warehouse teamed with remote plant. Medium-sized and small industrial marketers, and those whose volume does not justify daily or multiple-per-day shipments, may add a public or private warehouse near the customer to improve JIT service. Meanwhile, the marketer's plant remains 300 or more miles away.

Used as the final staging link, the public warehouse lets the marketer immediately relocate near JIT customers and establish a trial delivery program with minimum capital investment. A public warehouse can also help the marketer cut transportation costs without sacrificing customer service. The marketer ships large quantities to the warehouse, gaining economies of scale, but delivers small lots to the customer once or more each day.

By placing inventory near the customer's point-of-use, the marketer becomes even more responsive. And the warehouse doesn't increase inventory in the system if it replaces the supplier's existing distribution and inventory control system.

Because the traditional public warehouse was not designed to meet just-in-time customers' needs, a new kind of warehouse has emerged. Just-in-Time Warehousing, Whiting Public Warehouses, Incorporated, and Leaseway Transportation Corporation have developed "flow-through" or "just-in-time" warehouses.[3] Located near automotive-assembly plants, these facilities allow marketers to deliver parts to OEM lines on a jointly developed schedule. Local warehouses also let marketers combine shipments to reduce congestion at customers' receiving docks.

Despite these benefits, the use of public or private flow-through warehouses is not entirely consistent with just-in-time's goal of waste reduction. In addition to making it more difficult to remove inventory from the system, the warehouse introduces one more communication link between the marketer and OEM. This wastes managers' and line workers' time and increases the chance of a logistical error. However, warehousing may be worthwhile during a transitional period, such as the time required to develop a focused plant or nearby final processing.

Remote basic manufacturing, with final processing or assembly near the customer. Some industrial marketers, particularly those with final-stage processing or assembly that adds substantial bulk to their products, may prefer to transfer final processing to a facility near the customer. The marketer ships subassemblies and final-assembly parts to the nearby facility, avoiding the final products' "balloon freight" characteristic. This is quite rewarding if the customer buys several configurations of the final product, all assembled from standard parts or subassemblies.

The parts' density helps the marketer control transportation costs, and it may postpone final processing until the customer actually needs the product. The supplier "pulls" finished product from the satellite processing operation as needed and, if desired, in line sequence. Ideally, the marketer's final processing takes place at the customer's facility, in a leased area next to the point-of-use. This gives the supplier space with minimum investment. It is also the most efficient logistical arrangement, simulating the customer's in-house departments. Such arrangements also foster a closer relationship between the supplier and customer.

If an on-site arrangement isn't possible, the marketer may lease or buy a facility reasonably close to the customer's plant.

Focused plant near the customer. If the industrial marketer's remote location puts it at a competitive disadvantage, it should seriously consider relocating its processing facility. This is particularly true when the manufacturing process cannot be divided, as above.

Location is one of the JIT customer's most important considerations in selecting suppliers, and it becomes even more important as the OEM develops and fine-tunes its just-in-time manufacturing system. OEMs are increasingly establishing boundaries within which suppliers should—or must—be located. Chrysler has developed its supplier base with roughly 50% of components suppliers located within 250 miles of production. GM-Pontiac arranged its Fiero supplier base with 75% within 200 miles of the assembly plant.[4]

Not surprisingly, more industrial marketers are locating focused plants near major customer plants. Hoover Universal, a leading automotive-seating supplier, locates its plants within 50 miles of major customers. Hoover's focused plants are dedicated facilities that provide seats directly to the customer's point-of-use, in sequence. The focused plants require a four-hour lead time to delivery and a thirty-minute delivery window.[5] This may seem like a risky move, but if the supplier carefully selects its focused-plant customers, and they are OEMs with which it already has a strong relationship, plant relocation may be the wisest decision.

In deciding on location, the remote supplier must recognize that it affects both its own and the customer's organization. The marketer should weigh the advantages and disadvantages of each alternative, recognizing that location becomes more important as customers further reduce buffer stocks, lot sizes, and lead times. If the marketer is already a major supplier to a particular OEM, it should ask, "How well are we meeting customer needs with our present location, and how will this change over the next three to five years, based on the customer's plans?"

If the marketer is trying to become a major supplier but is in a remote location, it may consider relocating. Assuming it can meet the customer's performance specifications, the marketer should ask: "If we move, will the locational advantage be enough to substantially boost sales to the customer?" and "How do we know this shift will happen, and last?"

For a remote out-supplier competing with a remote in-supplier, relocation may be the strategic weapon needed to land the account. On the other hand, the remote in-supplier's competitive position may deteriorate if a competitor located nearer the OEM becomes better at meeting the customer's performance requirements.

ORDER PROCESSING

Order processing is the physical distribution system's "nerve center." Customer orders activate the logistics system, and the speed and quality of the customer-marketer information flow continuously affect the distribution system.

From the customer's point of view, the order cycle begins with placing an order and ends when it puts ordered goods into stock or production. The time needed for each order-cycle activity in the traditional marketing system, shown in Table 9-2, is based on a comprehensive customer service study of manufacturing operations conducted for the National Council of Physical Distribution Management by Bernard Lalonde and Paul Zinszer, and published in *Customer Service: Meaning and Measurement.*[6]

The elapsed time between order placement and order receipt depends on how the customer transmits the order. The Lalonde/Zinszer study shows that sales reps deliver about one-tenth of all orders; customers phone in about one-third and mail in another one-third; and about one-fifth are transmitted electronically by the customer.

Generally, the ordering mode's speed influences order processing's variability vis a vis delivery time. Slow, unpredictable ordering methods, including the mail, are not a good way to serve JIT customers. Because the time it takes to transmit orders by mail or sales rep is unpredictable, the customer doesn't know when deliveries will arrive and must keep large buffer stocks, just in case.

In the order cycle, the marketer controls order processing and picking/packing. With conventional order processing, the marketer checks the inventory to see if the material is available for shipment. If not, it is

TABLE 9-2 Traditional Customer Order Cycle

Activity	Average Time Required (days)	Who Controls Activity
Customer: Places order	1.9	Customer
Marketer: Receives order		
Processes order	2.1	Marketer
Picks and packs order	2.2	Marketer
Ships order		
Customer: Receives order	4.1	Marketer/Customer plus Carrier
	Total = 10.3 days	

scheduled for production and the order is acknowledged. If it is in stock, the system initiates order acknowledgment, invoicing, and the development of shipping documentation and picking and packing instructions for the marketer's warehouse. The Lalonde/Zinszer study indicates that, on average, this process takes 4.3 days if the material is in stock.

The time elapsing between order shipment and customer receipt averages 4.1 days, making transit the most time-consuming order activity. Transit time depends on the distance between the marketer and customer, and the transportation mode. With "inbound" transportation control, the customer takes charge of transportation. With "outbound" control, the supplier takes charge. But once the customer and supplier choose a mode, the carrier assumes primary control. The carrier may be a unit of the customer or marketer company. More frequently, it's an independent transportation firm.

An order cycle of ten days or more is clearly unacceptable for OEMs using just-in-time manufacturing techniques. Industrial marketers, particularly those aspiring to world-class status, must substantially reduce order-cycle time. The marketer takes a giant step toward world-class status when it reduces the order cycle's variability and compresses how long it takes. The customer doesn't want to be surprised during the order cycle, by timing or anything influencing production. Error-free processing should occur in each step of the cycle. That means:

- Error-free order transmission, with the customer specifying correct part numbers, quantities, and shipping/arrival times.

- Error-free processing, in which the supplier produces or draws from stock the correct part numbers and quantities. The supplier also packs and ships the order for damage-free delivery and invoices the customer correctly.

- Error- and damage-free handling and transportation from the supplier's shipping dock to the customer's point-of-use.

To reduce order-cycle time and boost the quality of order-cycle activities, the marketer may adapt Shigeo Shingo's system for minimizing production setup time, which he describes in *A Revolution in Manufacturing: The SMED System* (single minute exchange of die system).[7] To do so, the supplier:

- Separates internal and external order-cycle activities, continuing to control the former. An external organization, such as the customer or carrier, controls the latter.

- Converts the external activities into internally controlled or internally influenced tasks.

- Streamlines internal and external activities through internal analysis and improvements and close cooperation and counsel with relevant outsiders. These activities are order transmission, order processing, and order shipment, which includes materials handling and transportation.

Because the JIT concepts naturally streamline operations—particularly customer-supplier interactions like those in the order cycle—the JIT order cycle is quite different from the conventional model. As Table 9-3 illustrates, the cycle's time and cost decrease as the marketer's control or influence over order-cycle activities increases. That calls for the spirit of cooperation and trust discussed in Chapter 4.

TABLE 9-3   The JIT Customer Order Cycle

Activity	Average Time Required	Who Controls Activity
Customer: Places order	1 hour	Customer, but influenced by marketer (EDI)
Marketer: Receives order		
Processes order	nominal (hours?)	Internal: marketer
Picks and packs order	eliminated	Internal
Ships order to customer	1–2 days	Marketer control or influence
Customer: Receives order	_____	
	Total = 1–2 days*	

*Same-day delivery if marketer is 50–100 miles from customer.

ORDER TRANSMISSION

This activity can significantly reduce the order cycle's time and improve its accuracy. The OEM generally controls order transmission, but the marketer can strongly influence how orders are transmitted. The traditional approaches—mailing and phoning in orders and having salespeople pick them up—waste too much time and just aren't accurate enough. Many JIT producers recognize these pitfalls, as our survey of just-in-time OEM producers shows.

Table 9-4 shows that by 1985 a major shift had occurred: customers' main order-transmission tools were no longer mail and phone, but phone and computer. In general, the respondents planned to use computers and were devising ways to do so. Suppliers are influencing this choice by

TABLE 9-4   Effect of Just-in-Time Systems on Customer Order Transmission*

Primary Mode of Transmission	Percent Using Mode (%)		
	Traditionally (before JIT)	Currently	Next 3–5 years
Single Modes:			
Mail	51	2	—
Phone	3	23	3
Computer	13	33	81
Combination of Modes:			
Mail-phone	33	13	—
Mail-computer	—	7	—
Phone-computer	—	4	16
Mail-phone-computer	—	18	—
	100%	100%	100%

*Source: Survey of Automotive Industry Final Product Assemblers, conducted in 1985 by Charles O'Neal, Professor of Marketing, University of Evansville.

working closely with customers to develop hardware and software that streamline computer transmission.

Electronic Data Interchange (EDI) is an increasingly popular way of communicating via computer. Anything written on standard business forms, including purchase orders, releases, acknowledgments, invoices, shipping notices, planning schedules, and status reports, may be electronically transmitted. EDI offers the industrial marketer and customer several benefits, including the following:

• Less paperwork, because no hard copy is needed.
• More accurate transmitted information, because EDI eliminates much of the human error of keypunching, transcribing, and recording.
• A shorter order cycle, because communications are directly placed and received.
• Improved operations planning, thanks to more timely and accurate order information.

To encourage a customer to order electronically, the marketer may place a computer terminal in that OEM's purchasing office. The terminal is connected to the marketer's mainframe computer, and the customer may check product availability, pricing, and order status, as well as place orders. This kind of proprietary system is a step removed from true EDI and only works for OEM customers dealing with a few suppliers.

Standard EDI systems offer computer-to-computer, or "core-to-core," linkage. The marketer and customer each maintains an "electronic mailbox" and communicates by leaving messages in the mailboxes. To safeguard proprietary information, the partners may design the system with areas inaccessible to the other party.

As electronic data interchange has become more popular, standards for EDI equipment and software have started to emerge. The Automotive Industry Action Group took the initiative in 1985 to set such standards for automotive industry suppliers and customers. The goal was more effective, efficient communications.

Putting systems such as EDI in place, and training employees to use them, are the first steps toward reducing order-transmission time. The second phase is procedural: the customer must tell the supplier its materials requirements well in advance. The industrial marketer needs to know the customer's materials requirements, *and* quantities, *and* shipping frequency. If the customer provides this information well before its need, even in preliminary form, the supplier can plan capacity and materials requirements to minimize waste.

As the time comes for the supplier's production and shipment, the customer must provide precise, fixed schedules for its own production plans. The lead time for those precise schedules should be at least as long as the supplier's order cycle, including the marketer's production time. The customer modifies the advance schedules on a "rolling" basis, so changes only affect the supplier's production plans outside the immediate order cycle.

Rather than using traditional purchase orders, the customer releases materials weekly, daily, or several times a day, against a very precise schedule. If the customer uses EDI to request goods, transmission time virtually disappears, or drops to minutes at most. The system reduces elapsed time dramatically and practically eliminates human error in transmission.

Together with other JIT practices, the above system eliminates or significantly reduces much order processing. For example, the supplier need not delay processing for a customer credit check. A check is unnecessary because the supplier only selects customers with good credit. And the supplier can schedule production well before the actual release, preparing finished materials for delivery precisely as needed. Knowing the customer's fixed schedule makes such performance possible.

In addition, the supplier need not formally acknowledge orders. The supplier and customer do discuss problems or changes occurring within the "fixed" period that could keep the marketer from meeting the revised schedule, however.

The marketer may also streamline customer invoicing by making it part of the EDI release system. The customer and supplier prearrange an invoicing schedule, possibly consolidating invoices to make them less frequent than shipments. Even better, the customer and supplier may be able to persuade their banks to handle payments electronically.

MATERIALS HANDLING

Conventional manufacturing produces batches of product to fill actual orders and hoped-for orders from established customers. The supplier puts the goods in stock and waits for the order-receipt or order-release date. When it's appropriate, the supplier releases the order for shipment and forwards it to the warehouse. Warehouse personnel pick from stock and pack the order for shipment. This system is dangerously error prone. Orders may be shipped with the wrong parts or quantities, and goods may be damaged as they're picked, packed, and moved to the shipping dock.

The just-in-time system, properly implemented, eliminates nearly all order picking and packing. Rather than processing the product in advance and warehousing it, the supplier produces it daily, or several times per day, with final processing adjacent to the shipping dock. Operators put the product in the staging area at the shipping dock as it comes off the line, and execute the final process just before the just-in-time carrier's scheduled pickup.

Small-lot production and frequent pickups eliminate a tremendous amount of waste and curtail materials-handling and storage-related damage. The supplier can use storage space productively. And it requires less materials-handling equipment and fewer materials handlers and order pickers and packers. Most important, the marketer enhances its product quality by eliminating opportunities for loss, damage, and picking/packing errors.

TRANSPORTATION

The final link in the customer order cycle is transporting the finished product to the customer's plant. This is a task that eats up time and money—more so than any other activity in the cycle. Yet it is crucial to product and service quality. In the conventional order cycle, transportation consumes about 40% of the cycle's total time. This gives world-class marketers a huge opportunity for improvement. By using just-in-time dedicated carriers, suppliers can provide next-day delivery of truckload quantites within a 500- to 800-mile radius. And the supplier can creatively consolidate LTL quantities for second-day delivery.

The JIT customer and supplier have three options for controlling transportation. These are: marketer, or outbound, control; customer, or inbound, control; and shared control. (See Fig. 9-2.) In theory, the decision is simple: select the approach that meets customer needs at minimum total cost. In practice, it means the marketer and customer carefully negotiate control-related terms such as FOB (freight on board) point and freight

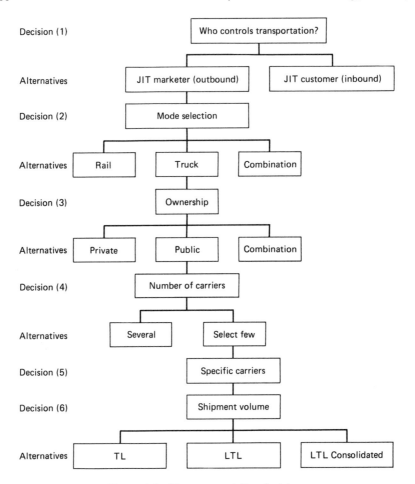

Figure 9-2   Key transportation decisions.

payment. Of course, there is no single "right answer." The control choice varies with the customer's timing, quality, and total-cost requirements.

Cost, transit time, consistent arrival times, and damage-free shipments all figure in the control decision. And timeliness, quality, rate structure, information access, interaction ability, and procedural requirements all affect total cost.

The overall transportation objective is to develop a three-way partnership among the marketer, carrier, and customer. In determining which organization should take the lead role in negotiating terms with carriers, the buyer and seller look at: the marketer's and customer's relative size, the overall volume of shipments that potential carriers handle, and the historic relationship between prospective carriers and the two organizations.

For example, if the supplier does not ship significant volumes to several customers, it's in a weaker negotiating position than the OEM customer that receives shipments from various suppliers—all shipped via one travel corridor and handled by a single carrier. That customer's ability to "bundle" multiple-supplier shipments and gain favorable rates makes it the better choice for controlling carrier negotiations. In such a scenario, the customer may arrange for consolidation of LTL shipments originating at separate points served by the carrier. This solution may provide the cost advantage of full truckloads.

In contrast, if the JIT marketer is a large multi-plant organization serving common customers, it may be better positioned than the customer to negotiate favorable terms with carriers.

Under certain circumstances, product flow may justify private carriage, controlled by either the marketer or the customer. This depends on the volume and regularity of shipments between the two organizations, the number of other suppliers or customers generating consistent product flow, and the need for greater control over product movement.

In reaching the transportation-control decision, the customer and supplier must study their entire transportation flow, not just the volume moving between them. Representatives of the two organizations should jointly analyze both companies' inbound and outbound flows to determine which company is in the better position to control transportation. Consequently, the marketer takes control with some customers but not others. Either way, the marketer influences the decision by working cooperatively with the customer.

Mode Selection

The just-in-time marketer needs to move increasingly smaller lots more frequently, faster than competitors, with precise and consistent arrivals, and at lowest total cost. No single transportation mode can do all that, but a mixed group can. Air freight provides fastest transit time; rail, lowest cost; and motor freight, high quantities and consistent deliveries, at least in truckload quantities. Each mode has a place in the JIT system.

Air-freight carriers such as Federal Express, Profit Express, and Emery Worldwide play a crucial role, filling the gap when the normal system breaks down. This is particularly important during the JIT start-up phase, which may take a year or more. In the ideal JIT system, the customer and supplier do not need such emergency transportation. As they fine-tune the system, they rely less on stopgap methods.

In some cases, air freight is the normal transportation mode. It may be the most economical, considering *total* cost, if distances are great and the product has a high value-to-bulk ratio. Apple Computer, for example, uses Skyway Systems Airfreight to airfreight and truck computer components.[8] Similarly, a Columbus, Indiana-based marketer uses Burlington

Northern Airfreight to supply Hewlett-Packard's Greeley, Colorado, facility with electronic components. Multi-tier air rates based on same-day, next-day, and fourth-day delivery times help the marketer control costs.[9]

Rail transportation also has a place in the just-in-time system but often loses out to faster, more consistent transportation modes. Historically, OEMs preferred rail transport for bulky materials with relatively low unit value, shipped in large volumes over long distances. The automotive industry, for example, has relied heavily on rail transportation. In fact, most automotive-assembly plants' receiving areas were designed primarily to accommodate rail freight. The rail lines have tried to upgrade service by converting from eighty- to fifteen-car trains and traveling point-to-point, without moving through "classification yards." But they're losing the battle.

Our study of automotive-industry JIT suppliers revealed that they historically shipped half of their volume by rail. By 1985, that had dropped to 25% and was expected to fall to 20%. Respondents said a major problem with rail transportation, in addition to lengthy transit times, is uncertain arrival time. Just-in-time producers cannot function successfully with such variability in the system.

Trucking is the JIT marketer's natural transportation choice. Motor-freight carriers are successfully adapting to the just-in-time system's requirements. This mode's advantages include smaller vehicles, compared with rail cars; door-to-door delivery; reduced transit time; and more certain arrival times. Even auto makers are relying more on trucking. General Motors' Buick City plant in Flint, Michigan, for example, uses motor freight exclusively for inbound freight and has provided 300 truck docks to accommodate deliveries.[10] Robin Transport's long-term contract with GM's Orion, Michigan, plant illustrates the consistency motor freight can provide. This trucking firm delivers fifteen loads per day with a ten-minute time window. It is penalized if it exceeds that window more than 3% of the time.[11]

New truck designs allow trucking firms to provide small trailers, called "pups," to match suppliers' small lots. They are also starting to use flexible-sided side-loading trailers to expedite loading and unloading. At GM's Fisher Body plant, side loading has improved dockside materials flow dramatically. Dock workers can unload a forty-five-foot trailer in ten minutes or less and may load and unload simultaneously.[12]

Leaseway uses flexible-sided trailers to improve its JIT delivery service in moving automobile seats from Richmond, Virginia, to Cleveland, Ohio.[13] With standard trailers, unloading shipments took four to five hours per truck. Now, thanks to special racks in the trucks, Leaseway can unload the padding with forklifts in less than twenty-five minutes. Quick loading and unloading is critical as pickups and deliveries become more frequent and lot sizes shrink.

Ownership

The basic question facing OEMs and their suppliers is whether to own and operate a private truck fleet or to engage independent transportation companies. Transportation deregulation makes the question more complex. The lines between private and public transportation are blurring as private carriers add for-hire services. Single-source leasing through which the private carrier may acquire drivers and equipment from a single source for thirty days or more, and trip leasing, in which the private carrier leases drivers and equipment to a for-hire carrier for thirty days or less, have also reshaped the motor-freight industry.

Becoming a private carrier requires a careful cost-benefit analysis. There are many potential advantages, including: greater control, security, and flexibility; decreased packing requirements; easier tracing; and higher service quality. But going private also incurs substantial capital expenses or leasing costs, plus administrative overhead. And it implies loss and damage responsibility and requires relevant management skills.

Rather than a clear-cut yes-or-no answer, the cost-benefit analysis may suggest combining private and public transportation. With such a scheme, the public carrier contracts for "dedicated carriage" and essentially serves as a private carrier for some routes. The conditions influencing the OEM's and supplier's choice of carriage are diverse, but the basic criteria are cost and the potential quality of transportation service.

Number of Carriers

The decision on number of carriers is very important and resembles the JIT purchaser's decision of how many suppliers to use. Industrial marketers and their customers have historically used many carriers, conducting individual transactions rather than long-term agreements. But the just-in-time concept, with its "partnership" or "marriage" relationship, precludes using many carriers.

Recent transportation decisions by leading firms with just-in-time programs illustrate the point. Outboard Marine Corporation, in developing JIT programs at eleven plants, reduced the number of LTL carriers serving the company from fifty-five to thirteen.[14] It cited the difficulty of communicating its needs to fifty-five carriers. GM's Buick City facility cut back its sixty-carrier base to five.[15] Those carriers serve particular geographic regions and meet very stringent service requirements.

By using fewer carriers, JIT customers and suppliers may obtain volume discounts; reduce loss and damage; improve communications, pickup performance and claims handling; and reduce transit times.

Selecting the Specific Carrier

The JIT carrier evaluation and selection process is very similar to the OEM's supplier evaluation process described in Chapter 4. Because carriers strongly affect the industrial marketer's customer service, carrier selection must be a deliberate, open, and objective process. Although the marketer doesn't usually choose one systemwide carrier, it may select one dedicated carrier to serve a specific customer or customers. The marketer, customer, and carrier develop a three-way partnership—in stark contrast to the traditional approach (see Fig. 9-3).

To participate successfully in a JIT relationship, the carrier must have:

• **A strong performance record.** The carrier's record indicates what users may expect in the future. The performance history includes transit times, loss and damage experience, volumes the carrier has handled, and deliver-time consistency. The carrier should have a companywide goal of continuous improvement of performance in each of these areas.

• **Facilities and equipment.** The carrier's facilities and equipment should give it the speed, flexibility, and precision to meet performance specifications. It needs equipment that matches the lot sizes to be shipped. And the carrier's terminal design should allow it to break bulk and consolidate or interchange shipments efficiently.

• **Technology.** Ideally, the carrier should have state-of-the-art transportation equipment, operations, procedures, and communications. These include EDI systems, through which the industrial marketer and its customer may exchange status reports, tracing and rate information, and more.

• **An appropriate management attitude.** This is probably the most important characteristic. The carrier's managers and all employees

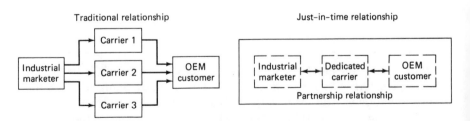

Figure 9-3 The traditional vs JIT industrial marketer-carrier-customer relationship.

should put the customer first. They should have a sense of urgency and be committed to serving customers as well as they can. The carrier's management culture should be compatible with that of the industrial marketer and its customers.

Shipment Size

Conventional industrial marketers are not terribly concerned about shipment size. To gain high-volume rates, suppliers historically shipped truckload or carload quantities to major OEM customers, even though it meant stockpiling substantial finished-goods inventories to provide customers with the right product mix. Suppliers made these "stocking shipments" weekly or even less frequently.

As OEM customers launch just-in-time manufacturing programs, stocking shipments are incompatible. The customer requires small lots and more frequent shipments from suppliers. If the industrial marketer is able to become a favored or sole supplier, the more frequent shipments may still be truckload quantities. This may continue indefinitely for major-share suppliers selling important products to high-volume customers.

For example, the Davidson Panel Instrument Division of Davidson Rubber Company, cited earlier, ships by carload to non-JIT customers and by truckload to JIT customers in the Detroit area. The division makes four deliveries daily to the JIT customers: 9 A.M., 1 P.M., 5 P.M., and 9 P.M.[16]

In lower volume situations, a supplier's shipments are in much less than truckload quantities. This means substantially higher transportation costs and slower deliveries, unless the supplier makes creative arrangements with the carrier to compensate for shipment downsizing. Note that suppliers may gain a substantial discount from usual LTL rates by contracting with one carrier for all their LTL volume. The carrier grants the discount to gain the volume commitment.

The supplier or JIT customer can further reduce costs and improve service through consolidation and/or co-loading. With the latter, the shipper works out a cooperative arrangement with a nearby company to share trailer space on LTL shipments going to the same place. Chrysler has developed a co-loading shipping and receiving system in which one supplier may fill a truck headed for various Chrysler plants, or several neighboring suppliers may jointly fill a truck going to one Chrysler plant. Deere and Company uses private carriage to make milk runs for suppliers within 100 miles of its quad-city (Illinois) facilities.[17]

Carriers are also consolidating and co-loading. Leaseway, with its Red Ball Service, picks up LTL shipments from multiple suppliers and moves them to the OEM customer's assembly plant the next morning.[18]

These are just a few of the creative solutions industrial marketers and OEMs have developed to minimize transportation costs while maintaining and improving service levels.

Transportation Company Response

The transportation industry, particularly motor freight, is aggressively responding to the just-in-time challenge. Trucking firms are learning how JIT works, or is supposed to work, and are developing equipment, procedures, and systems to meet its needs. In 1987, the American Trucking Association launched a series of regional JIT workshops encouraging participants to exchange tradition for adaptability and open communications. The workshops stress the need for exceptional cooperation between groups that have not always cooperated in the past.

One carrier that has performed outstandingly in the JIT environment is Customized Transportation Inc. (CTI), of Jacksonville, Florida. In 1985, GM-Delco recognized CTI's performance with an award for its performance in delivering modular struts. CTI delivers 132 parts for 117 car models, which lets Delco maintain virtually zero inventory.[19]

CTI moves the parts from the Dayton, Ohio, production line to its 50,000-square foot flow-through warehouse in Howell, Michigan, thirty miles from Delco's plant. Delco electronically notifies the CTI warehouse when a particular car model will be coming out of the paint process. CTI then picks the needed parts, loads a twenty-eight-foot trailer, and delivers the items to Delco's Lansing, Michigan, plant one and a half hours before they're required. The parts move directly to Delco's assembly line. None of the 500,000-plus parts CTI has delivered this way have been out of sequence.

Systems like CTI's require extemely close coordination and communication between supplier, carrier, and customer. Most leading carriers, including CTI, Roadway Express, Consolidated Freightways, PIE Nationwide, Duff Truck Lines, and Carolina Freight Carriers Corporation, are developing advanced EDI systems that allow frequent, timely communication.

INVENTORY

Although just-in-time is a philosophy that must pervade the entire organization to succeed, many see it as an inventory system. This is because a JIT program may dramatically affect inventories at all levels. OEMs in several industries have proved the point. Between 1981 and 1985, the "Big Three" auto makers held an average of $538 in inventory for each vehicle they produced. General Motors held an average of $598; Chrysler, $552; and Ford, $465. Nissan Motor Manufacturing Corporation, in contrast, held $92 per vehicle. Toyota Motor Corporation, the grandfather of just-in-time, held only $46.[20]

Harley-Davidson Corporation, after embarking on a just-in-time program in the early 1980s, increased work-in-process (WIP) inventory turns from 5.9 to 10.8 within eighteen months. By 1988, the company had cut in-process inventory value from $23 million to $8.5 million and had plans to increase WIP inventory turns to twenty.

Deere and Company's Dubuque (Iowa) Works, which produces off-highway equipment, has reduced crankshaft-machining process inventory from a thirty- to a three-day supply. Similarly, the plant now keeps a three-day supply of small crawler tractor chain instead of a thirteen-day supply, and a one-day supply of large crawler roller frames instead of two weeks worth.

Omark Industries' Mesabi, Minnesota, twist-drill plant has reduced large-drill inventory 92%, and its Oroville, California, firearms-reloading equipment plant has cut inventories in half. The company's Beaverton, Oregon, saw-chain plant outperformed a three-year plan to reduce inventories 40%, by reducing them 55% over five months. And IBM Corporation's Raleigh, North Carolina, display product operation increased inventory turns for its Model 3178 display terminal by at least five times with a just-in-time system.[21]

The list goes on and on. As a final example, consider Ford. Between 1978 and 1985, the company halved the number of days of in-process inventory held. By 1985, two Ford plants could meet or beat the Japanese auto makers on days' supply of in-process inventory. These two plants also achieved the *highest quality* and *best efficiency* in Ford's history—and exceeded capacity.[22]

The industrial marketer striving for world-class status may think the just-in-time philosophy's goals of quality and efficient inventory use are incompatible. How can it dramatically reduce inventory and still maintain the desired quality level? It helps to think of inventory as a liability whose primary function is to cover up problems.

Inventory may be categorized as: cycle stock, in-transit stock, buffer or safety stock, speculative stock, and dead stock. Manufacturers have historically held these five kinds of inventory "just-in-case," to cover up problems. Let's consider each kind of stock.

Cycle stock. Cycle stock is the materials inventory needed to meet assured production demands, which exist when the supplier can accurately predict quantity requirements and replenishment times. Cycle stock is largely a function of the production lot size.

U.S. manufacturers typically produce large lots to reduce unit cost. Say a customer orders 1,000 units of each of four separate component models. The most "efficient" manufacturing approach is to order or make materials for the 4,000 units and commence production, upon delivery of materials, for the first product in the manufacturing sequence. Production continues until the 1,000 units are produced, and the manfacturer holds these finished products in inventory while producing the other three models. The company then ships the entire batch of 4,000 units, taking advantage of low CL or TL freight rates.

The average cycle stock (beginning stock plus ending stock divided by two) is half of 4,000 units, or 2,000 units, assuming production began when the manufacturer received *all* materials. For each individual model, cycle stock is 500 units, or 1,000 divided by two. Any finished models are considered finished-goods inventory, an added expense.

In-transit stock.   In-transit stock includes the supplier's finished goods en route to the OEM, and the OEM's products en route to its customer. The producing organization usually includes only one of these in its costs, depending on the terms of purchase and sale. Either way, in-transit inventory represents a substantial investment: product transit may require three to five working days, or longer for LTL/LCL shipments.

Safety stocks.   Safety, or buffer, stocks complement cycle stock, and may include raw material, work-in-process, and finished goods' inventories. Buffer stock covers quality and disruption/delay problems with materials and goods-in-process, as well as short-range variations in customer demand.

Speculative stocks.   Speculative stocks are materials and supplies inventories the buyer holds for reasons unrelated to demand. For example, the producer may order large quantities of certain components to receive quantity discounts or to guard against price increases and shortages.

Dead stocks.   Dead stocks are finished goods with low, or no, demand over a long period, as well as obsolete inventory.

The need for these kinds of inventory changes radically with JIT. Because cycle stock is a function of lot size, the manufacturer immediately reduces cycle stock when it reduces lot size. Lot-size reduction also reduces in-process inventory and the raw materials inventory needed to support production. Just-in-time's ultimate goal is to reduce lot size to one unit and reduce inventory to zero.

The manufacturer may reduce in-transit inventories by working closely with the carrier, suppliers, and customers. Together, these groups develop a logistics system that minimizes transit times through precise pickup and delivery time windows, dedicated just-in-time transportation, and creative consolidation practices. Each day or hour they reduce transit time correspondingly reduces inventory cost and responsibility.

Buffer stocks are the worst waste culprits, because they conceal operational problems. Many Japanese firms view such problems as "treasures," because they pose opportunities for improved efficiency. The built-in "slack" in most U.S. companies provides the same oppportunity. Manufacturers carry excessive inventories to protect against the consequences of machine breakdowns, defective materials, processing errors, supply interruptions, and variable transit times.

The just-in-time system's goal is to eliminate these problems. It can significantly reduce them all. Programs that focus on preventive maintenance, quality at the source, "doing it right the first time," and total quality control have greatly reduced inventory and improved quality at many firms. Several of the companies cited have virtually eliminated transit-time variability through careful scheduling, open communications, and close cooperation among all involved parties.

Speculative stock and dead stock have no place in a just-in-time system. Because the industrial marketer and its customer openly share cost information, quantity requirements, and more, there is no reason to produce even one extra unit. Once the supplier knows how much demand exists, it can stop producing goods to meet possible demand and eliminate products that no one wants.

The OEM converting to just-in-time usually reduces raw materials inventory as one of the first steps. This increases the raw materials supplier's importance to the customer and makes the supplier more responsible for timely, accurate shipments. It may also increase the supplier's finished-goods inventory, shifting buffer stocks back one link in the supply chain.

Our study of first-tier JIT suppliers serving final-product assemblers in the automotive industry confirmed this phenomenon. About 40% of the suppliers reported that their finished-goods inventory was higher immediately after their customers reduced raw materials inventory. Only 17% reported lower finished-goods inventory, and 43% maintained the same level. Looking two to three years ahead, 55% said finished-goods levels will decrease; 21% said inventories will be much lower. Only 19% expected inventories to remain at a higher level.

Industrial marketers can help their customers reduce raw materials inventory and also keep it from backing up in the supply channel. This requires a two-pronged initiative. First, the marketer must work closely with the customer to determine its exact materials requirements for the short term. It also needs sound estimates of long-term requirements. The "short term" is at least as long as the order cycle, which includes the supplier's production period. The supplier may also help the customer improve its demand forecasting and communicate demand requirements better.

Second, the marketer must develop an in-house just-in-time system synchronized with the customer's system. This sharply reduces the supplier's production cycle, allowing greater production flexibility and eliminating the need for large cycle stocks and buffer stocks. In moving toward JIT, the industrial marketer works with its own suppliers to reduce lead times and inventories and to further improve product quality.

JIT marketers and their customers also work to reduce in-transit stocks. Inventory that is not currently in transit to the point-of-use or undergoing small-lot processing does not add value to the final product. It is waste.

Multi-level inventory reduction offers tremendous opportunities for cost savings, operational efficiency, and quality improvement. And the rewards are not limited to Japanese companies. Many U.S. organizations, including those discussed earlier, are reaping the same benefits.

MATERIALS HANDLING

"Materials handling" may not sound exciting, but it plays a vital role in inventory reduction and can help the industrial marketer increase productivity and improve quality. Materials handling is a significant cost contributor in any manufacturing operation, and the JIT marketer must scrutinize the portion of it that moves product from the point of final production to the OEM's point-of-use.

Point 1 in Figure 9-4 represents the industrial marketer, whose manufacturing line is laid out with final processing adjacent to the shipping dock. If the company has several manufacturing lines, it may dedicate shipping docks to one or more of them.

After manufacturing and before carrier pickup, the supplier packs its products in standard, reusable plastic shipping containers. These make counting and handling easier, and they protect the product. The containers should either collapse or nest, for cost-efficient return shipment. They may also be bar-coded with lot information for easy identification and use in the EDI system. If the supplier palletizes the containers, it should use standard-size pallets, also bar-coded.

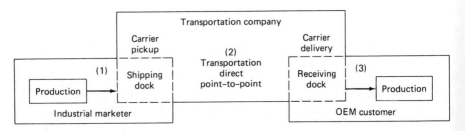

Figure 9-4   Just-in-time materials handling.

The supplier stages packed and palletized lots at the appropriate shipping dock for carrier pickup. The supplier and carrier synchronize the pickup with the supplier's manufacturing schedule to keep finished goods and the carrier's equipment from sitting idle.

Point 2 of Fig. 9-4 represents the carrier company. The carrier selects equipment compatible with the production lot's size and bulk. If it frequently picks up similar lots from that marketer, and if the destination is not far, the carrier may choose flexible-sided equipment for quick loading and unloading. The driver "cuts" the bill of lading electronically, using an EDI system that links the carrier with the marketer and OEM customer.

The supplier loads the lot immediately and it moves directly from the shipping dock to the OEM customer's receiving dock, if carrying a full trailer load. If it is an LTL shipment, the carrier makes additional pickups to form a consolidated trailer load. The carrier does not rehandle prior loads when loading successive lots.

Point 3 of Fig. 9-4 represents the OEM customer. The carrier delivers its load to the customer's receiving dock precisely as scheduled. Receiving personnel scan the bar codes as the material is unloaded. From there the goods move directly to the point-of-use, adjacent to the receiving area. OEMs commonly use multiple receiving areas to reduce congestion, staging, and the distance to point-of-use. The carrier picks up reusable containers for the return trip.

Although the system described in Fig. 9-4 is interorganizational, it resembles in-house systems in which a department provides materials for further processing. Only the distances are generally greater. The system conforms to sound materials-handling practice by doing the following:

- Eliminating handling whenever possible by removing buffer stocks and keeping active inventories to a minimum. No one rehandles inventory in this system.
- Minimizing how far the stock moves within the supplier and customer plants. The marketer completes the manufacturing process near its shipping area and transports finished product directly to the customer's receiving area, which is near the point-of-use.
- Minimizing goods-in-process and handling costs by reducing the lot size and handling materials only once.
- Ensuring uniform product flow, free from bottlenecks. Continuous small-lot scheduling and production, with precisely timed pickup and delivery, circumvents the congestion or delay caused by unpredictable carrier performance.
- Minimizing losses from waste, breakage, and theft, because only minimal product quantities are processed or accumulated. Expert

handling by motivated and trained materials handlers within the marketer, carrier, and customer organization, together with standard, reusable plastic containers, substantially reduces loss and damage.

Some leading JIT producers incorporate many of this system's features into their operations. Some are redesigning their facilities to be more like Japanese plants, with multiple receiving and shipping docks. The Automotive Industry Action Group promotes the use of standard reusable containers and bar coding, and some auto makers now require these. Chrysler specifies returnable containers for all JIT materials unless other methods are more cost effective.[23] And General Motors-Chevrolet-Pontiac-Canada requires bar-coded labels on all incoming containers.[24]

Physical distribution offers industrial marketers a great opportunity for quality and cost improvements. Clearly, the effort must be cooperative, with the supplier, carrier, and customer working as intimate partners.

The marketer striving for world-class status initiates the system. By integrating innovative locational, order processing, inventory planning, transportation, and materials-handling strategies into its overall marketing program, it gains a distinct competitive advantage.

NOTES

1. Lewis Stowe, "A Remote Just-in-Time Supplier Success Story," *Proceedings of the 1986 Annual Conference of Association for Manufacturing Excellence.*

2. Based on personal conversations and correspondence with Eaton Corporation, Axle and Brake Division representatives.

3. For example, see: Scott Whiting, "Public Warehousing and the Just-in-Time Production System," *Marketing Review,* 1983; Brian Moskal, "Warehouse on Wheels," *Industry Week,* April 2, 1984, p. 24.

4. Joan Feldman, "Transportation Changes—Just-in-Time," *Handling and Shipping Management,* September 1984, pp. 46–50.

5. E. J. Muller and J. Gordon, "Profiles in Conformance," *Distribution,* August 1986, pp. 26–38.

6. Bernard Lalonde and Paul Zinszer, *Customer Service: Meaning and Measurement* (Chicago: National Council of Physical Distribution Management, 1976).

7. Shigeo Shingo, *A Revolution in Manufacturing: The SMED System* (Stamford: The Productivity Press, 1985).

8. "A Place to Park That's Cheap, Fast, and Safe!" *Distribution,* August 7, 1986, pp. 46–55.

9. Margaret Bierman, "Flying for Just-in-Time," *Handling and Shipping Management*, October 1984, pp. 44–48.

10. "Transportation Changes—Just-in-Time," *Handling and Shipping Management*, September 1984, pp. 46–50.

11. Ibid., p. 50.

12. "Side Loading Trailers Speed Shipping and Receiving," *Modern Materials Handling*, April 9, 1984, pp. 58–59.

13. "Flexible-sided Trailers Expedite JIT Freight," *Handling and Shipping Management*, January 1985, p. 13.

14. Brian Moskal, "Delivering Just-in-Time," *Industry Week*, October 1, 1984, pp. 44–48.

15. Russell Miller, "Buick City," *Management Review*, March 1985, pp. 34–37.

16. Lewis Stowe, "A Remote Just-in-Time Supplier Success Story." *Proceedings of the 1986 Annual Conference of Association for Manufacturing Excellence.*

17. "How Co-Loading, Other Tricks Can Save You Money," *Purchasing*, July 11, 1985.

18. For example, see: Walter Weart and Edward Marian, "Everybody Out of the Pool," *Distribution*, May 1985, pp. 50–62; "Shippers Jump into the Pool," *Traffic Management*, February 1986, pp. 52–61; and Paul Fulchino, "Assembly and Distribution: A New Outlook," *Handling and Shipping Management*, November 1984, pp. 85–90.

19. "JIT Puts Accent on Partnership," *Traffic Management*, February 1986, pp. 47–49.

20. Bryan Berry, "Sagas of Success: Making Just-in-Time Work," *Automotive Industries*, February 1987, pp. 72–74.

21. Data on Harley-Davidson, Deere and Company, Omark Industries, and IBM Corporation inventory reductions taken from Association for Manufacturing Excellence Workshop Reports.

22. "No More Business As Usual: Ford's Production Philosophy," *Automotive Industries*, April 1985, pp. 42–44.

23. Bill Maraschiello, "JIT and the Receiving Room," *Handling and Shipping Management*, August 1986, pp. 36–38.

24. Joseph Callahan, "Automotive Bar Codes Take Off," *Automotive Industries*, June 1984, pp. 57–59.

Chapter 10

Communications Strategy

Effective communication is the glue that bonds the just-in-time marketer and customer together in a long-term relationship. It drives the integration of all the narrower relationships. These focus on product, service, delivery, and price, and support an overall marketing strategy. Because the JIT marketer's communication strategy establishes customer expectations and positions the firm in the marketplace, it is crucial to customer satisfaction. Communication is the heart of successful just-in-time marketing.

But marketing communications are not always effective, as illustrated in Fig. 10-1. Although this exaggerates the situation, it's a common problem.

Some of the primary characteristics of effective JIT communications are shown in Table 10-1.

These characteristics are a few of the reasons just-in-time relationships are so challenging to develop. They cut across the grain of the traditional communications process. But the marketer who recognizes the significance of these characteristics and assimilates them into its corporate culture will enjoy a distinct competitive advantage with key accounts.

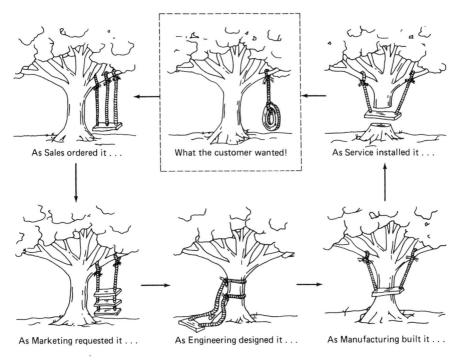

As Sales ordered it . . .   What the customer wanted!   As Service installed it . . .

As Marketing requested it . . .   As Engineering designed it . . .   As Manufacturing built it . . .

Figure 10-1 Marketing communications often leave something to be desired.

TABLE 10-1   Characteristics of Effective JIT Communications

Communications Are:	They Focus On:
Customer-focused	Customer benefits and problem solving
Comprehensive	Reaching all individuals who need to know
Personal	Face-to-face interaction for maximum effectiveness
Open	Free exchange of sensitive information with attitude of co-operation and trust
Responsive	Processes designed for flexibility and fast response in learning and meeting changing needs
Frequent	Constant flow of operational information to develop and support strategic processes
Two-way	Emphasis on listening and learning from each other
Multi-level	Vertical and horizontal communications to cut through the hierarchy and between organizations
Mutli-functional	Breaking down functional barriers, internally and between organizations
Real time	Electronic data interchange, when relevant

STAGES IN THE JIT COMMUNICATIONS PROCESS

The JIT communications process, which is critical to the just-in-time marketer's success, is extremely complex. It's a three-stage process that gets more complex as the supplier–customer relationship develops. The first stage covers promotional communications; the second, operational communications; and the third, feedback communications. Let's look at each.

Stage 1: Promotional Communications

The marketer's goal in this stage is to identify key customers and prospects and determine their basic needs and the distinct competencies it may use to best meet those needs. The supplier's goal is a long-term relationship with each key account. Marketing's role during this stage is to initiate promotional communication and lead in team development, customer assessment, and negotiations.

Stage 2: Operational Communications

The goal here is to provide a network for exchanging data needed to implement the JIT agreement. The goal in this stage is to ease the flow of timely information among the operational units of both organizations, including the commercial, technical, operational, and logistical teams. The marketing team's role in Stage 2 is to facilitate and coordinate this process and initiate related communications.

Stage 3: Feedback Communications

In this stage, communications center on actual performance results of critical processes and how they compare with expectations. The goal is to find variations from expectations and devise corrective actions that minimize waste. The marketing organization, as team leader for marketing-related feedback communications, coordinates this process.

The remainder of this chapter will focus on promotional and operational communications, and Chapter 11 will tackle feedback communications.

PROMOTIONAL COMMUNICATIONS: PICKING A PARTNER

Chapter 4 stressed the importance of self-assessment and customer assessment in identifying candidates with the most promise for long-term JIT relationships. And Chapter 6 explained the importance of focusing on

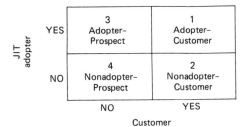

Figure 10-2 JIT relationship candidates.

individual accounts rather than market segments or customer groups. Communication plays a vital role in those activities.

Ideally, the market and account analysis produce four categories of OEM-customer candidates to whom the marketer may direct promotional communications. (See Fig. 10-2.)

To develop long-term agreements with customers in each category, the marketer needs four somewhat different strategies.

Adopter-Customer

The marketer has an advantage with these accounts because they're already customers and the supplier has contacts within their buying organizations. The marketer already provides some JIT service to adopter-customers but may not have a long-term agreement with them yet. These accounts may be at any stage of development with JIT manufacturing, ranging from "just starting" to "world-class."

If the account's JIT processes are fairly well developed, and its benchmark quality and productivity measures position it as "best in the class," the marketer takes the role of student. This customer becomes the tutor or trainer as the marketer moves to match the customer on similar performance measures. As a learner, the marketer listens carefully, not just to the customer's needs and requirements, but to its recommendations on how to meet these requirements. The marketer also carefully observes each of the critical processes the customer has nurtured to the benchmark position.

These advanced accounts, which include firms such as Ford, Xerox, Omark, Motorola, Toyota, Harley-Davidson, and Honda, are committed to JIT/TQC/TPI. They have committed significant human and financial resources to all parts of the process, including upgrading supplier quality. The learner strategy is natural when marketing to them. The key to success is to more than meet their needs. The marketer cooperates and participates actively and develops and implements processes that elevate it to world-class status.

These accounts are *winners,* and they are searching for suppliers that can match their quality levels and join with them to serve the final customer. JIT OEM customers negotiate long-term agreements with suppliers that either prove they can do this *or* have a philosophy of continuous improvement that will soon lead them to this position.

The marketer can also work cooperatively with JIT/TQC adopters who are not as far along. In this case, the two organizations mutually advance their processes in the drive toward joint world-class status. The marketer and account alternate in the trainer-learner roles, drawing on their individual abilities to strengthen each other. These accounts are not at the point of negotiating long-term agreements with suppliers, because they don't yet feel comfortable with single sources. They are still learning to negotiate from an attitude of partnership rather than with the old adversarial point of view.

The marketer's role is to help the account in this transition, drawing on its own experiences with world-class customers. As the marketer works closely with key individuals and teams in this kind of account, it earns a preferential position and an excellent chance of becoming one of the customer's first long-term partners.

Nonadopter-Customer

These are accounts that have not yet adopted the JIT/TQC philosophy but which the marketer has identified as strong candidates for long-term partnerships. These customers have been successful, because they enjoy a unique market advantage based either on cost position or product differentiation through proprietary processes.

The marketer may notice a subtle movement by the account as it starts the transition to JIT/TQC processes. By bringing the JIT message to the account's key managers and operational personnel—a message of opportunity for further growth and profitability despite the increasingly competitive environment—the marketer may even have played a role in the account's decision to adopt the JIT approach. As an in-supplier with established JIT/TQC process capabilities, the JIT marketer is perfectly situated to serve as trainer during this transition.

Typically, the two organizations already enjoy a mutually satisfying relationship, and the marketer has many key contacts with the account. Its challenge is to draw on its experience to help the account develop and implement the new philosophy. The marketer's biggest contribution may be to participate in drawing up a plan that relies on a range of external resources for education, training, and development. As the account moves toward implementation, which includes long-term agreements and single sourcing, the marketer is well-positioned to be chosen as a long-term partner.

Adopter-Prospect

These accounts present a much greater challenge than the first two categories. Because the marketer does not currently supply them (an out-supplier), it must win them over. The supplier isn't nearly as knowledgeable about the account and doesn't know who the key individuals are or what their needs are. Its earlier assessment may be helpful but certainly won't be enough to provide all the necessary data on the account. On the up side, the supplier and account do have something significant in common: a commitment to JIT/TQC.

The marketer must really do its homework to win these accounts. It already knows its product is strategically important to the customer; that was a key consideration in the earlier assessment of candidates. The important question is, how satisfied is the account with its current supplier(s)? The marketer needs to look at two kinds of information to answer that: feedback from the prospect and data on its own competitors.

The marketer begins by identifying the individuals within the account who influence supplier selection, including those involved in the technical, logistical, manufacturing, and service aspects of procurement. The marketer then analyzes its key competitors' actual performance levels and capabilities in each of the critical areas and compares them with its own.

Armed with competitive data, the marketer can approach the key buying influences to find out how satisfied they are with current suppliers. Actual performance data on those competitors is extremely useful and the marketer may ask the account for it, but it probably won't be forthcoming until the marketer and account have developed a solid rapport. This investigative process yields one of two outcomes. Supplier performance is either below the account's expectations, failing to meet its requirements, or it's satisfactory.

The first outcome provides an obvious opportunity for the marketer, assuming it can outperform competitors and has evidence to back that up. The markter's task is to persuade the prospect to let it prove its capabilities. The account probably has no long-term agreement with its current supplier. If it had, the performance problem wouldn't have happened at all—not without the supplier breaking its back to correct it.

The second outcome is tougher to deal with. But dislodging an in-supplier whose performance meets the prospect's expectations isn't impossible. From the competitive analysis, the marketer knows something about its competitors and their strengths. It knows whether it can outperform the in-supplier on any important characteristics and also remain competitive on secondary characteristics. If the marketer can't do those things, it has no case to present. But if it can beat the competition on even one critical characteristic, there's a fighting chance.

The key point is that prospects are satisfied with current supplier performance because it meets their expectations. This may well be because they don't know that another supplier could consistently perform at a higher, more desirable level. The out-supplier may be able to provide better quality or deliver shipments with more precise timing, for example. This supplier may even be able to boost quality and/or delivery reliability.

Any OEM prospect currently implementing a JIT/TQC system should be eager to hear from prospective suppliers with legitimate claims in these areas. The marketer's goal is to demonstrate the advantages of the higher level performance to the prospect *and* to the final customer.

Nonadopter-Prospect

These accounts are well-recognized in their fields and are solidly positioned because of competitive advantages they've been able to sustain in spite of traditional management and operational philosophies. They currently face one of three scenarios. Either they're maintaining market share and profit because global competition hasn't yet overwhelmed their market; they have a proprietary offering, which has forestalled such competition so far; or their share and profit is deteriorating. The marketer's strategy varies with the scenario.

These accounts, which tend to use multiple rather than single sources, may present less challenge than the adopter prospects. Their performance criteria are less demanding and they usually negotiate shorter term agreements with suppliers.

The most challenging nonadopter-prospects are those with stable market share and acceptable profit levels. Their business expectations are already being met, and the lack of a major threat or crisis works in favor of in-suppliers. An appropriate strategy here is for the marketer to approach buying influences within the account who are not satisfied with current performance or who realize a competitive threat lies ahead, and to suggest growth opportunities.

These account contacts make excellent team members and can help the marketer get to the other buying influences. Such prospects usually aren't fully aware of the markter's JIT capabilities or JIT/TQC's potential benefits. If the marketer's representatives can win over even one or two key buying influences, they can arrange for the marketers' team to tell the full JIT story to appropriate top managers.

The marketer's mission with these accounts is to present the JIT case for their consideration and, when they commit to the philosophy, act as trainer and facilitator. Becoming a supplier on a test basis shouldn't pose a problem, as these prospects are not typically locked into a long-term single source agreement with a competing supplier. As always, the marketer needs to know precisely what the competitors' performance levels are and the areas in which it, as a newcomer, excels. The latter become the marketer's key selling points.

The marketer's strategy is to move carefully in bringing the account up to speed with the JIT/TQC philosophy. It works with great deliberation to become a key supplier, using its JIT capabilities as needed to meet the account's requirements. The marketer may also recommend and/or help the account evaluate other noncompeting suppliers as the prospect starts to implement JIT processes.

With nonadopter-prospects whose performance is deteriorating, the transition to in-supplier may happen more quickly—if it's possible for the account to recover its previous position. In such cases, the prospect probably lost its leadership position by ignoring, or failing to recognize, the global competitive threat. These accounts are open to change. They may even be eager for help in getting back on track.

The JIT marketer is in a prime position to launch a two-pronged strategy to close the gap between the nonadopter-prospect's expectations and market performance. The markter's mission is the same as with the other kinds of accounts: help the prospect develop JIT/TQC programs and move into the position of major supplier.

Timing is more important with these accounts than with the others. Everything must move faster to get the prospect up and running with JIT processes as soon as possible. This dictates education and training by immersion, beginning with the account's chief executive and other top managers. Persuading the prospect to commit the significant resources needed to finance this transition is also important and must be emphasized when educating the top executives. The marketer starts off as a trainer for these accounts, but evolves into a supplier-partner as the customers become sophisticated enough to require its full JIT arsenal.

In each of these four cases, the marketer's strategy is to develop a strong relationship with the account. The starting point is different with each kind of customer, but the ultimate goal the same: to become a long-term partner. The previous discussion focused on face-to-face personal interactions with the account, primarily in the form of direct sales. But relationship marketing also includes other forms of communication. Promotional messages are one of the most important.

RELATIONSHIP MARKETING

Theodore Levitt has made some insightful observations on the long-term buyer-seller relationship.[1] He believes the relationship seldom ends when the sale is made. In fact, it intensifies. The sale simply completes the courtship, allowing the marriage to start. And the marriage's success depends on how well the seller manages the relationship.

Levitt points out that the more complex the buyer-seller relationship is, in terms of software, operating procedures, management routines,
and the like, the longer it takes to develop and the greater the customer's
anxieties and *expectations*. The customer purchases *expectations of benefits* purposely or inadvertently promised by the supplier.

Barbara Jackson adds that relationship marketing is a general management activity in which all functions should participate. Success requires deploying and coordinating a wide range of tools and people from
the marketer's organization.[2] As Jackson points out, organizational purchasers willing to make a long-term commitment usually focus on one of
the following in making their commitment.[3]

1. **Technology.** This focuses on how the supplier's product technology
   provides desired benefits. The buyer may deal with multiple suppliers if they are equally able to provide the technology.
2. **Vendor.** In this case, the buyer ties itself to a specific supplier, not a
   product or technology. The benefits of dealing with that supplier may
   extend well beyond the virtues of its specific product or technology.
3. **Product.** Here the buyer focuses on the particular product and its
   attributes.
4. **Person.** For this buyer, the supplier's representatives are pivotal.
   The customer values their helpfulness, talent, expertise, and other
   personal traits. In such cases, the representatives may be providing
   customized service.

It is in the JIT industrial marketer's best interest to persuade accounts to focus on the supplier organization—the vendor—rather than
technology, products, or people. This allows the marketer to highlight its
total offering, including strengths in technology, operations, logistics, and
customer relations.

Promotional communications can help shift customers to a supplier-
focused position. These communications are a strategic tool in developing
strong, lasting relationships with individual accounts.

Complementing the product and distribution strategies, which the
marketer uses to develop a distinctive offering, and the pricing strategy,
which helps it set a value-based price, promotional communications position the offering in the minds of the account's key purchasing influences.
The position reflects the offering's superiority over competitive products
in some important respects.

To strategically position the offering, the marketer must answer a
series of questions. Most important, *who* are the targets, *how* do we reach
them, and *what* message do we communicate?

The following sections answer these three key questions.

KEY BUYING INFLUENCES: "WHO ARE THE TARGETS?"

The "buying center" concept captures the complexity of industrial buying decisions. Individuals who significantly influence the purchase decision or the choice of suppliers participate in the buying center. Many researchers have tackled this topic since the late 1960s.[4]

Identifying these key influences certainly isn't easy. In fact, identifying them accurately and understanding the role each plays in supplier selection are significant stumbling blocks for even the best marketers. Robert Miller and Stephen Heiman, in *Strategic Selling,* recommend that the marketer look first for roles, not people.[5] It then looks for the people playing those roles, regardless of title. These researchers' incisive analysis of the buying center defines three critical roles: technical buying influences, economic buying influences, and users.

1. **Technical buying influences.** "Does it meet the specs?" is the key question in this group. Often, several individuals play different technical-influence roles within the JIT OEM account. Typically, they evaluate supplier candidates based on measurable specifications that go beyond product specs to include all aspects of the offering that could affect the buyer: price, delivery, credit terms, legal requirements, and the like. Technical buying influences are lodged throughout the organization. They reside in purchasing, design and process engineering, manufacturing, materials management, maintenance, finance, the legal department, and so on.

Though these individuals may not have final approval authority, they strongly influence those who do. They may screen out potential suppliers altogether. Technical buying influences tend to be gatekeepers of supplier and product information, and the final decision maker generally respects their recommendations.

2. **Users** ask the question, "Will it make my performance look better?" They're the people who use or oversee the use of the offering being purchased. Their role is to assess how the item will affect the task at hand. They ask tough nuts-and-bolts questions about the offering's reliability; ease of handling, assembly or use; and the maintenance it requires. They're most interested in how it will affect their jobs—and how much it will improve their department's performance.

3. **Economic buying influences** want to know, "How will it affect the bottom line?" They wield final approval authority and are generally high in the buying organization. Just how high depends on the procure-

ment's dollar value and the individual's previous experience with the offering and the potential supplier. The economic buying influence's primary concern is how the purchasing decision will influence the organization's income statement.

Identifying key buying influences within an account can be relatively simple or extremely difficult. In some cases, the marketer already knows exactly who they are. These are the accounts with which it has enjoyed a close relationship for a long time and whose organizational structure, culture, and decision processes it understands.

This doesn't mean the marketer can sit back and relax or consider relationships with these accounts "business as usual." Original equipment manufacturing is a rapidly changing business, and an industrial marketer's past success with an OEM doesn't ensure future success. Customers are constantly changing, and on many different levels: personnel, technology, organizational structure, processes, competition, and even in their expectations. The marketer must constantly monitor its key accounts for changes that could affect the buyer-seller relationship, and it must respond when changes occur.

At the other extreme is the account for whom the marketer is an out-supplier. The marketer knows little about who, within this customer's organization, plays an important role in selecting suppliers. Based on the preliminary assessment, this account is a candidate for a long-term relationship with the marketer. But the supplier must do its homework to determine key purchasing influences.

Between the two customer extremes are many current and potential accounts. The marketer may know a little or a lot about their buying influences, depending on the customer.

The marketer's best bet for learning about these influences and developing the buyer-seller relationship is to find a "coach." That's a person either at the account, in the marketer's organization, or outside both firms, who can bridge the buyer-seller gap.[6] Coaches understand how the account makes purchasing decisions and who's involved in the process. They want to help the marketer because of a rewarding relationship with it in the past or present.

The coach could be a satisfied customer, a member of the prospect's buying center, or someone on the marketer side who was or is deeply involved with the account in some way. In addition to helping the marketer identify key influences, the coach may suggest effective approaches to the customer or arrange introductions to key individuals in the buying center. If the coach is part of the buying center, he or she is positioned to directly, positively influence others on the customer side.

SELECTING THE MEDIA: "HOW DO WE REACH THEM?"

Having identified the key buying influences in each account, the marketer faces another tough job: deciding how to communicate "the message" to them. There's an almost infinite number of media combinations. Figure 10-3 portrays the primary media the JIT industrial marketer may choose. In combination, they are the promotional communications mix.

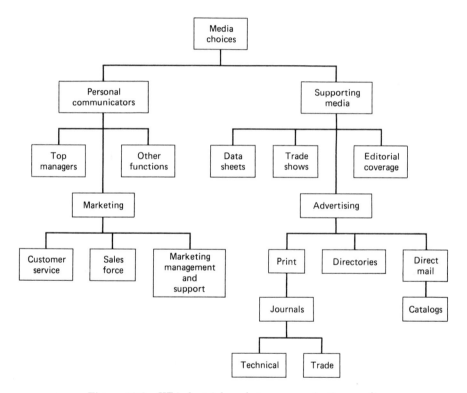

Figure 10-3   JIT industrial marketer communications media.

Most professional marketers are well aware of each medium and how to use it. What they may not know is the role of each in the JIT marketer's communications strategy. As Fig. 10-3 indicates, JIT marketers don't rely solely on salespeople or advertising managers for communications. In the just-in-time environment, communication is a total organizational process that includes many individuals, in functions at every level from the CEO down.

PERSONAL COMMUNICATORS

The unique character of the JIT industrial marketer's mission dictates extensive personal communication. This marketer is selling *need satisfaction*, in the guise of a product, to targeted accounts. Its goal is to satisfy a bundle of needs, including those centered in product quality, delivery, service, supplier reputation, and relationships.

The offering's complexity, together with the intricacy of the account's buying center, demands face-to-face communication. But the sales representative alone cannot convey the whole message. That requires a multifunctional team led by the sales rep. (For more on the marketing team's makeup and function, see Chapter 4.)

The openness and honesty so necessary in JIT marketing can also cause trouble if the marketer isn't careful. The supplier needs to sell the customer or prospect on a long-term partnership, but in so doing it must be extremely careful *not to oversell.*

Consider an account that requires incoming product quality in the 200 to 300 defective parts per million (DPM) range. Marketer A promises to deliver at a 225 DPM rate, and one of A's key competitors, marketer B, promises a 275 DPM rate. The account has different expectations based on the two suppliers' quotations. When deliveries start, marketer A's quality is at 250 DPM, and B's is at 270 DPM. The customer is dissatisfied with A's performance because it falls below the expectation A created with its 225 DPM promise. B's defect rate is higher, but the customer is more satisfied because B met—and exceeded—the expectation it created.

This is not a minor point. Quality is truly in the mind of the beholder.

So, although the marketer's goal is to develop and sustain long-term relationships, or strategic partnerships, with key accounts, short-term performance strongly affects whether or not it can do so. Long-term agreements are risky for both partners. Day-to-day performance is what ultimately bonds the two together in an ongoing relationship. A single tactical blunder may cause the prospective partner to doubt the relationship's viability. The successful JIT industrial marketer builds long-term partnerships by proving a series of satisfying short-term transactions across the spectrum of buyer-seller interactions.

Because the sales rep plays the strongest role in providng customer satisfaction, the representative acts as the marketing team leader. To lead the team successfully, the rep must understand the technical, operational, and logistical aspects of the buyer-seller relationship and be able to nurture that relationship.

• **Technical competence.** Reps must understand the JIT/TQC technical processes involved in the design and development of their own product *and* the customer's prouct into which it will be incorporated. They must also be able to interpret specifications and technical drawings and talk comfortably with engineers in both organizations.

• **Operational competence.** The rep must also understand the JIT/TQC manufacturing processes used to produce both organizations' products. Reps should feel "at home" in a JIT manufacturing environment and be able to communicate the basics of the environment to nonadopter accounts and prospects.

• **Logistical competence.** Another requirement is understanding the materials management and distribution concepts supporting the JIT/TQC philosophy. The rep should be able to comfortably communicate these to nonadopters.

• **Relational competence.** Finally, reps must be able to nurture parallel vertical relationships within their own organization and in the customer organization. They must also be able to forge horizontal relationships between people in support functions in both firms. Long-term relationships require a strong web of vertical and horizontal relationships. The sales representative is the cement that binds these relationships.

All of the marketer's personnel, not just the sales reps, should view every interaction with accounts and prospects as an opportunity to satisfy the customer's needs and build a relationship. Each person that contacts the customer, either directly or indirectly, must assume the role of customer representative and make every effort to provide outstanding customer service.

Top managers' involvement in the negotiation and implementation stages of customer agreements reinforces the marketer's commitment to developing high-quality, long-term relationships. The marketer's executives may leverage their influence with their peers in the customer organization. At the other vertical extreme, factory personnel must interact with customer production and materials managers to understand the user environment and establish strong working relationships.

Unfortunately, functional barriers within the marketer's organization remain the greatest barriers to that kind of teamwork and to effective JIT/TQC management in general. As explained earlier, internal marketing is crucial to break down those barriers.

Phil Ensor coined the expression "functional silo syndrome" to describe this problem.[7] In his view, the primary symptoms of the problem are as follows:

• A top-down authoritarian management style lacking trust and delegation.

- A deeply layered vertical hierarchy, or silo, designed to maintain top managers' control and minimize trust and problem solving by workers.
- Narrow, boring, specialized jobs designed for easy supervision rather than challenge and fulfillment.
- A confrontational, legalistic relationship between management and unions rather than mutual goal setting.

Functional silo syndrome promotes slow learning, mistrust, a lack of mutual concern, and gaping functional separation that keeps employees from understanding the big picture and effectively solving the organization's real problems. It certainly doesn't help the marketer develop a world-class capability. Marketing plays a key role in tearing down the functional silos so organizational teams can identify and serve customer needs.

SUPPORTING MEDIA

Although personal communication plays the biggest role in conveying the marketing message to the customer's buying influences, other media play important supporting roles. When selected intelligently and timed for exposure, print and direct mail advertising can make personal selling much more effective and efficient. Data sheets, trade shows, and editorial coverage are also important in the communications mix.

Print advertising.   Print advertising, the most prominent of these communication vehicles, can be used to reach key buying influences who are either unknown or inaccessible to the JIT marketer. Research reveals that on average, salespeople reach only three or four of every ten buying influences.[8] Print advertising can help reach the others by creating awareness of the marketer, its reputation or record, and its offering. The goal is to pique the prospect's interest enough to make further information necessary. Print ads "presell," making personal or telephone selling much more productive.

There are many print vehicles in which the marketer may advertise. Trade papers and journals are ideal for reaching purchasing, materials management, and operational personnel. Similarly, ads in technical journals can reach engineers and technical individuals in other functions.

Directories.   Directories are another advertising option. They're usually quite credible and some buyers or gatekeepers use them as primary data sources. A good example is the *Thomas Register,* which claims to generate hundreds of millions of dollars in daily direct response sales for its advertisers. This directory consists of nineteen volumes and includes listings from thousands of industrial firms and product headings.[9]

Direct mail advertising. Direct mail advertising may influence the customer or prospect even more than a print ad. Its advantage lies in the ability to target accounts—with minimal waste. For that reason, direct mail is relatively low cost. It may also be timed precisely to reinforce other communications, specifically from the sales force. And direct mail pieces can be complete enough to communicate the message in some detail. Of course, to do this kind of advertising, the marketer needs the names, titles, addresses, and functions of the target influences.

Catalogs. Catalogs are a twist on direct mail advertising and are a good way to reach purchasing professionals. This vehicle gives the marketer a way to communicate product comparisons, applications, and prices. Catalogs may serve as a "gate opener" if they reach a chief gate keeper.

Trade shows. Trade shows also offer several advantages. The exposition medium can be quite fruitful for the JIT industrial marketer that is developing new products but hasn't identified prospects outside the existing customer base. For that marketer especially, trade shows are more economical than personal selling. Expositions also give the marketer a chance to examine competitive products and meet buying center members who would otherwise be inaccessible. It's important for the marketer to set specific goals for the show up front and to confirm that attendees are qualified buyers—or at least purchasing influences. Otherwise exhibiting is a waste of time, people, and money.

Technical specifications. Technical specifications, or data sheets, are yet another medium. Data sheets can be powerful sales tools in the absence of a sales rep. They can be used to augment communications at trade shows or to follow up inquiries stimulated by print ads. Depending on the objective, the marketer may even include data sheets in a direct mailing. The sheets should include key selling points and other technical data relevant to the prospect's application. Copy and graphics should be clear and persuasive, boosting the offering's credibility.

Editorial coverage. Editorial coverage, or publicity, is a good medium to communicate the offering's features and benefits. It doesn't cost much but is the most credible medium and may convey the strongest message. Editorial coverage in trade and technical publications often generates sales leads. Some periodicals even include "reader information numbers" at the end of each article to encourage that response. Articles in respected trade publications carry a lot of weight with industrial purchasers facing a buying decision.

In addition to coverage in stories that include several suppliers, the marketer may want to place by-lined articles in appropriate technical journals. These pieces, written by technical specialists in the marketer's organization, position the authors as authorities and the firm as a leader in its field. By-lined articles add credibility to the marketer and its offering.[10]

FOCUSING THE COMMUNICATIONS STRATEGY

To be effective, marketing communications must cover all *economic, technical,* and *user* influences. Combinations of the media discussed above, teamed with appropriate messages, can meet that strategic objective. In each case, the medium and message must square with the influence's focus. The following suggests how to reach and persuade economic, technical, and user influences.

Economic Buying Influence

Because the main focus for this group is "the bottom line," the marketer's message should explain how the purchase decision will improve the buying organization's financial performance. The marketer may point out how its higher quality offering can lower customers' costs. It should support the claim with performance data.

In addition to personal selling, the marketer may use print and direct mail advertising and editorial coverage to reach the economic buying influence. The sales team must include peers of the influence, such as the marketer's chief financial officer or marketing director. The sales rep makes the introductions and the higher level individual, chosen for compatibility and effectiveness, does the selling.

If possible, the sales team should invite the influence to visit the marketer's plant and/or offices. Tours are a good way for the marketer to showcase its personnel, facilities, and processes. Ideally, the prospect's key technical and operational managers also go on the tour. Such visits underscore the marketer's commitment to the JIT/TQC approach and reinforce its credibility. These are both important to develop long-term relationships with customers.

Supporting the direct sales effort are advertising and public relations. Selective direct mailings can sustain the prospect's interest and involvement and reinforce the marketer's reputation and performance claim. Similarly, selective advertising and editorial coverage in business or financial publications may be useful if the size and focus of the customer base justifies the expenditure.

Technical Buying Influence

These influences focus on "the offering." Therefore, messages should convince them that the marketer can provide an offering conforming to their specifications. Supporting this contention, the marketer points out that its offering is designed for assembly, desired performance, reliability, durability, and serviceability; that it can deliver within the desired time window; that its costs are competitive with the best in the class; that it adheres to a continuous improvement philosophy; that it has an infrastructure supporting the quality claims; and that its processes and personnel are market-driven.

The most important medium used to communicate this message to the technical influence is personal selling. The sales rep is the primary contact with the prospect's purchasing group and leads the sales team in identifying other key influences. The rep introduces the marketer's technical and operational team members to their counterparts on the customer side and prepares them for direct contact. Visits to the marketer's facilities are crucial to convince technical buying influences that the supplier can conform to their specifications, and to assure them of its commitment to continuous improvement.

Supporting media cover a broad spectrum, including all of those cited earlier. The marketer should communicate through trade journals, catalogs, directories, and via direct mail. By-lined articles in technical journals are an important tool, as are trade shows aimed at purchasing and technical or engineering personnel.

User Buying Influence

The focus here is "the user's job." The message must convince these influences that the marketer's offering will make their operations more productive. Emphasis is on the offering's design for assembly, and its ease of use in the customer's manufacturing process.

Again, personal selling is an important communication tool. The sales rep makes the initial customer contact, and the marketer's application and process engineering reps follow up with support and continuing contact. Select production employees from the marketer's organization exchange information with customer personnel to understand how the customer uses the product and to communicate the marketer's ability to meet the customer's needs.

The marketer can be much more selective in choosing supporting media for this group. Direct mail pieces may include testimonials from satisfied users with applications similar to those of prospects. Print advertising and by-lined articles in trade journals may help the marketer reach the more inaccessible users.

The importance of sustained contact, particularly personal communication, with the various kinds of influences cannot be overemphasized. Today's buying influence may be gone tomorrow. Unless the marketer maintains continous communication, such changes create gaps in its communications network.

In communicating with all the influences, the marketer emphasizes how its offering would affect not only the customer's organizational performance, but the influence's personal goals. The first task is fairly straightforward. But to do the latter, the marketer must understand the influences and their personal priorities—recognition, greater freedom, trust, personal productivity. The marketer's communications must assure the buying influence that selecting this offering will enhance his or her personal position on those dimensions.

IMPORTANCE OF EFFECTIVE LISTENING

Clearly, personal communications play a critical role in the JIT industrial marketer's communications mix. The marketer has much to tell the customer and even more to learn. Monitoring the customer continuously at all its levels is crucial for the marketer to develop and sustain a satisfying long-term partnership. Effective listening, a rare practice that isn't often mentioned in training programs, plays a key part in monitoring. Easton Atwater, in *I Hear You,* makes some excellent points about effective listening. Let's consider some of them.[11]

There are several reasons for ineffective listening. The poor listener may be too busy talking. Put two such individuals together and they talk *at* each other, communicating only nominally. In this "duolog," conversation is a competitive exercise.

Or, the individual may mistakenly think that listening just means not talking. Or the poor listener may be preoccupied with private feelings and needs and hear only what he or she wants to hear. People don't want to hear some things, especially if they're emotionally involved in the issue.

Too often, the individual just doesn't know how to listen. Most of us grew up in an environment of competitive talking and never learned how to listen well.

The tendency to be judgmental also interferes with listening. If listeners disapprove of others' statements, they may screen them out. Listening is an active process. To do it well, the listener must want to listen. That means:

• Sharing the responsibility for the communication.
• Being physically attentive.

- Concentrating on what the speaker is saying.
- Listening for the total meaning.
- Observing nonverbal signals.
- Expressing empathy to put the speaker at ease and learn the real message.

The JIT industrial marketer whose representatives listen well can secure more accurate information about accounts and better understand their needs. And that's a competitive advantage in developing and sustaining long-term relationships.

OPERATIONAL COMMUNICATIONS

After the JIT industrial marketer and OEM customer establish a purchasing agreement, they must develop an operational communications system. Although that extends well beyond the marketing function's responsibility, it can strongly affect relationships with customers, which is marketing's responsibility.

The marketer must establish three levels of communication with the JIT OEM customer to minimize the number of operational surprises. The levels represent the long-range, intermediate, and short-term planning stages.

1. **Long-range** product and production plans look at what kinds of products the customer will produce in the future and include multiyear production volume forecasts. This information helps the JIT marketer plan capacity for components it currently supplies. It can also use the data to alert its marketing, design engineering, product planning, and operational and technical representatives about the customer's plans for new products and modifications to existing products.

2. **Intermediate-range** plans include projections and schedules for three to twelve months into the future. Such data give the JIT marketer specific information for this period, helping it set tentative production schedules and plan materials and manpower requirements.

3. **Immediate** production schedules and data on material releases are crucial and must be directed to production schedulers and materials planners. They describe the exact quantities the OEM will produce, including precise production periods. The OEM's production during part of this period—perhaps the immediate ten to twenty days—is fixed. Its production beyond that period varies within reasonable limits. The fixed

portion, or "line set," grants the marketer *demand certainty* for that period. The immediate production schedule should be a "rolling" schedule that's updated frequently, preferable daily. Actual releases may be drawn, or pulled, from the JIT marketer's production several times daily in response to the customer's electronically transmitted requests.

The three-tiered production planning schedule lets the JIT marketer provide *its* key JIT suppliers with comparable production forecasts. And as the system develops, those suppliers pass similar information on to their own suppliers. The demand certainty built into the system eventually synchronizes all the supply links in the marketing chain. As procurement and production cycle times reach the line-set time period, suppliers can virtually eliminate materials inventories. Productivity increases, because no supplier manufactures products without a firm "order," and those orders are only for the products needed. This kind of planning removes guesswork and surprises from the production process.

ELECTRONIC DATA INTERCHANGE

Clearly, JIT operational communications must be computer driven. Electronic data interchange (EDI), discussed in Chapter 9, is the most appropriate computer linkage. Leading JIT industrial marketers and their customers are rapidly adopting EDI technology. The automotive industry, with the Automotive Industry Action Group as a catalyst, has significantly influenced this movement. Major automobile producers now require their first-tier suppliers to develop an EDI capability that meets AIAG's industry standard.

EDI has been around since the 1960s, but has only been an important tool for marketer-customer communications since the mid-1980s. The technology comes in many forms. A common approach is for the marketer to provide the customer with a proprietary terminal for placing orders and getting transaction-related information. The terminal only permits communication with the marketer who provided it, and the buyer's computer is not linked with the marketer at all.[12]

This is not true EDI, because only the marketer's computer is involved. It does provide greater speed and accuracy than traditional systems. But if the customer relies on several suppliers, it will need several terminals, and probably different ordering formats. This approach does not automatically integrate the details of order transactions into the customer's information system.

True EDI is computer-to-computer linkage. This can be done either directly, with the marketer's computer communicating directly with the customer's, or indirectly, through a third-party network. In either case, the marketer and customer both have electronic mailboxes from which they retrieve electronic messages. Up-front security measures safeguard both parties' internal files unless they purposely make them available to outsiders. This protects the confidentiality of proprietary data.

JIT marketers' and customers' need to communicate logistical and technical data fast, often, and accurately makes EDI essential for success, particularly as the JIT relationship progresses. Their EDI system should be able to handle:

- On-line transmittal of basic orders and order revisions.
- Line-set transactions, including the customer's actual production schedule translated into the marketer's part numbers, customer inventory position, and the like.
- Advance shipping notices. This electronically provides the customer with all pertinent shipping data: bill of lading, carrier, part number, quantity, date and time shipped, and so on.
- Bill of material inquiries. The customer may look directly into the marketer's bill-of-material data base to determine the current product configuration.
- Purchase order transmittal. The purchase order is the basic document against which the marketer draws individual releases.
- Order acknowledgment. The marketer may acknowledge receiving the customer's orders, and the customer may acknowledge releases received, verifying prices and citing scheduled shipping dates and similar data.
- Invoice transmittal. The marketer may transmit invoices for released materials on-line, eliminating the hard copy.
- Order status inquiries. The customer may find out if a specific order is in process, and how close to completion, to determine if and when to expect the material.
- Inventory status inquiries. This lets the buyer inquire directly about the availability of material for purchase. The customer's lead time and when it could accommodate the delivery may be included in the inquiry.
- Inventory allocation updates. This process removes committed material from the "available" category to avoid allocating the same material to several customers.
- Price inquiries. The customer may determine current prices on-line.

EDI's major advantages are *speed* and *accuracy*. Both eliminate waste in the communications process. The faster speed of communications significantly affects lead time, boosting the marketer's flexibility and responsiveness when the inevitable changes in demand schedules pop up. Accuracy, a by-product of reduced human error, reduces the cost of communications by cutting data rekeying and other rework. The ability to call up data on-line is also a great help to both firms in short-term planning and decision making.

The impact of an EDI communications system cuts across most of the organizations' functional units: purchasing, sales, and marketing, engineering, manufacturing, distribution, and finance. The system reduces production and distribution lead times, and at the same time streamlines cash flow through the electronic transmission of invoices and payments. In the long run, EDI benefits each organization, freeing people to tackle more productive and challenging tasks.

NOTES

1. Theodore Levitt, *The Marketing Imagination* (New York: The Free Press, 1986).
2. Barbara Jackson, *Winning and Keeping Industrial Customers* (Lexington, Mass.: D. C. Health and Co., 1985).
3. Ibid., pp. 65–93.
4. Examples of this research include: Frederick Webster and Yoram Wind, "A General Model of Organizational Buying Behavior," *Journal of Marketing,* April 1972, pp. 12–19; Thomas Bonoma, "Major Sales: Who Really does the Buying?" *Harvard Business Review,* May–June 1982, pp. 111–19; Rowland Moriarty, *Industrial Buying Behavior* (Lexington, Mass.: Lexington Books, 1983); Wesley Johnston and Thomas Bonoma, "The Buying Center: Structure and Interaction Patterns," *Journal of Marketing,* Summer 1987, pp. 143–56.
5. Robert Miller and Stephen Heiman, *Strategic Selling* (New York: Warner Books, 1985).
6. Ibid., pp. 83–86.
7. Phil Ensor, "The Functional Silo Syndrome," *Target,* Spring 1988, p. 16.
8. Frederick Webster, *Industrial Marketing Strategy* (New York: John Wiley & Sons, 1984).
9. "*Thomas Register* Ranks as King of Catalogs," *Advertising Age,* March 7, 1985, p. 54.
10. Jerome Williams, "Industrial Publicity: One of the Best Promotional Tools," *Industrial Marketing Management,* vol. 12, 1983, pp. 207–11.
11. Easton Atwater, *I Hear You* (Englewood Cliffs, NJ: Prentice Hall, 1981).
12. Margaret Emmelhainz, *Electronic Data Interchange in Purchasing* (Oradell, N.J.: National Association of Purchasing Management, 1986). Note: The National Association of Purchasing Management published an information kit, *Electronic Data Interchange,* in Janaury 1988. It includes serveral articles on EDI.

PART IV: ADDITIONAL SUGGESTED READINGS

CHAPTER 6 DEVELOPING A WINNING JIT MARKETING STRATEGY

Kate Bertrand, "The Just-in-Time Mandate," *Business Marketing,* November 1986, pp. 45–55.

———, "Marketers Discover What 'Quality' Really Means," *Business Marketing,* April 1987, pp. 58–72.

Shirley Cayer, "World Class Suppliers Don't Grow on Trees," *Purchasing,* August 25, 1988, pp. 45–49.

William Golomski, "Quality Improvement of Marketing," *Quality Progress,* June 1986, pp. 24–26.

Barbara Jackson, *Winning and Keeping Industrial Customers* (Lexington, Mass.: Lexington Books, 1985).

Bob Kukla, "Meeting Customer Needs," *Quality Progress,* June 1986, pp. 15–18.

Charles O'Neal, "Customer-Supplier Relationships for Just-in-Time," *Journal of Computer Integrated Manufacturing Management,* Spring 1986, pp. 33–40.

———, "Just-in-Time Supplier Strategies," *Distribution Management,* Auerbach Publications, 1985.

Charles O'Neal and William Lafief, "Marketing's Leadership Role in Implementing the Marketing Concept through Total Quality Control," *1988 AMA Educators Proceedings,* p. 59.

Michael Porter, *Competitive Advantage: Creating and Sustaining Superior Performance* (New York: The Free Press, 1985).

George Stalk, Jr., "Time—The Next Source of Competitive Advantage," *Harvard Business Review,* July–August 1988, pp. 41–51.

CHAPTER 7 PRODUCT STRATEGY

J. Anklesaria and David Burt, "Personal Factors in the Purchasing-Engineering Interface," *Journal of Purchasing and Materials Management,* Winter 1987, pp. 9–17.

Somerby Dowst, "Product Reliability Depends on Purchased Goods' Quality," *Purchasing,* December 13, 1984, p. 43.

Somerby Dowst, William Semich and Ernest Rais, "Design Report: The Purchasing Connection," *Purchasing,* June 13, 1985, pp. 81–111.

Lance Ealey, "Taguchi Methods: The Thought Behind the System," *Automotive Industries,* February 1988, pp. 68–70.

David Garvin, *Managing Quality: The Strategic and Competitive Edge* (New York: The Free Press, 1988).

Berton Gunter, "A Perspective on the Taguchi Methods," *Quality Progress,* June 1987, pp. 44–52.

John McElroy, "Defining Statistical Quality Control, " *Automotive Industries,* October 1984, pp. 73–75.

———, "Supplier Viewpoint: Planning for the Long Haul," *Automotive Industries,* December 1986, pp. 63–87.

Ronald Moem and Thomas Nolan, "Process Improvement," *Quality Progress,* September 1987, pp. 62–68.

John O'Connor, "Yes, There Are New Things to Say about Value Analysis," *Purchasing,* March 28, 1985, p. 49.

Otis Port, "How to Make it Right the First Time," *Business Week,* June 8, 1987, pp. 142–43.

William Semich, "The Costs of Quality," *Purchasing,* November 5, 1987, pp. 61–63.

L. P. Sullivan, "The Power of Taguchi Methods," *Quality Progress,* June 1987, pp. 76–79.

Lea Tonkin, "John Deere Harvests the Fruits of VA," *Purchasing,* June 16, 1988, pp. 82–87.

CHAPTER 8 PRICING STRATEGY

H. Thomas Johnson, "Activity-Based Information: A Blueprint for World-Class Management Accounting," *Management Accounting,* June 1988, pp. 23–30.

H. Thomas Johnson and Robert Kaplan, *Relevance Lost: The Rise and Fall of Management Accounting* (Boston: Harvard Business School Press, 1987).

Robert McIhattan, "How Cost Management Systems Can Support the JIT Philosophy," *Management Accounting,* September 1987, pp. 20–26.

Robert Monczka and Steven Trecha, "Cost-Based Supplier Performance Evaluation," *Journal of Purchasing and Materials Management,* Spring 1988, pp. 2–7.

Michael Morris and Mary Joyce, "How Marketers Evaluate Price Sensitivity," *Industrial Marketing Management,* vol. 17, 1988, pp. 169–76.

Richard Newman and Joseph Scodro, "Price Analysis for Negotiation," *Journal of Purchasing and Materials Management,* May 1988, pp. 8–14.

Douglas Williams, "Supplier Viewpoint: Learning New Contract Rules," *Automotive Industries,* December 1986, p. 61.

CHAPTER 9 PHYSICAL DISTRIBUTION STRATEGY

Susan Avery, "Truckers Take to the Road with JIT," *Purchasing,* October 10, 1985, pp. 70–73.

Ted Drozdowski, "JIT: Twelve Things Carriers Need to Know Before the Trucks Start Rolling," *Purchasing,* April 24, 1986, pp. 53–55.

"Electronic Data Interchange: Taming the Paper Tiger," *Traffic Management,* February 1986, pp. 44–45.

Matt Gallaher, "A Just-in-Time Call for Logistics Action," *Target,* Fall 1986, p. 15.

"How Co-Loading, Other Tricks Can Save Your Company Money," *Purchasing,* July 11, 1985, pp. 45–47.

"In Search of (Carrier) Excellence," *Traffic Management,* May 1984, pp. 32–39.

"JIT Puts Accent on Partnership," *Traffic Management,* February 1986, pp. 47–49.

E. J. Muller and Roger Schreffler, "Nummi: How Toyota/GM Makes Cars by Crossing the Pacific, Just in Time," *Distribution,* October 1986, pp. 53–59.

Francis Quinn, "How to Gain the JIT Advantage," *Traffic Management,* February 1987, pp. 39–52.

———, "Just-in-Time: No Room for Error," *Traffic Management,* September 1984, pp. 28–34.

Amy Rogers, "Buyers Look to Trucking Services to Make JIT Work," *Purchasing,* April 24, 1986, pp. 36–46.

CHAPTER 10 COMMUNICATIONS STRATEGY

Leon Brodeur, "Streamlining Tire Distribution," *Purchasing,* Presidential Issue 1983–1984, pp. 20–26.

Joseph Callahan, "AIAG Pushes Computerized Communications," *Automotive Industries,* September 1984, p. 94.

Al Furst, "JIT: Spreading the Gospel at Fluke," *Electronic Business,* April 1, 1986, pp. 82–83.

John McElroy, "Steel Service Roundtable: Just-in-Time/Just in Turmoil," *Automotive Industries,* September 1985, pp. 61–62.

Ernest Raia, "Just-in-Time USA," *Purchasing,* February 13, 1986, pp. 48–62.

Arjan Sadhwani and M. H. Sarhan, "Electronic Systems Enhance JIT Operations," *Management Accounting,* December 1987, pp. 27–30.

Robert Spekman and Wesley Johnston, "Relationship Management: Managing the Selling and Buying Interface," *Journal of Business Research,* vol. 14, 1986, pp. 519–31.

James Stock and Douglas Lambert, *Strategic Logistics Management* (Homewood, Ill.: Richard D. Irwin, 1987).

Lea Tonkin, "JIT and the Trucker: New Responsibilities and Challenge," *Target,* Fall 1986, pp. 16–17.

Craig Waters, "Profit and Loss," *Inc.,* April 1985, pp. 103–12.

Bob Woods, "Selling Parts with Service," *Sales and Marketing Management,* July 4, 1983, pp. 29–32.

Frank Yanacek, "Just-One—More-Time," *Handling and Shipping Management,* May 1987, pp. 47–48.

Part V

Replaying the Game Tapes

Chapter 11

Monitoring the System

INTRODUCTION

Writing the playbook and developing a game plan are crucial for a marketer to field a winning team in the increasingly competitive global marketplace. But they alone are not enough to assure continuous improvement in marketing performance.

The firm may get a feel for its competitive standing by tallying wins and losses in individual skirmishes with key competitors. But, valuable as that market share and profitability information is, it provides no insight into *why* the marketer performed as it did. Nor does it suggest how the marketer could improve further.

The game tapes fill this gap. They give the marketer immediate feedback on strategy and execution. The tapes monitor the implementation of key JIT marketing processes, providing the coaching staff and players with valuable information.

While monitoring and evaluation of JIT industrial marketer's performances includes several of the elements of traditional marketer performance evaluation, the process is more formalized and much more rigorous. The JIT marketer must:

1. Determine customer needs by working closely with key members of the account's buying team.
2. Convert these needs into offering characteristics through product design, processing, delivery, service, and relationships with customer personnel.
3. Develop conformance measurements by deciding, together with the customer, the relevant attributes and dimensions that affect product performance, and gauges that correspond to them.
4. Establish, with the customer, target values for each of these attributes and dimensions.
5. Monitor actual performance on the key attributes and dimensions, measuring conformance to the target values and variability within the specified limits.
6. Develop and implement a program for continuous improvement, with the goal of reducing variability from the target values.

The monitored areas relate directly to key JIT goals. The marketer's objective is to provide: a quality offering every time, using frequent deliveries of small lots, with exact quantities delivered precisely as needed, at lowest total cost and in the context of a satisfying customer relationship.

Representatives from many of the marketer's functional departments help monitor these characteristics. The primary responsibilities are described in Table 11-1.

As the table shows, the marketer's various departments are responsible for the offering's performance on the dimensions they control. For example, design engineers and manufacturing managers share primary responsibility for the basic product's reliability and durability. This approach is consistent with the philosophy of quality function deployment. (See Chapter 7.)

The functional unit works closely with the customer, as part of the marketing strategy team, to define key requirements and characteristics and to establish target values. The functional units are responsible for meeting these targets. The marketing department coordinates the activities for which it is not primarily responsible.

If more than one of the marketer's functional units influence the offering's performance on a dimension, they share the responsibility for conforming to the customer's requirements in that area. Consider the various departments in the value-adding chain of an automobile door-hinge marketer. In its own way, each contributes to the product's performance, measured by ease of closure. The following describe the functions of the marketer's various departments.

- **Design engineers** are responsible for designing a functional hinge assembly. And, together with their peers on the customer side, the

TABLE 11-1 **Marketer's Functional Responsibility for Monitoring Performance**

| | Inbound Logistics (Materials Management) | Operation | | Marketing | Outbound Logistics Distribution | Post-sale Service |
		Design Engineering	Manufacturing			
Offering's Quality Characteristics						
Basic Product						
Performance		P*	P*	C*	*	*
Features		P*		C*		
Reliability		P*	P*	C*		*
Durability		P*	P*	C*		*
Serviceability		P*		C*		
Conformance	P*		*	*	*	
Augmented Product						
Delivery			*	P*	P*	
Service				P*	*	P*
Relationship	*	*	*	P*	*	*

P*: Primary responsibility
C*: Coordinating responsibility
 *: Substantial involvement

marketer's design engineers must select appropriate materials and design individual components that are reliable.

- **Purchasing department,** and the second-tier supplier's logistics personnel, control how well purchased materials and components conform to specifications and how much they vary within specified tolerances.

- **Manufacturing function** is responsible for producing hinge assemblies that consistently conform to customer specifications, and for reducing variability within the specifications. To meet these goals, the marketer's operational managers may need to refine the manufacturing process.

- **Logistics personnel and carriers** are in charge of maintaining the hinge assembly in its original condition throughout post-production handling, packaging, transportation, and delivery. They are also responsible for delivering the item at the exact time required.

- **Application and technical service specialists** are responsible for post-transaction service requirements. They help the customer integrate the hinge assembly into its manufacturing process.

- **Field service unit** is in charge of technical service, specifically warranty repairs, caused by defects related to the marketer's cumulative process.

Each of these functions is responsible for maintaining the marketer's overall process within the planned cost/price structure and for nurturing the supplier-customer relationship. In each case, the "customer" is the department that will add value to the offering after the current unit finishes working on it. Specifications for each of these internal customers are based on the external customer's requirements.

The door-hinge example deals mainly with physical product flow in the value-adding process. There is a parallel flow of communications that includes personal communications, either via phone or in person; written, or hard-copy, interactions; and paperless electronic communications. The quality of all these communications is as important as the physical product's quality and correlates strongly with it.

WHAT PERFORMANCE MEASURES?

Performance measures are crucial in a monitoring system. The marketer must capture each quality characteristic with a performance measure to evaluate actual performance against the target value on that dimension.

Sound simple? Unfortunately, it's not. And it's not usually done very well—if at all.

Robert Howell and Stephen Sourcy make this point rather forcefully.[1] They point out that although many U.S. manufacturers are dramatically changing how they operate their factories, with more emphasis on customer responsiveness, product line profitability, product profit contribution, operating effectiveness, and asset management, they have no effective management reporting system to evaluate overall performance and identify opportunities for action.

They observe major weaknesses in extant monitoring systems. Specifically, the systems produce reports that are irrelevant to managers' needs, and half the reports produced either aren't used or are redundant. They found, for example, that in about half of most manufacturing firms, reporting schedules focus on labor efficiency and utlization. Yet labor content represents only 5% to 10% of the product's total cost. Production managers are much more concerned about quality, delivery, scrap, inventory, and cycle time than labor utlization.

Note that quality heads that list. Performance measures, like everything else in the JIT environment, must focus on quality. In a 1987 *Purchasing* survey, OEMs cited quality as their primary concern, rating it 9.58 on a scale of one to ten.[2] Because quality is a function of *all* the offering's characteristics, including intangibles such as delivery and service, monitoring or evaluation systems must look at how each characteristic meets customer expectations.

Performance measurement tends to be situation specific. It depends on the customer's application of the product, what characteristics the customer values, the supplier's process capability, competitive intensity, and more. However, some performance measures are fairly universal. (See Table 11-2.)

Some industrial marketers are already using these and other performance measures. Let's look at each characteristic more carefully.

Performance. Performance is the product's primary operating characteristic and is probably the most frequently measured. It requires a target value against which to compare actual results. For example, the marketer may measure the force required to close the door hinge using pounds of pressure, or evaluate its quietness of operation in decibels.

Features. Features describe the product's secondary characteristics. For example, the hinge pin may include an automatic centering feature that makes the pin easy to assemble into the customer's product. Performance measures reflect the pin's success rate in the customer's manufacturing operation, perhaps in defects per million units processed.

TABLE 11-2   Performance Measures of Offering Quality

Offering Characteristic	Dimension to be Measured	Performance Measure (illust.)
Basic Product		
Performance	primary operating characteristics	primary spec. vs actual (speed/RPM; quietness/ decibels)
Features	secondary (bells and whistles)	feature spec. vs actual: automatic centering; errors per million
Reliability	probability of failure (time period)	mean time between failures; failure rate
Durability	product life	expected life vs actual
Serviceability	ease/speed of repair	mean time to repair
Conformance	meeting specifications/ variability	defectives per million (DPM); range of deviation
Augmented Product		
Delivery	lot size	% of shipments meeting size specs; % deviation
	quantity precision	% of shipments with variation; % of variation within lot
	timeliness	% of shipments within time window; % of variation from target
	condition	% of shipments error-free; # of errors/ shipment; mean errors/ shipment
Service		
Logistical (customer service)	order processing	% of orders error-free; mean errors/order; mean time for processing
	transaction-related communications	mean response time for requests
Technical		man-hours of assistance;
-Pre-production	design/value engineering	value of contribution
-Production	production-application/ value analysis	value of contribution
-Post-production	field service	time required; callbacks required
Relationship		
Internal	attitudes	customer satisfaction scaling
External	attitudes	customer satisfaction scaling

Reliability.   Reliability measures the probability of failure, within a specified time period, for products that may be repaired and returned to normal operation. For such products, mean time between failures (MTBF) is a common measurement. (See Chapter 8 for more on MTBF.) For products that cannot be repaired and reused, such as components and parts, "failure rate" is the measure of reliability.

Durability.   Durability is closely related to reliability. It is interpreted as the product's useful life and may be further defined vis a vis the operating environment. Durability is measured in terms of expected life versus actual life, based on time in use, or hours of operation.

Serviceability.   Serviceability considers the post-sale characteristic of servicing the product when it breaks down. A common measure here is mean time to repair, which covers ease of repair and the service person's technical competence. (See Chapter 8 for more on MTTR).

Conformance.   Conformance cuts across each of the other characteristics. It measures the degree to which each of them matches the customer's specifications, and how much the offering varies from target when it does meet the specs. Measuring overall conformance is redundant if the marketer measures the conformance of each product characteristic individually.

Delivery.   Delivery is a characteristic that comprises four important dimensions: lot size, quantity precision, timeliness, and product condition.

• **Lot size** is increasingly important to the JIT OEM, whose batch sizes are shrinking. It's also difficult for the JIT industrial marketer to provide smaller and smaller lot sizes without incurring higher costs for purchasing, processing, delivery, and the rest. Lot-size measures should quantify the percent of delivered lots that match the lot size specified. A further measure is the extent of lot-size variation versus the lot size requested. This second measure focuses on planned differences—shipments for which the marketer was aware of lot-size variation from the target.

• **Quantity precision,** in contrast, determines unplanned variations, or concealed errors. It reveals missing or excess units in delivered lots. Precision measures look at the number of lots in which there is a variation, compared to total lots shipped; whether there were too few or too many units in the lot; and the degree of variation.

• **Timeliness** is a measure that reflects the importance of precise delivery timing. The customer specifies its delivery time window with a target value for the time preferred and a range on either side. Measures look at how each delivery deviates from the target value.

• **Condition** refers to the condition in which the product is delivered. It reflects problems such as product damage and incorrect part numbers. These are significant factors that make the product unfit for immediate further processing. Condition measures quantify the number of deliveries received in "perfect" condition, possibly considering quantity precision. This dimension should also be measured by the average number of errors per delivery or per a statistically valid number of deliveries.

Service.   Service can be separated into two categories: logistical service and technical service. Each of these, in turn, may be broken down further.

Logistical, or customer, service, covers order processing and transaction-related communications. Order processing is measured in two dimensions, accuracy and speed. JIT customers want error-free order processing, or as close to it as possible. The marketer, to measure its accuracy in processing orders, may measure the percentage of all orders it processes without errors, or the average number of errors per order or per a statistically valid number of orders. To measure order-processing speed, the marketer clocks the time it takes to process the paperwork for orders or measures the period between order placement and delivery. It then compares the results with the target values and calculates variability.

Transaction-related communications are less defined and harder to measure. These interactions include order status requests, inventory level inquiries, price inquiries, and expediting requests. The marketer may select the most important of these, measuring actual performance against target response times. Or, it may opt to measure its responses in aggregrate, using a more subjective rating scale.

Technical service includes three categories, each related to the customer unit for which the service is performed. The three are: pre-production, production, and post-production service.

Pre-production service is technical assistance the industrial marketer gives the customer's design and product development units. It includes help with initial product or prototype designs, and value-engineering assistance to improve the designs. The marketer may measure its performance in this area by the number of technical assistance hours it provides, or by the value of its pre-production service to the customer. The latter may be measured financially, if data are available, or subjectively.

Production service is technical assistance given to the customer's manufacturing unit as it places the product into production, and as it manufactures. The first is application engineering; the second includes process engineering and value analysis. Measuring performance on production service takes two separate measures: the number of technical assistance hours provided, and the service's financial contribution, based on cost reduction and/or increased sales made possible by productivity and product improvements.

Post-production service comes after the OEM sells its product. This is field service that includes the JIT marketer because of its special expertise, or for help solving problems its components and assemblies caused after becoming part of the OEM's offering. Unlike the other kinds of technical service, less post-production service is better than more. It is good for the JIT marketer to provide plenty of technical assistance while the OEM is designing its product and during the value-analysis phase, but final customers shouldn't need much service. If they do, there are problems with the marketer's offering that should have been detected earlier. The goal is to minimize the need for post-production service, measured in actual technical assistance hours versus a target value. Other measures are hours per call and callbacks for the same problem. These also measure service technicians' competence.

Relationships.   Relationships, the final category, are vital to a satisfying long-term relationship. External and internal relationships are equally important, although the external tend to draw more attention. Both kinds of relationship may be measured directly or indirectly.

All of the preceding measurements indirectly measure relationship quality. When the JIT industrial marketer closely meets the OEM customer's product, delivery and service requirements, the marketer-customer relationship tends to be close, with open, frequent communications and mutual understanding. Often, when a marketer departs markedly from the OEM's requirements, it's because this kind of give and take is missing. The OEM may interpret its supplier's deviations from target as quality problems. That weakens the relationship further. The JIT industrial marketer needs to cover both bases by providing a quality offering *and* monitoring its internal and external relationships. It can do the latter through periodic customer-satisfaction surveys. These go to relevant functional units and general managers in the JIT marketer's own organization and in the OEM customer's firm.

Table 11-3 summarizes the overall monitoring process. It shows the offering characteristic to be monitored, the customer and marketer units doing the monitoring, and the marketer and customer units requiring feedback for evaluation and corrective action.

To monitor the first characteristic in Table 11-3, product conformance, the JIT marketer's manufacturing unit first feeds *forward* the process data that confirm conformance. This allows deliveries to the OEM customer on a direct-to-assembly basis. The OEM feeds information back

TABLE 11-3 Summary of the Monitoring Process

JIT Industrial Marketer's Unit		Offering Characteristic Being Monitored		OEM Customer's Unit
Marketing-sales		Total process coordinator		Purchasing
		PRODUCT		
		Conformance		
Manufacturing	== >	Feedforward	== >	Materials management
Marketing	< ==	Feedback	< ==	Materials management
Manufacturing		Features		Manufacturing
Manufacturing		Reliability		Manufacturing
Product engineering		Product life/durability		Field service
Product engineering		Serviceability		Field service
Product engineering		Performance		Manufacturing
Application engineering		Performance		Field service
		DELIVERY		
Distribution		Lot size		Materials management
Manufacturing		Quantity precision		Materials management
Distribution		Quantity precision		Materials management
Distribution		Timeliness*		Materials management
Distribution		Condition*		Materials management
		SERVICE		
Distribution-customer service		Order processing		Materials management purchasing
Distribution-customer service		Transaction-comunication		Materials management purchasing
R&D design engineering		Technical: Pre-production		R&D/design engineering
Application engineering		Technical: Production		Process engineering
Process engineering		Technical: Production		Manufacturing
Technical services		Technical: Post-production		Field service
		RELATIONSHIPS		
Marketing				Purchasing
Distribution				Materials management
R&D/design engineering				R&D/design engineering
Manufacturing				Manufacturing
Process engineering				Process engineering
Marketing				Distribution
Marketing				Marketing
Technical service				Field service

*transportation-carrier performance is integrated into the monitoring of this characterstic to the supplier either on each lot received, to confirm the quality status, or based on defective units. A preferable approach is for the OEM and marketer to exchange data when they see the offering's characteristics moving toward the limits of nonconformance.

The two organizations' marketing and purchasing units coordinate monitoring efforts. They keep track of the status of each offering characteristic throughout the value-adding process. They also keep feedback information flowing and make sure problems are swiftly corrected.

TOOLS FOR MONITORING PERFORMANCE

Speedy, accurate feedback information on performance is extremely important to the just-in-time industrial marketer. Together with the OEM customer, it quickly detects and corrects deviations from expected levels to preserve the system's integrity. In this process, statistical process control and electronic data interchange are helpful tools.

Statistical Process Control (SPC)

Earlier chapters looked at SPC as a control tool in the manufacturing process, but it can also play in important role in monitoring postproduction processes. The following illustrates how the marketer and OEM customer may use SPC.

Product delivery—logistical performance—is the most error-prone value-adding activity.[3] As such, it requires a strong system to monitor, evaluate, and control its quality. That describes SPC. As previously discussed, delivery includes: timeliness, lot size, quantity precision, and condition. SPC-based control mechanisms that include target values and acceptable limits for each characteristic may be used to measure each.

As an illustration, consider timeliness of delivery. First, the marketer, customer, and carrier set an acceptable delivery time window: Daily deliveries scheduled for 10 A.M. and 2 P.M. are acceptable if received between 9 A.M. and 11 A.M. and 1 A.M. and 3 P.M. This is a simplified explanation; several nontechnical books explain the details of calculating SPC parameters.[4] (For a general discussion of these, see Chapter 9.) Control charts for monitoring performance are shown in Fig. 11-1.

The marketer tests its process's capability before monitoring begins, and removes causes of delivery variation. With SPC, sample performance data are selected, plotted on the X and R control charts, and checked for conformance. In this case, sample data are the recorded observations of four actual deliveries. The X value refers to average arrival time, and R reflects the range of delivery times.

If the actual performance data fall within the upper and lower con-

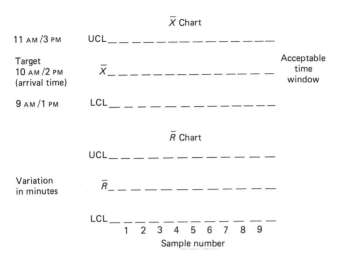

Figure 11-1 The X and R control charts used to monitor quality.

trol limits (UCL and LCL), the process is "in control." The next step is to reduce the process's variability and make deliveries conform better to the target values, keeping possible cost trade-offs in mind. The cost to improve performance shouldn't exceed the benefit of more precise deliveries.

To monitor performance in cases like this, where the occurrence happens infrequently (only twice daily), an alternative is to record every occurrence, plot it on the X chart and compare it with the specifications. An R chart isn't necessary because each plotted data point includes only one observation.

This approach can be used to monitor performance on lot size, quantity precision, and condition of shipments. It's also a a way to evaluate delivery communications, based on incidence of improper bills of lading, transportation billing errors, and the like.

SPC may be used to monitor service characteristics such as order processing, based on order-cycle times, entry errors, and filling errors. It can also evaluate technical service, especially field service. Measures there include the number of calls in a specified time period, the mean time to repair, and callbacks for the same problem.

Electronic Data Interchange

The need for quick, accurate feedback information precludes traditional communication methods for monitoring. A real-time tool such as EDI is essential.

The JIT industrial marketer and its carriers and customers must plan and develop the EDI system together. Functional units that will be affected by the system's performance lead the charge. To monitor delivery performance, the marketer's logistics team, the carrier, and the customer participate. When evaluating service performance, the parties involved depend on the kind of service: logistical or technical pre-production, production, or post-production service. A computer network linking the units involved in these activities, and software that provides timely, accurate, and meaningful performance data, are essential.

The EDI system is also useful for in-house monitoring. Supplier-to-user departments need feedback on their performance. This monitoring must be timely and systematic, using objective quantified measurements as much as possible.

The responsibility for monitoring service rests heavily with the JIT customer organization. It, together with the carrier, generates much of the information used in monitoring. Monitoring service is like monitoring product quality—in reverse.

Product quality conformance is a "feed-forward" process, in which the marketer gives the customer proof of process capability, and of the offering's conformance, when it delivers the product. Or the marketer may electronically transmit the SPC data before the shipment arrives. This system, in which the supplier is primarily responsible for providing the data, provides quality-assured product to the customer. In contrast, post-production delivery and service processes depend on "feed*back*" systems, with the carrier and customer primarily responsible for supplying the performance data.

Effective monitoring requires a close working relationship among all involved. They must share responsibility, costs, and performance data. The ever-present guidelines apply: Focus on the vital few—those characteristics that significantly affect the offering's quality—and keep it simple!

The monitoring process's bottom line is to assure everyone that the marketer's offering conforms to the customer's requirements. That means sharing data that permit systematic reduction of variation from target values.

EFFECTIVE MONITORING REDUCES WASTE

The JIT offering that conforms to customer requirements can be maintained through an effective monitoring system and people dedicated to the task. The payoff may be tremendous, measured both in cost reduction and increased revenue from quality-differentiated products.

A before-and-after schematic demonstrating the potential of a solid JIT/TQC/TPI process is shown in Fig. 11-2.

The JIT approach reduces the fourteen steps in the traditional post-production process to five. Most of the fourteen don't add value to the

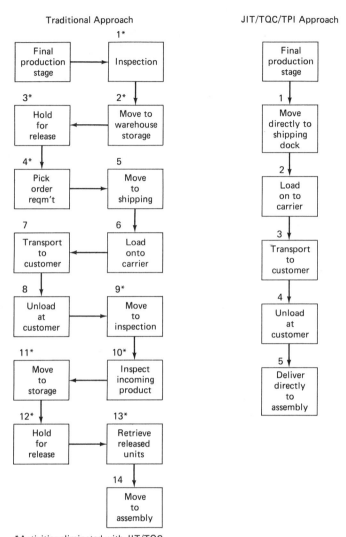

Traditional Approach · JIT/TQC/TPI Approach

*Activities eliminated with JIT/TQC

Figure 11-2 The waste reduction potential of JIT/TQC/TPI.

marketer's offering and become unnecessary as it synchronizes its processes with those of major OEM customers. For example, a final inspection is no longer needed: The SPC system verifies product conformance. Preparing the offering for storage, and inventorying and retrieving it, are also unnecessary. The marketer can move its product from the last manufacturing point directly to the shipping dock. There, shipments are staged for loading or loaded directly into the carrier's trailer.

The customer enjoys a similar streamlining. It may eliminate incoming inspection and materials inventorying. And it can move incoming materials directly to the manufacturing line, located near the receiving dock. Eliminating these non-value adding activities is reason enough to adopt the just-in-time philosophy, but it's only the tip of the iceberg.

JIT's more significant contributions come in the pre-production joint design phase. That's when products are designed into the OEM's product for high performance, serviceability, and ease of manufacture at the customer end. This produces shorter lead times to production for the supplier, and to delivery for the customer. It also reduces or eliminates engineering changes after the marketer's product is in production; substantially lowers production costs, because the product is designed with standardization and simplicity as major goals; and yields a product whose field performance meets the customer's *customers'* durability standards. If the component or assembly does fail, competent service technicians may easily fix it.

JIT marketers and OEM customers that can visualize and apply the JIT/TQC/TPI philosophy in their linked value-adding chains can't help but succeed in the global marketplace.

NOTES

1. Robert Howell and Stephen Sourcy, "Management Reporting in the New Manufacturing Environment," *Management Accounting,* February 1988, pp. 22–29.
2. Somerby Dowst, "CEO Report: Wanted: Suppliers Adept at Turning Corners," *Purchasing,* January 29, 1987, pp. 69–74.
3. "What's your Problem? Well, There's Delivery Management. . . ," *Purchasing,* April 28, 1988, pp. 18–19.
4. For example, see: J. M. Groocock, *The Chain of Quality* (New York: John Wiley and Sons, 1986), pp. 233–34; and Richard Schonberger, *Operations Management* (Plano, Texas: Business Publications, 1985), pp. 469–85.

Part VI

A Preview of Next Season

Chapter 12

Looking Ahead

Among U.S. manufacturers, which only started practicing the just-in-time/total quality philosophy in the late 1970s, JIT/TQC is still in its infancy. The pioneers that developed and implemented these processes are now achieving impressive results. And a second wave of firms, still in the embryonic stage with the new approach, seems certain to obtain similar results. Meanwhile, many producers are still in a "wait-and-see" mode. Based on results to date, JIT/TQC is clearly a winning strategy *if* the industrial marketer develops and implements it well.

Too often, the industrial marketer trails the JIT customer in developing processes that optimize the two organizations' lead times, costs, quality levels, and market share. This is especially true of second- and third-tier suppliers. Unfortunately, marketers that put off developing their JIT/TQC capabilities will lose out as customers, and prospects choose more progressive suppliers. With an increasingly competitive environment promoting survival of the fittest, it's the marketers that are developing, implementing, and actively marketing their JIT capabilities that will prosper.

By adopting the JIT/TQC philosophy, the marketer boosts its own productivity. But more important, it becomes much more attractive to OEM customers who want long-term partnerships. By taking the initia-

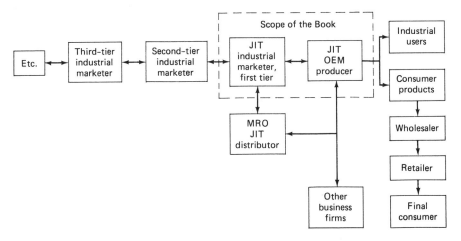

Figure 12-1 Extension of the JIT/TQC philosophy.

tive and developing JIT capabilities in parallel with, or even before the customer, just-in-time marketers can help their industrial customers become globally competitive more quickly. Putting off JIT partnerships jeopardizes both firms' "world-class" potential.

In the late 1980s and 1990s, one link in the industrial value chain— the interface of first-tier industrial marketers and final-product OEMs— is particularly well positioned to enjoy the benefits of joint JIT/TQC processes. Eventually, firms preceding and following this link will adopt the same processes. The upshot will be entire industries geared toward efficient, effective global competition. (See Fig. 12-1.)

LOOKING UPSTREAM

The industrial marketer serving the final-product OEM is often several steps removed from suppliers of assemblies, subassemblies, components, parts, and materials. But each of these links in the value chain strongly affects the final offering, vis a vis cycle time, quality, and cost.

The value chain is only as strong as its weakest link. The component's quality cannot exceed the quality of materials from which it is formed; the component supplier's cycle time constrains that of the subassembly producer; and the cost of materials, parts, components, and subassemblies governs the final assembly's cost.

The ideal JIT/TQC system extends backward to the raw materials source, with partnerships between linking members. The partners carefully spell out their requirements, based on the final customer's needs. The ideal communication system includes direct computer linkage between members at all levels of the industry value chain. This lets the final-product OEM communicate its requirements throughout the supply channel in real time, and avoids supply delays and messages garbled in transmission.

In addition to improving quality and speeding communications, such an ideal system would greatly reduce surprises and crises. This is starting to happen between first-tier suppliers and OEMs, and is gradually moving upstream to include second-tier suppliers.

LOOKING DOWNSTREAM

The mature downstream application of JIT is the U.S. supermarket. This supply channel was a major influence in the Japanese move to the just-in-time approach. Supermarkets draw thousands of products, as needed, from many sources on a daily or weekly schedule. Thanks to extremely high inventory turnover, the markets enjoy an acceptable return investment with roughly a 1% profit margin on sales.

In contrast, just-in-*case* marketing is the norm for many retailers. For example, automobile retailers stockpile hundreds of cars—various models with assorted options—for weeks or even months, waiting for the customer whose requirements happen to match one of those cars' exact specifications. Consider the apparel shop or department store that buys seasonal merchandise at least six months in advance; its suppliers must cut and sew the garments for delivery several weeks before the season starts. Once delivered, the retailer holds the goods in stock, on the floor, for weeks or months, as sales clerks try to match merchandise with customers.

In both cases, marketing is reduced to a virtual game of chance. The customer's cost is tremendous because of huge inventory-carrying charges and frequent supply/demand mismatches. The manufacturer, retailer, and final customer all pay a premium for the system's inefficiency.

Can JIT/TQC save the day? Probably. But traditional attitudes and practices must be flipped. That's a formidable task, but there are a few glimmers of hope.

Jeanne Boyle, principal of Stone Management Corporation, sees profound changes starting in the retail business. She calls this new approach "just-in-time inventorying, American style, retail-tailored."[1] Several large, state-of-the-art stores have hired consultants to put JIT systems in place. According to Boyle, the big stores will force this change because most smaller merchants can't believe just-in-time is for them. The supply side has traditionally driven retailing. Suppliers provided product at a certain time, and retailers could take it or leave it. It was a true push-through approach.

Boyle says the current system makes retailers buy products they don't need and store products they can't sell. She believes JIT will ultimately separate the winners from the losers at both the retailer and vendor level.

Consider the prospective car buyer who walks into a showroom equipped with a large-screen video display with features and specifications of each car model available to the dealer. The showroom includes a few demonstration models to give the prospect a chance to kick the tires, sit in the driver's seat, and test drive. What's missing is a huge parking lot stocked with several million dollars worth of inventory.

Using the video display, the prospect may call up any number of brand-model variations, with specifications, sticker information, and lead-time to delivery. End-user orders would pull automobiles through the system, kanban style. The benefit to the prospective customer is the car of choice at a savings of $500 to $1,000—the inventory-carrying cost savings. The cost to the customer is waiting a week for delivery.

As in the retail trade, the new approach would require radical changes in the way cars are bought and sold. But meeting the short cycle time needed for such a scenario is increasingly less of a problem. Auto makers and their suppliers are quickly developing the ability to deliver with short lead times.

LOOKING AT MRO PROCUREMENT

The just-in-time approach affects the OEM's procurement of MRO supplies, or products bought for maintenance, repair, and operations, just as it affects purchases of production materials. MRO materials are a significant expense for the typical industrial firm. A recent *Purchasing* survey showed that MRO procurement represents about a third of the work load for respondents' purchasing departments and about 13% of total dollar purchases.[2] Respondents said they buy most MRO goods from industrial distributors, particularly local distributors.

JIT purists would frown on the use of such indirect sales channels, because they add waste to the process by inflating lead times and inventory in the system. But with MRO products, small lot sizes and the huge volume of part numbers usually make direct sales prohibitively expensive. Can any JIT concepts work in MRO procurement? The answer is a qualified yes. The following examples illustrate the possibilities.

Sandia National Laboratories, which buys $60 million worth of MRO goods annually, launched a JIT program for those purchases in late 1985. The program's goals were to:[3]

• Eliminate MRO inventory and the 20,000-square-foot warehouse that held it.

- Cut purchasing, vendor, receiving, and billing paperwork to a minimum.
- Restructure the receiving system for MRO purchases.
- Provide considerably better service for all MRO goods purchased by Sandia including next-day delivery on stock items and five-day delivery on other goods.
- Improve the quality of MRO goods received.
- Procure MRO goods at prices considerably lower than what Sandia traditionally paid.

These goals are certainly consistent with the JIT philosophy: reduced waste and costs through greater efficiency and higher quality. Within two years, Sandia achieved dramatic results. The company:[4]

- Emptied its 20,000-square-foot warehouse and reconditioned it for office use.
- Saved $4.2 million on goods covered by systems contracts.
- Eliminated the $7.2 million average inventory carried in its warehouse.
- Eliminated warehouse and servicing tasks for labor savings of about $2.3 million per year.
- Improved the service level for internal users of MRO goods.

These benefits didn't just happen. They came out of a well-planned program fully supported by top management. Sandia separated MRO items into "product families" that it could purchase from single distributors. The firm sought out and evaluated qualified suppliers for each product family using a priority system based on the amount of warehouse space and goods consumed. The Number 1 product family, office supplies, represented about $1.2 million in annual volume.

Sandia sent requests for quotations to qualifying distributors in each product family and used two key criteria to evaluate responding suppliers. First, it looked at whether the supplier could fill the contract, delivering stock items within twenty-four hours 95% of the time and responding to emergencies within two hours. This criterion was weighted at 60% of the supplier-selection decision. The other factor, weighted at 40%, centered on the supplier's quoted price. Sandia's evaluation team included purchasing representatives, users, and technical specialists.

Upon choosing a distributor as the single source for a product family, the firm negotiated a three-year contract that included two successive one-year options. These long-term relationships motivate distributors to improve their productivity and develop value analysis programs. The new system cost roughly $600,000 and is expected to save about $8 million per year when fully in place.

The JIT-MRO system at Packard Electric, a division of GM, is like Sandia's. It includes:[5]

- Three-year contracts rather than the traditional one-year agreements.
- Single sourcing, with suppliers totally responsible for inventory.
- Twice-a-day deliveries to Packard's plants via common carrier.
- Paperless purchasing, using dedicated phone lines.

Packard's long-term goal is to achieve an inventory-free, paperless system, based on total cost rather than price, for all purchased items. When the division undertook the project, its MRO inventory was roughly twenty-seven days' worth, or more than $3 million.

It started by choosing twenty "core" suppliers—local distributors—based within fifteen miles of its Warren, Michigan, plant. These suppliers jointly hired a local trucking firm to deliver twice daily to Packard facilities in the Warren area. To gain access to products they don't stock, the core distributors piggybacked with more distant suppliers. The program has been quite successful, helping Packard reduce inventory and shorten lead times. The division's ultimate goal is zero MRO inventory.

Reliance Electric Company; Miller Electric Manufacturing Company; U.S. Borax and Chemical Company; Lydall, Inc.; Jamesburg Corporation; Dow Chemical; and New United Motor Manufacturing Inc. (NUMMI), a GM-Toyota joint venture in Fremont, California, have also developed JIT-MRO programs. Overall, NUMMI's MRO stocks are 25% of what they would be at a typical auto plant. Stocks for some items are only 5% to 10% of the typical level.[6]

THE DISTRIBUTOR AS PARTNER

The MRO customer interested in developing a JIT program must develop close relationships with supplier-distributors. These partnerships are much like those between JIT industrial marketers and their OEM customers. The MRO buyer must agree to buy a family of products sourced by the distributor. Meanwhile, the distributor commits to certain levels of price, delivery service, and quality.

Both partners win with this relationship. The customer wins through increased product quality and major reductions in inventory, paperwork, and acquisitions costs. The distributor wins through a more predictable and higher volume of business, better use of internal buying-supplying systems, improved inventory turns, and stable customer relationships.[7]

Developing partnerships with key MRO customers positions the distributor to do the same with its manufacturer-suppliers. As the MRO customer's partner, the distributor is a substantial purchaser of product families; has a stable, long-term requirement for these products; and has reliable internal and interorganizational systems. This is all very attractive to potential partners in the distributor's supplier base. Anything the distributor does to develop partnerships with its manufacturer-suppliers further enhances the MRO offering's value to the final-product OEM.

A CALL TO ACTION

The bottom line with JIT/TQC, whether in the procurement of MRO or production materials, is that it contributes to U.S. industrial firms' global competitiveness.

Traditional practices are no longer good enough. Industrial marketing has entered a new era, one that demands change. Changes in corporate philosophy and culture are needed, and so is a change in personal attitudes. Chief executives, senior and middle managers, line operators, and support staff members must all realign their thinking. Organizational policies, strategies, and practices must change. Functional silos must go. None of this is easy; everyone resists change. It's particularly hard if the organization is performing reasonably well.

However, regaining lost market share is several times more difficult and expensive than maintaining it. In the long run, taking the initiative is much more rewarding than just reacting.

The success of firms that have studied and applied the concepts of just-in-time, total quality, and total people involvement are real. And they are noteworthy. Almost all the leaders are final-product OEMs: Omark, Hewlett-Packard, Xerox, Motorola, Harley-Davidson, Ford, GM, Chrysler, Toyota, and IBM, to name a few.

Unfortunately, the final-product OEM's performance is closely tied to that of its suppliers. The ability of first-, second-, and third-tier suppliers to truly meet the OEM's requirements shapes the ability of the OEM to do the same for the final customer. Generally speaking, these links in the value chain need strengthening. But taking control is not the OEM customer's sole responsibility, as it has so often been in the past. These changes are just too expensive in time, money, and human resources for the OEM to shoulder alone.

Industrial marketers serving OEMs should follow the customer's lead or even take the initiative to develop in-house capabilities that match those of the more innovative OEMs. These customers, in turn, should become intimately involved with their suppliers—who are doing the same with their own suppliers. The upshot is a new level of competi-

tiveness for every link in the value chain. Time is too precious for marketers to wait for "reverse thrust" from the final-product OEM to transform
the system. Every link in the chain, starting with the basic materials
supplier, is responsible for fueling the JIT/TQC process.

For industrial marketers and OEM customers that want to develop
or implement JIT/TQC processes, assistance is readily available. There
are publications that cover virtually every aspect of the field, and some
consultants concentrate solely on this area. In addition, several professional and industry organizations, including the Association of Manufacturing Excellence, the Automotive Industry Action Group, the American
Supplier Institute, and the National Association of Purchasing Management, offer resources to interested organizations. Seminars, workshops,
monographs, and the like are also available, usually for a modest price.

One thing is clear. The competitive environment most firms face
today will not stabilize. More likely, the competition will accelerate. Organizations will not succeed tomorrow using today's methods. The successful industrial marketer of the future will be thoroughly grounded in
"teamsmanship." That covers relationships within the organization, between tightly coordinated functional units driven by customer needs, and
partnerships with customers and suppliers.

Each team will be well-informed, thanks to careful study of the just-
in-time, total quality, and total people involvement playbook. Coaches
committed to total customer satisfaction will prepare and encourage their
players to continuously improve team performance. Players and coaches
alike will be prepared to take on the best-of-the-best in the global arena.
Why not join them?

NOTES

1. "American-Style Just-in-Time Retail—Tailored," *Stores,* May 1986, p. 58.
2. Somerby Dowst, "Surveying the MRO Scene," *Purchasing,* April 28, 1988, pp.
   74–81.
3. James Morgan, "Who Says Just-in-Time Buying Is only for Production?" *Purchasing,* February 13, 1986, pp. 66–71.
4. "Sandia Bucks Low-Bid Ritual," *Purchasing,* September 24, 1987, pp. 20–21.
5. Ernest Raia, "Just-in-Time Just in Time," *Purchasing,* May 9, 1985, pp. 81–84.
6. Somerby Dowst, "MRO and JIT: How the Pros Pull Them Together," *Purchasing,* May 22, 1986, pp. 62–68.
7. "Partnership Is a Strategy—Not a Gizmo for Selling MRO," *Purchasing,* April
   28, 1988, pp. 60–71.

Index